Mines of Plumas County, California

Compiled by the staff of
the California State Mining Bureau

with an introduction by Kerby Jackson

This work contains material that was originally published in 1918.

Introduction

It has been over ninety five years since the California State Mining Bureau released its "Mines and Mineral Resources of Plumas County, California" which detailed the mines of the famous gold fields of Plumas County.

Plumas County was first established in 1854 from a portion of Butte County. Another larger portion was taken from nearby Lassen County in 1864, also later annexing a portion of Sierra County into its boundaries. The mining camp of Quincy was its first county seat.

Mining had its beginnings in what became Plumas County in 1850 when large numbers of prospectors began to wander into the area in search of a fabled golden lake. Tales of the lake were fueled by stories of Thomas R. Stoddard who made claims that while wandering hungry through the wilderness, he had encountered gold nuggets littering the shores of a small lake. While coarse gold, including nice nuggets, had been previously found in the area and prospectors had been working to trace the color to its sources high in the hills, everything changed when Stoddard came wandering into what later became Downieville and told a wild about a secluded mountain lake who's shores and bottom was covered in hunks of gold. While even the miners of those very early years were skeptical of wild stories, where Stoddard's story differed from many, was that he had in his possession, a considerable poke of nuggets, which he claimed to have merely picked up by hand before a band of Indians had run him away from his discovery.

According to an account published years later by the San Francisco Call on September 8th, 1895, Stoddard "*had come over the Lassen trail with a party and that he and a companion had gone out for a hunt and losing their way had wandered for several days in the mountains to the northeast of Downieville; when shot at by Indians he claimed that he was wounded in the leg, and showed a scar as proof; that he ran for the hills, became separated from his companion and never saw him again; after some days he reached the Yuba and told his story, but it was late in the season, winter was coming on, and the fate of the Donner party had made men cautious, so he got no encouragement that fall.*
But in the spring the whole country having become enthused over the story, he had no trouble in getting up a party, and in May, 1850, he got twenty-five prospectors together and left Nevada City at their head, bound for Gold Lake. In the meantime immigrants were swarming in from every quarter and most of them were ready to believe anything told to them. … Under such circumstances an expedition like that headed by Stoddard could hardly fail to attract a great deal of attention, and the little company was followed by thousands from the day they started out. There are conflicting stories in some respects, but they all agree that it was one of the wildest of all the wild goose chases ever made. … Stoddard soon proved that he knew nothing of the country, and never found any gold lake, or any other lake, but the crowds that were following his party stuck to it like shadows, and vainly imagined that all the tramping to and fro in an apparently aimless manner was to throw them off the scent. They wandered into the Sierra Valley and into some of the smaller valleys north of it. Patience at last gave out and the anger of the camp increased to such an extent that it was voted to hang Stoddard. He was notified, and he begged so hard that the men agreed to give him one more day. That night he disappeared, and the little valley is known to this day as Last Chance."

Despite Stoddard's sudden flight, throngs of men continued the search for his illusive golden lake. Though a body of water matching his description was never found, the rush that Stoddard started resulted in dozens of legitimate gold discoveries in the mountains. Rich placer strikes were made at Nelson Creek, Poorman's Creek, Hopkins Creek, Onion Valley, Rich Bar and Butte Bar, while equally rich were bars located on the East Branch of the Feather River known as Rich Bar, Indian Bar, French Bar, Smith Bar, Junction Bar and Missouri Bar. Others included places known as the Frenchman's, Brown's Bar, Wyandotte and Muggins. At Nelson Creek, a party calling themselves the Wisconsin Company took out 93 odd pounds of placer gold in three weeks at a place they called Meeker Flat. Other rich discoveries continued to be made by small groups of miners until at least 1852.

By 1855, hydraulic mining had gotten its start in the area, most notably at Nelson Point, Sawpit Flat, Gopher Hill and Upper Spanish Creek.

According to most sources, Plumas County's recorded gold production up until 1959 was 1.67 million ounces, but even some USGS publications claim that actual production was closer to 4.5 million ounces.

Copper mining too, was of vast importance to Plumas County, which during the 1920's and 1930's led the rest of the state in its production. The famous Engle Mine, in only 15 years of operation, yielded over 117 million pounds of copper.

Today, modern day prospectors continue to flock to the streams and hills of Plumas County. Utilizing usually only small equipment, these modern day 49'ers continue to locate gold in the area and all signs are there that much more exists.

It has often been said that "*gold is where you find it*", but even beginning prospectors understand that their chances for finding something of value in the earth or in the streams of the Golden West are dramatically increased by going back to those places where gold and other minerals were once mined by our forerunners. Despite this, much of the contemporary information on local mining history that is currently available is mostly a result of mere local folklore and persistent rumors of major strikes, the details and facts of which, have long been distorted. Long gone are the old timers and with them, the days of first hand knowledge of the mines of the area and how they operated. Also long gone are most of their notes, their assay reports, their mine maps and personal scrapbooks, along with most of the surveys and reports that were performed for them by private and government geologists. Even published books such as this one are often retired to the local landfill or backyard burn pile by the descendents of those old timers and disappear at an alarming rate. Despite the fact that we live in the so-called "Information Age" where information is supposedly only the push of a button on a keyboard away, true insight into mining properties remains illusive and hard to come by, even to those of us who seek out this sort of information as if our lives depend upon it. Without this type of information readily available to the average independent miner, there is little hope that our metal mining industry will ever recover.

This important volume and others like it, are being presented in their entirety again, in the hope that the average prospector will no longer stumble through the overgrown hills and the tailing strewn creeks without being well informed enough to have a chance to succeed at his ventures.

Kerby Jackson
Josephine County, Oregon
April 2014

CONTENTS.

ILLUSTRATIONS.

PLUMAS COUNTY.

MINING DISTRICTS.

BUTTE VALLEY MINING DISTRICT.
Including Sunnyside.

Gold is the only metalliferous product of importance in the Butte Valley district. It has been produced from rich placer diggings in gravels of both recent and ancient streams. Considerable gold is also being recovered from quartz veins, and prospects for the future are promising.

The settlement of Butte Valley (sometimes known as Butt Valley) is situated at an elevation of 4600', ten miles by stage from Crescent Mills on the Indian Valley Railway. It is about ten miles by trail west of Greenville, and about nine miles by stage road south of Prattville. Prattville is sixteen miles by stage northwest of Greenville, which is ten miles northwest of Keddie, a station on the main line of the Western Pacific Railroad. During the winter months heavy falls of snow and rain make transportation difficult. The roads are good during the summer.

Timber consists of pine, fir, spruce and tamarack. Water is plentiful, since the North Fork Feather River, Indian Creek, Yellow Creek, and several small streams flow through the district.

History of mining.

A few relatively small deposits of ancient auriferous gravel have been mined in this district. Deposits of auriferous gravel occur in the recent beds of the North Fork Feather River, Indian Creek and Rush Creek. This gravel was once rich in gold, and was extensively mined. At some localities it has been worked over a number of times, and mining still continues. Very little mining of gold quartz deposits has been done, although there are several prospects.

Topography.

Dyer Peak, elevation 7400', in the northeastern part, is the highest point in the district. South of the peak there is a gradual slope to a broad-topped ridge, elevation 6400', lying between North Fork Feather River and Indian Creek. This ridge has a steep, northwesterly face where bordered by the North Fork Feather River, and is deeply cut by Indian Creek, which flows westerly. Red Hill rises to an elevation of a little over 6000' between North Fork Feather River and Indian Creek. The west side of Dyer Peak slopes precipitously to Big Meadows, which is a broad, flat area, lying at an elevation of about 4300'. The streams in this area head in broad shallow valleys, but as they approach North Fork Feather River they cut deep cañons. This whole region drains into North Fork Feather River, which heads in Big Meadows. Indian Creek drains all of the southern portion of the district and Yellow and Chip creeks western portions.

Bibliography.

U. S. Geol. Survey, Folio No. 15, 1895, Lassen Peak. U. S. Geol. Survey Bull. No. 353, 1908, Geology of the Taylorsville Region, California, by J. S. Diller.

Geology.

In the northeastern portion of the district, on the slopes of Dyer Peak, diabase and porphyrite are exposed. They lie in contact on the north with basalt; on the west with the alluvium of Big Meadows, and on the south with quartz-porphyry. The formations southeast of here all strike northwest, being overlain by basalt to the northwest in the regions of Prattville, Longville, Yellow Creek and Chip Creek. The formations in succession from northeast to southwest are peridotite, Arlington formation, diabase, Calaveras formation, diabase, Cedar formation, peridotite and Calaveras formation. The igneous rocks lie in narrow bands between the sedimentary formations.

The Grizzly formation is composed chiefly of slates; it is of Silurian age and is the oldest fossiliferous rock yet discovered in northern California. A small area occurs along the south contact of the quartz-porphyry with the peridotite. The Arlington formation, supposed to be of Devonian age, is composed of gray sandstone, slate and conglomerate. The Calaveras formation, belonging to the Carboniferous period, consists of comparatively small lenticular masses of quartzite, slate and limestone, cut by occasional auriferous quartz veins and areas of gabbro and other intrusive rocks. The Cedar formation, of the Juratrias period, consists of metamorphosed slates and limestone, in which auriferous quartz veins have been found.

The diorite of this district usually contains plagioclase, hornblende, black mica and quartz, and belongs to the quartz-mica-diorite series. The sedimentary rocks in contact with diorite are greatly altered. Peridotite is an intrusive rock originally composed of olivine, and, in many cases, pyroxene. When pyroxene becomes the predominant mineral the rock is called pyroxenite. Since its intrusion the olivine and some of the associated minerals have been altered to serpentine. Diabase and porphyrite are the other intrusive rocks of the Juratrias period; they have been subjected to great pressure, accompanied by an alteration of their mineral constituents. Andesites, which are characterized by the predominance of pyroxene, are called pyroxene andesites; in like manner some of the rocks are called hornblende andesites. Generally the andesites are older than the rhyolites, dacites and basalts. The rhyolites of this district are light-colored, usually lithoidal, and occasionally composed of perlitic glass. Basalt is the most common and widely distributed lava of the district, having escaped from many volcanic vents towards the end of the Neocene period; it flowed down the cañons cut in the older rocks, occasionally damming them up, and giving rise to fertile meadows.

The relation of land and sea in northern California and Oregon, was essentially the same throughout the Silurian, Devonian, Carboniferous and Juratrias periods; frequent oscillations of the land with reference to the sea level are recorded in the changes of sediments. These strata, originally deposited horizontal, have since been faulted and metamorphosed; the fractures have been filled with auriferous quartz veins. The deformation did not all occur at the same time; the first tilting took place before the oldest Triassic formation was deposited. The rocks were again folded during the Juratrias, at the close of which period the great deformation occurred which raised the whole of northern California above sea. In this district there were active volcanoes during the Carboniferous and Juratrias periods. Many of these older eruptions have been folded and displaced along with the sedimentary rocks. Later volcanic action occurred during Neocene time. To the younger flows of basalt this district is indebted for the development of its agricultural and grazing lands. Lava in many places dammed up the cañons, in which by gradual accumulation of gravel, sand, mud, infusorial earth and vegetable matter, beautiful meadows formed, as typified by Big Meadows, Humbug Valley and Butte Valley.

Mineral deposits.

By the disintegration of the auriferous slates of the Cedar and Calaveras formations gold has been furnished for placer mines in the Quaternary stream gravels of Indian Creek, Rush Creek, and the North Fork Feather River. The deposits in the region of Lot's diggings and Dutch Hill are typical occurrences of auriferous gravels of ancient streams. They have all been mined and the latter is said to have been rich. The gravel at Dutch Hill is about 1000' above the North Fork Feather River and at Lot's diggings near the latitude of the fortieth parallel, the gravel lies nearly 4000' above the level of the river where it cuts across the range. It is evident that there has been a great change in the drainage of the country since these gravels were deposited.

Lode mines and prospects in this district are limited to the auriferous slates, of which the Cedar formation and the Calaveras formation have been the most productive. Intermingled with the auriferous slates are eruptive rocks, and it has been found that the most promising prospects of the district are located near the borders of these eruptive masses. The ore bodies may be in the auriferous slates or the eruptive rock, but in either case they are not far from the contact. Among the quartz mines and prospects are the Savercool and Del Monte mines on both banks of the North Fork Feather River just to the north of Seneca, the Lictum and Plumas Amalgamated quartz mines in the Calaveras formation between Seneca and Indian Falls, and the Elizabeth Consolidated in the Cedar formation to the east of Red Hill. Considerable quantities of gold have already been taken out, and the future is promising.

CRESCENT MILLS MINING DISTRICT.
Including Greenville.

The leading mineral product of this district is gold, though some silver and copper are produced as by-products. The gold has come mainly from the Crescent Mills belt of quartz mines, but it has also been mined in the recent and ancient stream gravels. Exposures of iron ore occur in the district, but iron has not been exploited.

Crescent Mills is in the north central portion of Plumas County. It is a station on the Indian Valley Railroad, ten miles from Paxton, the junction. Greenville lies nearly four miles northwest of Crescent Mills.

Staging is difficult during the winter, as the heavy precipitation of rain and snow renders the roads bad, but during the summer months traveling is quite good.

The elevation of Crescent Mills is 3520', and that of Greenville 3580'. Both are situated on the west side of Indian Valley. During the winter months cold, wet weather is typical, but it is warm and dry as a rule during the summer.

Considerable timber is found covering the slopes and ridges surrounding Crescent Mills. Yellow and sugar pine with some fir, spruce and tamarack are common, and underbrush grows on the slopes.

Wolf Creek, draining the country north of Greenville, Dixie Creek to the south, and Indian Creek, comprise the natural water supply. In addition, a large reservoir, called Round Valley Reservoir, is situated at an elevation of 4480', about two miles south of Greenville and west of Crescent Mills.

History of mining.

The principal producing mines have been the Crescent Mills, Green Mountain, Indian Valley and McGill-Standart, which lie in the Crescent Mills mining belt. In October, 1914, there were but two active producers.

Placer mines in the auriferous gravels of present streams have been worked for some years. Near Arlington Bridge and Shoofly Bridge, both on Indian Creek southwest of Crescent Mills, mining is still going on. The annual yield, including placers in Light's Cañon and above Flournoy on Indian Creek, is about $10,000.

Some mining of auriferous gravels of ancient streams has been done. One placer, one-third of a mile northwest of Round Valley Reservoir, is said to have yielded $150,000.

The total production of the Crescent Mills belt is stated to have exceeded $6,650,000.

Bibliography.

Diller, J. S., Geology of the Taylorsville Region, Cal., U. S. Geol. Survey Bull. 353, 1908. Lindgren, W., Tertiary gravels of the Sierra Nevada, U. S. Geol. Survey Prof. Paper 73, pages 114–116. U. S. Geol. Survey Min. Resources, 1905, page 180. U. S. Geol. Survey Min. Resources, 1907, pt. I, page 219. U. S. Geol. Survey Min. Resources, 1908, pt. I, page 343, U. S. Geol. Survey Min. Resources, 1909, pt. I, page 281. U. S. Geol. Survey Topo. sheets, Indian Valley, Taylorsville, Honey Lake.

Topography.

The district is situated on what is generally known as the Grizzly Mountain block, which lies at the northern end of the Sierra Nevada, northeast of the main crest, and between it and the Diamond Mountain block.

The Grizzly block comprises the Grizzly Mountains and Keddie Ridge. In the Grizzly Mountains the crest line and escarpment are well marked, presenting a steep slope of over 3000' at the west end of Genesee Valley. The crest line sinks and curves toward the northwest; disappearing at Taylorsville into the Indian Valley, it rises

Photo No. 1. View across Indian Valley, showing Crescent Mills in center. Crescent Mine and Green Mountain Mine are on peak behind town.

again in Keddie Ridge and curves back to its northwest course. The broad gap in the crest occupied by Indian Valley is more than a mile in width. Keddie Ridge, which carries the crest beyond Indian Valley, extends for about fourteen miles both extremities, ending in plains.

The southwest slope of Grizzly Mountains is gentle. About Crescent Mills and Greenville, the block is broken down to the level of Indian Valley, which crosses the main crest. This gives especial prominence to the escarpment of Arlington Heights and Houghs Peak, which form a second crest. Beyond Round Valley Reservoir the slope is better preserved in the northwestern inclination of the divide between Indian Creek and the North Fork Feather River.

Indian Creek, flowing in a general southwesterly direction from Crescent Mills, has cut a deep notch through the Grizzly block, both sides of which slope gradually to the crest.

The district is completely drained by Indian Creek and its tributaries. Wolf Creek drains the northern portion, Dixie and Clear creeks the southern, and Houghs Creek the eastern part.

Geology.

In the northern portion of the district, extending from Keddie Peak westward, is a large exposure of Taylor meta-andesite. In contact with this on its southern width is an extensive area of meta-rhyolite, the latter completely enclosing the Greenville arm of Indian Valley. South of this meta-rhyolite is an exposure of Arlington formation having a northwest-southeast trend, and in contact on its northern edge with the meta-rhyolite and the alluvium deposits of Indian Valley. Bordering the Arlington formation on its southern edge, Taylor meta-andesite which trends generally northwest-southeast, is in turn bordered by a relatively large area of Shoofly formation. West of Indian Creek there are four small exposures of basalt and two of rhyolite. Two relatively small exposures of andesite are seen, one about one mile east of Arlington Bridge; one capping some auriferous gravels and in contact with the meta-rhyolite. Four small areas of serpentine, one on the northern edge of Round Valley Reservoir, are enclosed by meta-rhyolite. The serpentine on the north of Round Valley Reservoir is in contact with an exposure of granodiorite, which is fully enclosed by the meta-rhyolite. Another very small exposure of granodiorite is seen fully enclosed by serpentine in contact on all sides with the meta-rhyolite just to the northwest of Round Valley Reservoir. A fairly large area of Taylorsville formation lies about two miles west of Greenville, and another lies two miles southeast of the town, in contact with the alluvium deposits of

Indian Valley. Dikes of rhyolite are seen in two places, one about three-fourths of a mile due north of Round Valley Reservoir in the granodiorite, and three smaller ones in the Taylorsville formation west of Greenville. A small exposure of auriferous gravels is seen in the Shoofly formation, west of Indian Creek; another partially capped by andesite lies northeast of Greenville, and another is found about three miles northeast of Greenville in the meta-rhyolite.

The meta-rhyolite is a massive gray siliceous rock generally containing phenocrysts of quartz or feldspar in a uniformly fine, compact ground mass. It is of pre-Silurian age, and the oldest rock in the district. The next oldest is the Taylorsville formation of fine sediments, slates and thin-bedded sandstones of Devonian age. The Taylor meta-andesite is decidedly green in color and porphyritic when unaltered. This great mass, comprising a lava flow, lies conformably between the Arlington and the Shoofly beds. The igneous rocks of the late Jurassic or early Cretaceous include serpentine, granodiorite and rhyolite dikes. Most of the material included under the designation of serpentine is typical green serpentine. The rock called granodiorite is a light-colored and for the most part medium-grained rock, which looks like granite. The rhyolite dike rock varies from light gray to pale green and reddish brown, containing small phenocrysts of quartz, but is rarely porphyritic. These are all later than the formations with which they are in contact, and the latter are later than the granodiorite. During the Tertiary period a flow of rhyolite of Miocene age took place. This is a siliceous lava, generally light-colored or brownish and more or less porphyritic, with grains of quartz and sometimes with scattered crystals of feldspar or biotite. The andesite of the Pliocene period is a light gray lava more or less porphyritic in thin section. A felty dark gray ground mass encloses crystals of plagioclase, also hornblende, biotite and pyroxene in various proportions. The exposure east of Arlington Bridge is black, and breaks with irregular fracture. The andesite overlying the auriferous gravel, a mile northeast of Greenville, is richer in augite and poorer in amorphous matter than that near Arlington Bridge. The basalt, seen on the ridge west of Shoofly, in part covering rhyolite, belongs to the Quaternary period. It is a lava which is darker colored, more compact, and heavier than andesite and frequently contains visible grains of yellowish-green olivine.

On the valley border, one mile northeast of Greenville, there is a mass of gravel exposed along the road for over half a mile which may represent an early diversion of the Jura River. These gravels belong to the Quaternary period. The valley alluvium, also of the Quaternary, is the sediment which fills Indian Valley. It contains some gravel, but sand is more widely distributed and silt is the most common material, making an excellent soil for agriculture.

Mineral deposits.

Two types of auriferous gravels have been mined in this district: (1) the gravels of the present stream beds and the terraces near them; and (2) the gravels of ancient streams or high gravels.

Under the head of present stream gravels are small workings on one of the benches near Shoofly Bridge by water taken out of the narrows and having a fall of nearly 100'. Placer mining has also been carried on along the upper course of Wolf Creek.

A third of a mile northwest of Round Valley Reservoir a placer mine on the slope toward the reservoir is said to have yielded $150,000. Its richness was attributed to residual material from the veins of the Standart-McGill mine. This deposit comes under the head of ancient stream gravels.

The principal production from the district has come from the Crescent Mills belt, which extends from the neighborhood of Taylorsville N. 50° W. through the Crescent Mills and Greenville districts to Wolf Creek, a distance of about fifteen miles, with a width of a little over a mile. In the Crescent Mills district the metalliferous deposits are confined chiefly to the igneous rocks in more or less well-defined quartz veins running through the granodiorite. The veins run generally parallel to the course of the belt, but in a few cases there are small veins nearly at right angles to the others. The ore is auriferous pyrite, sometimes in small bodies, but generally disseminated in the narrow strip of sheared rock of the partially formed vein in which there is usually some quartz. The pyrite is nearly always changed to limonite, setting the gold free. In the Green Mountain mine, one mile west of Crescent Mills, one subordinate vein carries a small amount of chalcopyrite, but in general copper is absent.

EDMANTON MINING DISTRICT.

This district, including Meadow Valley, is typified by deposits of gold and manganese. The gold occurs both in river and lake gravels and also in vein deposits in a lode formation. The manganese is found in both vein and lode formations.

The district is located in the west-central portion of Plumas County. Edmanton is about thirteen miles by road west of Quincy. The latter is connected by the Quincy Western Railroad to the Western Pacific Railroad at Quincy Junction (Marston).

Road conditions, while fair in summer, are quite uncertain in the winter months, due to rain and snow.

The elevation of Edmanton is 4900', and the climate combines warm, dry summers with winters having considerable snow and rainfall.

The district is included in the Plumas National Forest and contains tamarack, fir, spruce, yellow and sugar pine.

The mineral of chief importance is gold, found in the Diadem lode, and also in auriferous gravels. Two veins of oxide of manganese are found near the Diadem lode, and also a well-defined vein of hematite and magnetite.

Several lakes in the northern part of the district and the headwaters of numerous small tributaries to the North and Middle Fork of the Feather River assure a good water supply, while considerable uncut forest furnishes plenty of fuel and timber.

History of mining.

The auriferous gravels of the Neocene period have been mined at the Monte Cristo claims, about two miles west of Edmanton, by means of a tunnel. Similar deposits have been noticed on the top of Spanish Peak, and also a mile and a half west of the peak. Two miles east of Buck's Ranch, pebbles like those at the Monte Cristo claim were noted, and about three miles southeast of Edmanton a large deposit of similar character is seen.

The Pleistocene lake gravels in the vicinity of Grub Flat have been mined over by hydraulicking.

The Diadem lode, composed of quartz veins in clay slate, containing rich selenides of gold and silver combined with lead and copper, has been exploited to a depth of over 300'.

Bibliography.

Harder, E. C., Manganese deposits of the U. S., U. S. Geol. Survey Bull. No. 380, 1909, pages 270–271. Lindgren, W., Tertiary gravels of the Sierra Nevada, Prof. Paper No. 73, 1911, pages 98–99. U. S. Geol. Survey, Mineral Resources, 1907, pt. I, page 101. U. S. Geol. Survey, Mineral Resources, 1909, pt. I, page 281. U. S. Geol. Survey, Folio 43, Bidwell Bar, 1898.

Topography.

The general character of the country in this district is mountainous. Edmanton is situated in Eagle Gulch, which traverses in a northeasterly direction a rather continuous range of high peaks trending northwest.

Buck's Ranch, approximately four miles southwest of Edmanton, is located in this same cañon, which has a gentle slope of about 300' downwards from Edmanton to Buck's Ranch.

From Edmanton, to the northwest, there is a gradual rise for three miles to the top of Spanish Peak, elevation 7047'. From Spanish

Peak northwest to Mt. Pleasant, for three miles, the top of the ridge is nearly level, Mt. Pleasant being 7111' in elevation.

On the eastern slope of the ridge, between Spanish Peak and Mt. Pleasant there is a chain of glacial lakes, connected by small tributary streams, flowing into Silver Creek, which, in turn, drains into Spanish Creek, thence into Indian Creek and the North Fork Feather River.

To the southeast of Edmanton there is a gradual rise to the top of a broad-topped plateau trending southeast. The general surface of this plateau is rather even, the few peaks being all of about 5500' altitude. As the plateau nears the cañon of the Middle Fork Feather River, there is an even, but somewhat steep drop of about 2500' It is drained on the southern side by Bear Creek and smaller tributaries, which flow into the Middle Fork Feather River. On the northern slopes it is drained by Rock Creek and tributaries, which flow into Spanish Creek, Meadow Valley and Grub Flat, about three miles northeast of Edmanton, having an average altitude of 3900'. Big Creek, flowing through Eagle Gulch, drains Meadow Valley and flows into Rock Creek and thence into Spanish Creek.

Geology.

The southern portion of the broad plateau region to the southeast of Edmanton, where cut through by the Middle Fork Feather River and Bear Creek, consists of the Calaveras formation. This extends northwesterly to Haskins Valley. North of the eastern portion of this belt of Calaveras formation is a broad capping of andesite of the Neocene period. This covers the broad plateau section to the southeast of Edmanton and extends north as far as Meadow Valley. West of the andesite capping and north of the Calaveras formation is a strip of granite formation of the bedrock series nearly two miles in width and extending westward about three miles, where it broadens out to the north, covering Spanish Peak ridge as far north as Mt. Pleasant and all the country to the west excepting Buck's Valley, Haskins Valley and a strip about two miles long by one-half of a mile wide on the top of Spanish Ridge, which is covered by an andesite capping.

On the north and east slope of Spanish Peak ridge is a series of fine moraines which form an area more than four miles long, as far south as Spanish Peak.

East of this morainal deposit is a narrow strip of Calaveras formation. This strip of Calaveras formation is in contact on the west with the granite from Spanish Peak southerly.

To the east of the last mentioned Calaveras formation is a strip of amphibolite schist, trending generally in a southeasterly direction. East of this comes a strip of Calaveras formation, and then serpentine.

Meadow Valley and Grub Flat are composed of gravel beds of the Pleistocene period.

The bedrock series embraces sedimentary rocks which were turned into a nearly vertical position during or before the post-Juratrias deformation, together with associated igneous rocks. The rocks of the Calaveras formation are metamorphosed sedimentary rocks of Carboniferous age. The amphibolites and amphibolite schists are metamorphosed igneous rocks. Serpentine comes under the head of the magnesian series, since magnesia is a prominent constituent. The granitoid rocks include the granites, granodiorites and quartz-diorites.

The superjacent series consists of late Cretaceous, Eocene, Neocene and Pleistocene sediments lying unconformably on the bedrock series.

During the Neocene period this district was a country of low relief, and the auriferous gravels were deposited by streams during this period.

Under the head of the superjacent volcanic rocks may be classed the basalts and andesites. These are of the Neocene and later periods.

There is a general fault zone trending to the southeast, running nearly six miles along the east side of Spanish Peak. There is also evidence of faulting along the Diadem lode at Edmanton; this is in the same general fault zone as that along Dogwood and Bear creeks and the east slope of Spanish Peak ridge. The displacements appear to have taken place after the last andesitic eruptions, either at the end of the Neocene or early in the Pleistocene.

Mineral deposits.

The gravel deposits of the district are mostly those of the Spanish Peak gravel channel. They are made up of pebbles of pyroxene-andesite, and were mined at the Monte Cristo claim at the south edge of the deposit. Another exposure is seen on the top of Spanish Peak itself, and again at a point one and one-half miles west of Spanish Peak, the gravel being capped by andesite breccia. Another exposure of gravel overlain by andesite breccia, is seen on the flat six miles southeast of Spanish Peak. The pebbles here are mainly of quartzite and other siliceous rocks.

The gravel beds of Grub Flat and vicinity are made up of Pleistocene lake gravels. A large area of the lower gravel beds have been hydraulicked. Underlying the well-rounded gravel northwest of Grub Flat is some decomposed 'cement' gravel, made up of small round, red, brown and white particles, between which decomposed tuff has been deposited.

The Diadem lode at Edmanton, with a strike of N. 37° W. and dipping 60° NE., has an average width of 60'. The vein matter is a highly ferruginous mass of material consisting of quartz, oxide of iron, chalcedony and manganese in clay slate. The lode has been exploited to a depth of 300'. Rich selenides of gold and silver combined with copper and lead are found.

There is a well-defined vein of hematite and magnetite paralleling the Diadem lode 400' westerly, and conforming to it in dip and strike. It may be traced for more than two miles and varies from 6" to 3' in thickness.

A vein of oxide of manganese occurs near the Diadem lode, and another deposit three-fourths of a mile due south is known as the Penrose lode. The latter has been traced northwesterly as far as Eagle Gulch. The manganese is in the form of pyrolusite and psilomelane.

About two miles west of Spanish Ranch post office and about three-fourths of a mile southwest of Meadow Valley bodies of chromic iron are found in place, and abundant pebbles of chromic iron are seen in the Meadow Valley Pleistocene conglomerate.

GENESEE MINING DISTRICT.

The mineral products of this district are gold and copper. Some placer mining for gold has been done in Tertiary gravels, but at present it is confined to the Quaternary stream gravels. Drift mining for gold and copper is carried on in the Genesee mining belt, extending N. 22° W. from Ward's Creek to Lights Cañon.

Genesee is situated about fourteen miles, by stage, from Crescent Mills, in approximately the central portion of Plumas County. Crescent Mills is on the Indian Valley Railroad, ten miles from Paxton, a main line station on the Western Pacific Railroad, and about twenty-nine miles, by stage, southwest of Susanville, county seat of Lassen County.

Travel by road during the winter months is difficult on account of heavy rain and snow fall, but during the summer months the roads are quite passable.

Genesee is situated at an elevation of 3690' on the southern end of Genesee Valley. The climate in summer is warm and dry, in winter cold and wet.

Timber is quite plentiful on the surrounding ridges. Spruce, fir, yellow pine, sugar pine and tamarack are found. The slopes are covered with brush, principally manzanita.

In the Genesee mining belt the ore, in some cases, is auriferous quartz and limonite, but in others it is chiefly bornite, chalcopyrite, chalcocite, or copper carbonates. Placer mining for gold has been carried on to some extent in the auriferous gravels of both ancient and recent streams.

Indian Creek, including its tributaries, assures a plentiful water supply to the whole district. Hosselkus Creek rising in the north and flowing southwesterly, Hungry Creek in the northeastern part, and Squaw Creek, Red Clover Creek, Wards Creek and Little Grizzly Creek, in the southern part, all of which flow into Indian Creek, cover the entire district.

The forest growth furnishes sufficient mining timber and fuel.

History of mining.

During the great gold excitement in California prospectors found their way into the mountains about Indian Valley as early as 1850. Many locations followed the discovery of the "Bullion Ledge," a short distance northwest of Greenville, in 1851. Gold was the primary object of search, but the discovery of rich copper ores in 1865 led to the erection of a small furnace, which maintained a sporadic activity for four years. The Gruss mine along Wards Creek on the border of Genesee Valley has been in operation for over twenty years. This is in the Genesee mining belt, in which in 1904 there were five active mines. The belt extends from Wards Creek, N. 22° W. to Lights Cañon. Conservative estimates placed the production of the Genesee belt at $450,000 up to 1904.

Bibliography.

Diller, J. S., Mineral Resources of the Indian Valley region, U. S. Geol. Survey Bull. 260, 1909, pages 45–49. Diller, J. S., Geology of the Taylorsville Region, U. S. Geol. Survey Bull. 353, pages 111–121. U. S. Geol. Survey Mineral Resources 1905, page 180. U. S. Geol. Survey Mineral Resources 1907, pt. I, page 219. U. S. Geol. Survey Topo. sheets Indian Valley, Genesee, Honey Lake.

Topography.

The district lies on the long and gentle southwest slope of the Diamond Mountain block, which extends from Honey Lake southwestward to the Grizzly Mountains. Its crest line lies close along its northeastern side, from McKesick Peak to Diamond Mountain. The slope to the southwest has the appearance of a plateau, the prominent features of Diamond Mountain block being the escarpment, the plateau slope and the valleys along its western border.

Kettle Rock Mountain is the greatest elevation in the district, being 7850' high, or about 2000' above the general level, but it rises for the most part by such gentle slopes that it is not out of harmony with the peneplain. The upper portions of the streams are in broad shallow valleys, but as they approach the middle portion of the block

2—46902

they cut deeper and deeper until they flow in cañons. The cañons of Indian and Squaw creeks above Flournoy are examples, and they open into a broad alluvial valley below. The general trend of the valley belt along the border of the Diamond Mountain block is southeast-northwest from Genesee Valley to Mountain Meadows. Genesee Valley has a breadth of from one-third to three-fourths of a mile and a length of nearly six miles northeast and southwest directly across the general trend of the valley belt. It is a flat alluvial plain on both sides of Indian Creek, with an irregular border from jutting spurs and lateral branches running up Red Clover, Wards, Hosselkus and Little Grizzly creeks. Between North Arm and Genesee Valley, there is a gap forming a broad depression in the ridge crest that joins Mount Jura and Kettle Rock. This gap is a remnant of the old valley of the Jura River. Southeast of Genesee Valley there is a gradual rise to a broad-topped plateau, cut with rather deep notches by the cañons of Little Grizzly, Wards and Red Clover creeks.

All of the drainage of the district goes into Indian Creek; Hosselkus Creek on the northwest, Indian Creek on the northeast, Red Clover, Wards and Little Grizzly creeks, on the south drain into Indian Creek, which in turn drains into the North Fork Feather River.

Geology.

The eastern portion of the district, except in the southeast corner, is composed of a large mass of granodiorite, which projects in on the north side of Genesee Valley to a point about two miles northeast of Genesee. A relatively large exposure of basalt is seen in the southeast. Lying north of Genesee Valley is a blunt wedge shaped area of Trail formation with a base about two miles in width along Hornfels Point. From Genesee Valley the Trail formation extends southeast to the basalt area above mentioned. Just to the south of this area of Trail formation is a small area of granodiorite. South of Genesee Valley, lying between Trail formation and basalt on its east and Robinson formation on its west, is a strip averaging about one-half mile wide of Kettle meta-andesite. North of Genesee Valley is a broad area of Kettle meta-andesite averaging about four miles in width and trending northwesterly. North of Genesee Valley and west of the granodiorite spur which lies north of Genesee Valley, is an exposure of Swearingen slate, in contact on its west with Robinson formation and Hosselkus limestone. South of Genesee Valley is a strip of Robinson formation, trending northwest and southeast, averaging a little less than one-half mile in width. North of Genesee Valley the Robinson formation is divided into two narrow belts by volcanic rocks, and is cut off by volcanic rocks about a mile south of

Lucky S. road, but reappears and shortly ends on the north side of a ravine leading down to Peters Creek. North of Genesee Valley, separating the Robinson formation, is a flow of Reeve meta-andesite trending northwest. This is a narrow belt with a considerable expansion about one and one-half miles north of Genesee Valley. It is cut off by Hull meta-andesite on the north. A second belt similar to the first, borders the Robinson formation on the west, but its long, slender, dike-like south end, penetrating the Taylor meta-andesite, does not reach Genesee Valley. South of Genesee Valley a small area of meta-andesite occurs east of Ward's Creek, in contact with Robinson formation. On both sides of Genesee Valley, trending northwest to a point about a mile south of Lucky S. road, where it is cut off by Hull meta-andesite, is a strip less than one-half mile in average width of Taylor meta-andesite. South of Genesee Valley a dike of Hull meta-andesite cuts the Peale formation into two narrow belts for a distance of about a mile and a half. West of the Peale formation and on both sides of Genesee Valley is an exposure of Hull meta-andesite. To the south of Genesee Valley it occupies a rather broad area in contact on the west with meta-rhyolite. North of Genesee Valley and lying to the east of the Hull meta-andesite is a deposit of Foreman formation, narrow near Genesee Valley and broadening out to a width of about two miles to the north of Taylor diggings. It is again interrupted by North Arm, whence it continues northwest to Mountain Meadows. On the west it is in contact with the Hinchman sandstone. Several small areas of andesite are seen in this district. One, about a mile long and less than one-half mile wide in its widest portion, lies on Hornfels Point; another, at the head of Foreman's Ravine, overlies a small area of auriferous gravels. South of South Fork Foreman's Ravine is an exposure of rhyolite, and another larger exposure occurs about a mile northeast of Taylor diggings. Several deposits of Tertiary auriferous gravels are seen: at Taylor diggings, a mile northeast of the summit of Mount Jura there is a relatively large exposure, and on the Lucky S. road a flat-topped mass of gravel caps the divide and main spur for over three miles. A small mass of gravel is seen on the Lucky S. road about two and one-half miles east of Hull diggings, and there are three flat-topped deposits at an elevation of from 5500' to 5800' capping the divide between Wards Creek and Little Grizzly Creek, southwest of Genesee Valley. Another mass is seen on the divide between Wards Creek and Red Clover Creek.

The oldest rock in the district, the meta-rhyolite, is a massive gray siliceous rock which generally contains phenocrysts of quartz or feldspar embedded in a uniformly fine, compact groundmass. It is of pre-Silurian age. The Peale formation, belonging to the Calaveras group of Carboniferous age, is a reddish to brown slaty shale, passing into tuffaceous sandstone and fine conglomerate. The Taylor meta-andesite, also of the Calaveras group, is a decidedly green rock and, in this district, has a pronounced porphyritic structure with phenocrysts of plagioclase or augite. The meta-andesite dips southwest beneath the Peale beds. The Kettle meta-andesite of the late Carboniferous is decidedly porphyritic, with many small phenocrysts of feldspar, some of hornblende and rarely quartz embedded in a reddish-brown or gray partially crystalline groundmass. The eruption of the great mass of Kettle meta-andesite probably occurred about the time the Robinson formation was deposited. The Reeve meta-andesite is composed of white crystals of plagioclase plentifully scattered in a compact dark groundmass. The relation of the Reeve meta-andesite to the Kettle meta-andesite is not clear, though it appears that the Kettle meta-andesite is the older. The Robinson formation includes a succession of variably sediments ranging from shale to conglomerate and composed chiefly of igneous material. The tuffaceous conglomerate and sandstone are composed almost wholly of volcanic material erupted in connection with the effusion of the mass of meta-andesite. It dips to the southwest between the Taylor meta-andesite, which was the source of its material. The Robinson beds evidently lie uncomfortably beneath all the later formations with which they come in contact. The Hosselkus limestone is dark blue on fresh fracture, weathers light gray and contains a few veins of white calcite. It is evident that in the Taylorsville region there is a decided interruption between the Hosselkus limestone and the Robinson formation. It is possible that their contact is a plane of displacement. The Swearinger formation is chiefly a dark slaty shale, sometimes more or less calcareous and again decidedly siliceous. The Swearinger slate and the Hosselkus limestone are everywhere conformable, the general dip is to the southwest beneath the Hosselkus limestone and shows that in the Taylorsville region the Jurassic has been overturned. The Trail formation, of Jurassic age, includes a mass of strata composed largely of slaty shales with some interbedded sandstones and conglomerates. The general dip of the formation is southwest, at an angle ranging from 35° to 80° and it passes beneath the Swearinger slate and Hosselkus limestone. The horizon of the Trail formation appears to be unconformably over the Swearinger slate. The Foreman formation is a succession of shale, sandstone and conglomerate in which the sediment is for the most part derived from rocks which are not clearly volcanic. The general strike of the Foreman formation is northwest, and the dip is to the southwest immediately beneath the Hinchman formation and all the other formations of Mount Jura which have been overturned. The

Hull meta-andesite of the late Jurassic is greenish to reddish in color. The prevailing type is essentially non-porphyritic and, in general, is only partially crystalline. The fact that it penetrates the Foreman beds to the northeast of Mount Jura, indicates that its eruption took place near the close of the Jurassic. The rock included under the head of granodiorite is a light-colored, and for the most part, medium-grained rock which looks like granite, composed chiefly of plagioclase and feldspar. Where the granodiorite comes in contact with the Swearinger slate and Trail formation, these have been converted into dark, flinty hornfels. The andesite is a light gray lava more or less porphyritic in thin section. It has a felty dark gray groundmass enclosing crystals of plagioclase and hornblende, biotite and pyroxene in smaller proportion. It occurs in sheets covering the older rocks, and is of Pliocene age. The basalt is a darker colored, more compact and heavier lava than the andesite, not plainly porphyritic, but frequently containing grains of yellowish green olivine. This basalt is made up of two lava flows of Quaternary age. The later basalt is dark gray, holocrystalline and rich in augite. The earlier is black and compact and contains much amorphous matter. Mount Ingalls was the vent for the flow in this district.

Mineral deposits.

The placer deposits of this district are of two kinds, Tertiary auriferous gravels and Quaternary stream gravels. Among the former are those of the Mount Jura divide, extending northeast from Mount Jura toward Kettle Rock. There are four areas, and the divide preserves a cross section of the ancient valley once occupied by Jura River. The two larger masses have been mined at Taylor and Hull diggings. These four areas were in all probability once connected. The gravels of the Mount Jura divide contain no pebbles of the Tertiary lavas. The pebbles of Tertiary rocks present are all of types that belong to the pre-Tertiary bedrock series. South of Genesee Valley, there are three flat-topped masses capping the divide between Wards and Little Grizzly creeks. These were mined at the old Peake diggings. In these gravels, pebbles of old rhyolite or quartzite like those of Grizzly Mountains are most abundant, with some of darker igneous rock and a few of granite. Pebbles 6" to 10" in diameter are common, but boulders as large as 2' are rare. Mining has been carried on in the present stream gravels of Indian Creek above Flournoy, and on Little Grizzly Creek, one of the strongest streams of the region. The entire annual yield of the placer mines within and bordering on the Indian Valley quadrangle, is probably somewhat less than $10,000.

Under the head of lode-mining, the mines of the Genesee belt are important. The most continuous activity in the district has been along Wards Creek on the border of Genesee Valley, where the Gruss mine has been in operation for over twenty years. This mine is on both sides of the contact between the Kettle meta-andesite and the slaty shale of the Robinson formation. In the shale the partially formed veins follow narrow sheer zones, in which there is some auriferous quartz associated with limonite. The adjacent meta-andesite is often decidedly slaty and its ores chiefly chalcopyrite or bornite, with copper carbonates near the surface. Near by is the Five Bears mine, in the Robinson slate, and this is much like the Gruss. The Green Ledge, Pilot, and others in the Kettle meta-andesite have small veins of quartz with bornite and some chalcocite. The veins are generally less than 5″ in thickness. Across Genesee Valley is the Cosmopolitan mine on the contact of the granodiorite with the Hosselkus limestone and Swearinger slate. The ore is chalcopyrite and bornite, forming solid bodies up to 15′ in thickness. On the surface the contact is marked by masses of garnet and epidote, which were not seen beneath, but in the Duncan mine the garnet and epidote are associated with the ore. The Bluebell mine is in the Hosselkus limestone near the contact, and from one of its shafts some tons of carbonate of copper have been brought up in connection with cave breccia.

In the Taylor gravel diggings some years ago a bed of coal about five feet thick, lying nearly flat beneath the auriferous gravels, and resting directly on the upturned edges of Jurassic sandstone, was laid bare. About one ton was mined for blacksmithing purposes.

GRANITE BASIN MINING DISTRICT.
Including Buckeye, Gold Lake and Merrimac.

The gold in this district is found principally in quartz veins in granite formations. Some gold has been taken from auriferous gravels of the Neocene period, both by hydraulicking and drift mining, and some from the gravel of the Little North Fork River.

The district is situated in the western portion of Plumas County and the eastern portion of Butte County. Buckeye, approximately the center of the district, is on the boundary line between Plumas and Butte counties. Buckeye is about six miles by trail due east of Big Bar, a station on the Western Pacific Railroad, and about thirteen miles by stage, northeast of Berry Creek, another station on the Western Pacific Railroad.

Considerable snow and a rather heavy rainfall in the winter months render the roads somewhat uncertain, but in the summer they are quite passable.

Buckeye is 5000' in elevation. Granite Basin is in the neighborhood of 4500', and Gold Lake and Merrimac 4250' and 3900', respectively. In the summer the climate is warm and dry, but the winters are quite rigorous.

Mine timber and fuel are obtained from the surrounding forest, which includes tamarack, yellow and sugar pine, fir and spruce.

The only mineral of importance is gold, which is mined both from gold-bearing quartz veins and by hydraulicking. At the Horseshoe mine, three miles southeast of Merrimac, the gravel of the Little North Fork River is washed.

French Creek, Little North Fork, and their tributaries on the south and west of the district and tributaries of the North Fork Feather River on the north furnish a plentiful water supply to the district.

History of mining.

The Reynolds mine, three miles northwest of Merrimac, was worked for some time, a quartz vein in granitoid quartz-diorite containing the gold values; and narrow quartz veins in the granite area known as Granite Basin have been worked. Some hydraulicking has been done to the east of Buckeye and one drift mine has been worked at Buckeye in the auriferous gravels.

Bibliography.

U. S. Geol. Survey Folio 43, Bidwell Bar, 1898.

Topography.

Granite Basin in the eastern portion of the district is a small granite area formed by erosion, and lying mostly between 4500' and 5000' altitude. Sloping gradually up to the north, there is formed a chain of hills, chief among which is Frenchman Hill, about three miles northeast of Granite Basin with an elevation of 5993', and Soapstone Hill, about three miles northwest of Granite Basin, with an elevation of 5500'. The general trend of this chain of hills is northeast. To the west there is an easy raise to an elevation of about 5000', cut by the cañon formed by Marble Creek, on the western part of which is situated Buckeye with an elevation of 5000'. About five miles due south of Granite Basin, two rather pronounced promontories are formed at the joining of Marble Creek, a tributary, and the Little North Fork River. East of the Little North Fork, which flows due south from Granite Basin, there is a fairly even slope to a broad low-sloping area in which is situated Gravel Range and China Gulch. West of the Plumas-Butte county line, the general slope of the whole district is to the southwest. The slope is even and slight to French Creek, which flows nearly due south throughout the district. This portion of the district is cut by numerous small tributary streams of

French Creek flowing in a general westerly and southwesterly direction.

The western portion of the district is drained by French Creek and its tributaries which flow into the North Fork Feather River. The northern part is drained by Grizzly Creek and tributaries, which in turn, flow into the North Fork Feather River. The Little North Fork and Marble Creek drain the southern and eastern portions, these flowing into the Middle Fork Feather River.

Geology.

Granite Basin is composed entirely of granite of the bedrock series. The exposure of this granite is somewhat circular with an average diameter of approximately two and one-half miles. It is surrounded by a wide area of amphibolite of the same series. In contact with the amphibolite to the northeast is a fairly large area of serpentine. Soapstone Hill, in the amphibolite area, is capped with serpentine, on the northeast of which is a small area of Calaveras formation. Bear Ranch Hill is capped with serpentine with a lens-shaped exposure of Calaveras formation about one-fourth of a mile by a mile and a half, to the east of and in contact with it. About a mile and a half to the east of Buckeye there is a small exposure of serpentine.

In contact with the whole amphibolite area, except for a small part about a mile and a half to the north of Buckeye where there is an exposure of older basalt, is an area of serpentine about one-half of a mile in width, broadening out both to the east and the west to a considerable extent. In the southeastern portion of the district the serpentine is in contact with an area of Calaveras formation about two by four miles. In contact with the Calaveras formation on the west is a comparatively narrow exposure of amphibolite, trending northerly. In contact with and on the west of the amphibolite is a large exposure of granite comprising the balance of the district and all of that section to the southwest of Buckeye, Merrimac and Gold Lake.

The older basalt is a sock-shaped exposure on the instep of which Buckeye is situated. There is another small exposure of this older basalt about one mile southeast of Buckeye.

The rocks forming the bedrock series are the Calaveras formation, the amphibolites and amphibolite-schists, the serpentines of the magnesian series, and the granites, granodiorites and quartz-diorites. Two relatively small exposures of the older basalt of the Neocene period, and a few deposits of auriferous gravels comprise the superjacent series.

Mineral deposits.

Of the three exposures of auriferous river gravels in the district, the one at Buckeye has been mined by drift mining. The others, one a mile southeast, and one a mile and a half east of Buckeye, have both been hydraulicked. All are capped by older basalt.

The Horseshoe mine, three miles southeast of Merrimac, is a present river gravel mine. A dam is built across the Little North Fork and the water turned into a flume. The gravel is then sluiced into the narrow gorge of the horseshoe, and allowed to accumulate during the summer. It is carried off during the winter months floods.

In the granitoid-quartz diorite three miles northwest of Merrimac some quartz veins have been found to contain considerable gold. The Reynolds mine was worked for some time.

In Granite Basin there are gold-bearing quartz veins that have been worked with profit. The veins have a general northeast-southwest trend. They are seldom over 2′ in width and stand either vertical or at a high angle. The ore contains auriferous pyrite as well as galena and zinc-blende, and is said to run $20 per ton. These veins have been worked at the Coquette and Robinson mines.

Limestone lenses found in the Calaveras formation east of Merrimac have not been exploited.

JOHNSVILLE MINING DISTRICT.

Including the region about Johnsville, Jamison, Mohawk and Long Valley.

In the large area included in this district gold is found in lodes and in both Tertiary and recent placers. The vein gold comes from the notable region about Plumas Eureka, in a belt continuous with the quartz-porphyry belt to the south in the Sierra City district. Placer gold is found farther north in the valleys drained by the Middle Fork Feather River.

The district is located in the south central portion of Plumas County. Johnsville is eight miles by road west of Blairsden on the Western Pacific Railroad, with which point it is connected by daily stage (except on Sunday) in good weather. The condition of the roads is fair in summer, but not dependable in winter.

The elevation of Johnsville is 5200′, and there is a heavy precipitation of rain and snow during the winter months, but the summers are warm and usually dry.

The region is not far from the border of the Tahoe National Forest, in which the chief growths are yellow and sugar pine, tamarack, fir and spruce.

Gold is the chief mineral product of economic importance at the present time. Many limestone masses and some marble occur within the district, and a little has been burned for lime. A deposit of magnetite occurs in the southern extremity of the district.

The water supply is good. Mohawk is on the Middle Fork Feather River, whose numerous small tributaries run throughout the district. Glacial lakes occur west and south of Johnsville.

Sufficient timber is furnished by the still uncut forest in the surrounding region.

History of mining.

The Pleistocene or recent river gravels in the Middle Fork.Feather River Valley were mined a long time ago, and in nearly all places were found to be rich in gold.

Considerable hydraulic mining has been done on gravel occurring at the south end of a spur from the andesite-covered Grizzly Mountains and at the Cascade mine. Tertiary gravels have been hydraulicked.

A gravel deposit four and one-half miles northeast of Johnsville was penetrated by Millers lower tunnel in the year 1890.

Bibliography.

Lindgren, W., Tertiary Gravels of the Sierra Nevada, U. S. Geol. Survey, Prof. Paper 73, page 111, 1911. U. S. Geol. Survey, Mineral Resources 1905, page 180. U. S. Geol. Survey, Mineral Resources 1906, page 192. U. S. Geol. Survey, Mineral Resources 1907, pt. I, page 218. U. S. Geol. Survey, Mineral Resources 1908, pt. I, page 844. U. S. Geol. Survey, Mineral Resources 1909, pt. I, page 281. U. S. Geol. Survey, Topo. sheet, Downieville. U. S. Geol. Survey, Geol. Folio 37, 1897.

Topography.

The general character of the country is mountainous. Johnsville and Plumas Eureka are situated near the base of the east slope of Eureka Peak, which has an elevation of 7490'. From Eureka Peak a ridge curves north for two miles and then northwest for four miles, the top being nearly level. South of Eureka Peak this ridge is broken by the cañon of Jamison Creek, from which it rises again to form Bunker Hill, 7400' in elevation. The ridge continues south, curving into the Downieville district.

East of Bunker Hill a number of highly elevated glacial lakes are connected by streams, which flow northeast into Jamison Creek, and thence into the Middle Fork Feather River.

For several miles east of Eureka Peak ridge the country flattens out, but is divided by many shallow stream depressions continuous with the cañons higher up on the ridge. Separating this locality from Long Valley on the north is Big Hill, five miles northwest of Johnsville, and 5700' in elevation. It is of very low slope from the south, but steeper on the north toward Middle Feather River and Long Valley. Big Hill also forms the divide between Little Poplar Valley on the west and Jamison Creek on the southeast.

East and north of Long Valley a high mountain chain runs in a northwest direction. The northern part of this chain is called the Grizzly Mountains, of which the highest peak is 7777′ in elevation. Several spurs radiate down to Long Valley.

In the south the mountains are less steep. Happy Valley extends east of Long Valley, separating the Grizzly Mountains ridge into a widspread system of spurs to the south. Mt. Jackson and Penman Peak occur on this system, the elevations being respectively 6625′ and 7280′. Mohawk Valley lies to the southwest. This is a broad level valley running northwest along the Middle Fork Feather River. The elevation of the valley is about 4500′ above sea level.

Geology.

The western portion of the district consists of folded slates and quartzites of Calaveras formation, generally of nearly vertical dip toward the east, and northerly strike.

Running through Eureka Peak and Bunker Hill the contact between the Calaveras formation and the quartz-porphyry belt is . continuous with that in the Sierra City district to the south. Except for one small patch, this quartz-porphyry belt does not appear again north of Eureka Peak until the base of the Grizzly Mountains, just north of Long Valley, is reached. From here the belt continues northwesterly, in contact with the Calaveras on each side.

West of Eureka Peak a body of intruded gabbro occurs in contact with the quartz-porphyry. Another body further south is possibly connected with the first under the intervening glacial detritus.

Photo No. 3. View showing character of the country south of Mount Elwell, in the vicinity of Gold Lake.

Augite-porphyrite extends north of Eureka Peak, in a belt superficially resembling the quartz-porphyry. This rock has a schistosity with a northwest strike and a dip of from 70° to 75° SE. It is in contact with the Calaveras formation on the west. Near Johnsville the belt is covered by glacial detritus, but south of Johnsville around Mt. Elwell and Long Lake it is five miles wide.

The quartz-porphyry and augite-porphyry were extended in Juratrias time or earlier, but have been compressed somewhat with the Calaveras formation. The augite-porphyry appears to be younger than the quartz-porphyry.

An area of Robinson formation, composed of tuff, trachyte, and red slate, occurs in the northern portion of the district, separated from the Calaveras formation by augite-porphyrite. The beds strike northeast and dip 60° E.

In contact with this on the south near the head of Grizzly Valley is an intruded body of granite-diorite. Granite-diorite bodies also occur at the head of Little Long Valley Creek, in Happy Valley, and in various other places at the edge of the andesite cap covering the large area north and south of Grizzly Valley, and it is probable that the entire cap is underlain largely by granodiorite.

An irregular shaped body of mica-schist is exposed near the upper end of Grizzly Valley, in contact with granodiorite and partially covered by alluvium and andesite. This formation is possibly a part of the Robinson, that has been thoroughly recrystallized to form schists.

Andesite, and some rhyolite and basalt, cover the uplands north of Mohawk Valley. These lavas are not extensive about Johnsville, but cover the region four miles to the west, and the peaks west of Eureka Peak.

A series of limestone masses occur on Eureka Peak and Bunker Hill in the Calaveras formation, crossing Nelson Creek Cañon, and a body of crystalline limestone occurs in Little Long Valley Creek Cañon.

The Calaveras formation is of Carboniferous age. The Robinson, also Carboniferous, is deposited on top of the Calaveras. At the end of the Paleozoic era these sediments were raised out of the sea, folded and compressed.

No sediments of the Juratrias period appear in the district, but during that time quartz-porphyry and augite-porphyrite were extended. At the end of the period these were folded and compressed with the previous sediments in the first great Sierra Nevada uplift. Extensive granodiorite intrusions, and also the gabbro, accompanied this movement.

Tertiary auriferous gravels accumulated in the Neocene epoch and toward its end separate flows of rhyolite, basalt and andesite took place.

Another uplift, accompanied by faulting with the downthrow on the eastern side, followed the volcanic activity. One line of faulting probably runs through the Mohawk Valley.

In early Pleistocene time scattered flows of basalt occurred, the lava following the river valleys eroded in the andesite. After this came a period of glaciation, shown by glacial detritus and lakes. The following period extends into the present time.

Mohawk Valley is the remains of a lake that filled the valley in Neocene and Pleistocene times. The lake obtained its maximum development after the andesite eruption, which appears to have formed it.

The rocks occurring within the district are Calaveras slate, quartzite, and limestone, Robinson tuff and red slate, mica schist, augite-porphyrite, quartz-porphyrite, gabbro, granodiorite, andesite, basalt and rhyolite.

Mineral deposits.

The most important mineral is gold, which occurs in quartz veins in the southern portion of the region about Eureka Peak, and in gravels of both Tertiary and recent streams in the central and northern portions.

On the steep eastern slope of the ridge four and one-half miles northeast of Johnsville, a large deposit of auriferous Tertiary gravel is exposed, surrounded by andesite breccia. Its altitude is about 6500'. A gravel deposit under the andesite was penetrated by Millers lower tunnel in the year 1890. The gravel was subangular, containing small fragments of blackened wood, and was evidently a gulch gravel. The bottom of the channel is 400' vertically below the top of the ridge.

A small deposit occurs at a point two and one-half miles northwest of Johnsville, on a bedrock of augite-porphyrite; some hydraulic mining has been done here.

In the extreme northern portion of the district, gravel deposits occur on two spurs of the Grizzly Mountains, about two and one-half miles southeast of Tower Rock. They are in a channel continuous with one in Honey Lake quadrangle, farther north. Gravel in this channel is again exposed at the Cascade gravel mine, on Little Grizzly Creek Cañon, thirteen miles north of Johnsville, and four and one-half miles southeast of Tower Rock. Calaveras formation composes the greater part of the bedrock, and rising ground to the south and west is covered by andesite breccia. Sandy layers are interstratified with the gravel. The deposit is 325′ thick. Large granodiorite boulders, presumably from the granodiorite region to the south, are found in the gravel and indicate that the river flowed north.

At the base of a spur from Grizzly Mountains on the northern slope of Little Long Valley there is another exposure of gravel, probably the southern continuation under the andesite of the Cascade mine channel. From the bedrock Calaveras formation and quartz-porphyry the elevation is 5600′ to 6000′. On the south end of the spur a large area has been hydraulicked.

Under the andesite and rhyolite of Lava Peak between Little Long Valley and Long Valley creeks the gravel is again exposed. On the spur south of Long Valley Creek there is a similar, but more extensive deposit, the elevation of some of this gravel being only 5000′.

The deposit of well-rounded gravel at the north end of Mohawk Valley, when in place, rests on Carboniferous slates. The low altitude, about 4500′, of the portion about the mouth of Cedar Creek is probably due to landslides. On the south it is in immediate contact with the Mohawk Lake beds. This and the gravel of the northern part of the channel are composed of pebbles with coarse sand and very little fine sediment, so it is probable that this channel has a steeper grade than the one in the southwest of the Downieville quadrangle.

The Plumas Eureka, one of the most notable lode mines in the Downieville quadrangle, occurs within this district on the eastern slope of Eureka Peak, one-half mile west of Johnsville. The vein matter in this mine is composed of firm white quartz containing a large percentage of pyrite, with galena and sphalerite. The gold

Photo No. 4.   View near Round Lake Mine, showing topography in Gold Lake district.

occurs both free in the quartz and in the pyrite, in about equal amounts. This mine has been worked profitably for many years, but is now almost completely exhausted. The Little Jamison quartz mine is one and one-fourth miles south of the Plumas Eureka. The country rock in this neighborhood is quartz-porphyry, gabbro and augite-porphyry. Much of the surrounding region is covered by glacial drift.

LA PORTE MINING DISTRICT.
Including the region about La Porte and American House.

This district has been the largest placer gold producer in Plumas County. The main Tertiary river channel west of the Neocene divide in the Downieville quadrangle runs through La Porte. As in the adjoining district, however, no gold is obtained from recent gravels or from quartz veins at present. La Porte is the principal shipping point of the region. It is estimated that at least $60,000,000 was forwarded from here from 1855 to 1871, including considerable gold obtained before 1855 from the present rivers.

La Porte is located in the southwestern corner of Plumas County, near the Sierra County line. It is fifty-one miles northeast of Oroville on the Western Pacific Railroad and the Southern Pacific Railroad in Butte County. A daily stage (except Sunday) runs from Oroville, omitting only the worst of the winter when the roads are not passable. There is also a daily stage from Marysville, sixty-five miles by road southwest of La Porte. Roads to the north connect La Porte with Quincy and with Clio.

The winter months are characterized by heavy rains and snow, but the summers are tolerably warm and dry. La Porte has an elevation of 5000'.

The district lies a short distance from the northern border of the Tahoe National Forest. Yellow pine, sugar pine, tamarack, fir and spruce compose the larger growths, and the steeper slopes are densely covered with manzanita and ceanothus brush.

Gold alone constitutes the mineral production of the district.

There is a good water supply. Slate Creek and its tributaries flow through the southern part, and the headwaters of the South Fork Feather River in the northern portion.

Electricity at a moderate price is available as a source of power.

History of mining.

In the La Porte district the greater part of the auriferous Tertiary river gravels have already been mined away. Together with Spanish-town, 10,400,000 cubic yards of gravel had been excavated up to the year 1891 and 800,000 cubic yards remained at that time as ultimately available.

The gravels of the entire region have been mined by hydraulicking and by drifting operations. In 1901 a tunnel was completed two miles northeast of La Porte, and the channel was mined successfully for some distance upstream.

About three miles northeasterly from La Porte the Feather Fork Gold Gravel Company has opened the channel by a long tunnel, the elevation of which was determined from borings. The channel was profitably drifted upon to a point where it widened out so that the gold was not sufficiently concentrated.

In 1905, La Porte produced $18,000 of placer gold; and in 1905, $6600 in Gibsonville. In 1909 La Porte and Gibsonville together produced $32,000.

Bibliography.

Lindgren, W., Tertiary Gravels of the Sierra Nevada, U. S. Geol. Survey, Prof. Paper 73, page 105, 1911. U. S. Geol. Survey, Mineral Resources 1907, pt. I, page 216. U. S. Geol. Survey, Mineral Resources 1908, pt. I, page 344. U. S. Geol. Survey, Mineral Resources 1909, pt. I, page 281. U. S. Geol. Survey, Topo. sheet, Downieville. U. S. Geol. Survey, Folio 37, 1897.

Topography.

The La Porte district is a sloping region of few hills, to the northwest of Slate Creek.

La Porte is situated at an elevation of 5000' on a gently sloping ravine of a tributary that runs southeast into Slate Creek. The latter, a branch of the North Fork Yuba River, flows southwestward. Slate Creek Cañon on the La Porte side is not steep, and is only about 800' deep.

North of La Porte the ground slopes gradually upward, until an elevation of 5500' is reached; then the grade increases to the top of Bald Mountain, 5918' in altitude and one mile north of La Porte. The southern slope of Bald Mountain forms a watershed for the creek running through La Porte, but on the northern slope tributaries of the South Fork Feather River flow north to meet the South Fork in Little Grass Valley. This broad level valley, running in a southwesterly direction, lies between the ridge west of Gibsonville and Whiskey Diggings on the southeast and Grass Valley Hill ridge on the northwest. The depth of the valley is about 800', and the distance between the ridges is two and one-half miles.

Lexington Hill, in the Bidwell Bar quadrangle west of Bald Mountain, is a little over 5800' in elevation. The two hills form a connecting link from Pilot Peak between the Gibsonville ridge and a similar continuous ridge in the Bidwell Bar quadrangle, on which American House is located. This ridge is parallel to the Mooreville ridge, but separated from it by Lost Creek Cañon.

Geology.

The greater part of the district within the Downieville quadrangle, excepting the southern area, is covered by andesite breccia or Pleistocene alluvium deposits. The broad Bald Mountain and Grass Valley Hill ridges are covered by andesite, while alluvium occupies the bottom of Little Grass Valley.

A belt of Calaveras slates and quartzites one mile wide runs northwestward through the district. On each side it is in contact with amphibolite, the western contact passing a little east of La Porte. The Calaveras formation is again exposed in Little Grass Valley north of the lava cap.

The amphibolite continues westward into the Bidwell Bar quadrangle. Lexington Hill is formed of amphibolite. West of this area of sediments, the amphibolite body continues until it comes in contact with the serpentine and with the great body of granite which is so prominent in the Bidwell Bar quadrangle. A long belt of the Calaveras formation, narrowing to less than one-fourth of a mile in the north, runs in a north-south direction one mile west of Lexington Hill.

The amphibolite appears to have been originally augite tuffs and surface lavas, but these have been altered, so that it now consists chiefly of green aluminous amphibole usually of the fine fibrous uralite type, but in part of a more coarsely fibrous, recrystallized variety.

The amphibolite and Calaveras formation extend downward indefinitely, and are continuous with the same formations in the Port Wine district in the south.

The Calaveras is the oldest formation in the district. During the Carboniferous period it was deposited as shale and sandstone. At the end of the Paleozoic era an uplift occurred which folded the strata somewhat, and at the end of the Juratrias the first great uplift of the Sierra Nevadas closely folded and compressed the sediments, and thus metamorphosed them into slates and quartzites.

During the Tertiary period erosion was at first rapid, but in the latter part, in the Neocene epoch, the country had been worn low, and the velocity of the various streams reduced so that auriferous gravels accumulated. These and the surrounding region were then covered by a mud flow of andesite breccia. The andesite flow in places covers some older massive basalt which preceded the andesite, and the basalt occasionally covers the auriferous gravels, but the basalt flow was not extensive.

At the end of the Neocene epoch the region was again elevated, the movement being accompanied by faulting and an increase in the rate of erosion.

Glacial detritus, which characterizes the Pleistocene period, is not found in the La Porte district.

The rocks which occur are: amphibolite, Calaveras slates, and quartzite, andesite and older basalt.

Mineral deposits.

Placer gold in Tertiary river gravels is the only mineral product of the district. No gold is produced from the gravel of modern rivers or from quartz veins at the present time.

The main river channel west of the old Neocene divide (Sierra Buttes) in the Downieville quadrangle runs through the district. The channel slopes southward from Hepsidam and Gibsonville, through La Porte and Secret diggings, then on to Scales, Indian Hill and Camptonville.

At La Porte the well-exposed white quartz gravel lies on a bedrock of amphibolite and the Calaveras formation. It may have come from quartz veins immediately adjacent and now exposed in the old river bed where the gravel has been hydraulicked away. The lower gravels were quite rich, averaging from $2 to $20 per cubic yard. A bank of gravel 250' by 100' and 30' high yielded gold at the rate of $20.87 per cubic yard.

Auriferous gravel occurs at Secret diggings on the main channel, one mile south of La Porte, and at Barnards, one mile farther southwest. The bedrock is in each case amphibolite and there is no andesite in the vicinity. Both deposits have been hydraulicked.

Dutch diggings are at the northwest end of the La Porte gravel deposit. Here the exposed channel is 500' wide, with steeply rising rims. On the southwest side the amphibolite rim rises several hundred feet probably without being influenced by faulting. Along the road northeast and southeast of Bald Mountain the amphibolite is exposed, showing that the northeast rim also rises sharply, in spite of the downthrow fault which occurs between here and Dutch diggings. The gravel banks show 80' of almost clean quartz gravel; even next to the bedrock few boulders occur over 6" in diameter. Fifty feet of sands and clays occur above the gravel, the clay being partly carbonaceous, evenly stratified and conformable on the gravel. Above the clays is a heavy cap of andesite tuff. Most of the gold was on bedrock or within 2' of it; that in the upper gravels was fine and flaky.

Two miles north of La Porte the Halsey bore hole showed the following strata. Starting with the lowest first: 5' quartz gravel, 10' gravel and clay, 2' gravel, 14' gravel and clay, 98' quartz gravel, and 316' of volcanic sand, clay and lava.

Near the Clay Bank tunnel, half a mile southeast of La Porte, there was only 14' of gravel, covered by 167' of clay. Above the clay in places a heavy body of gravel lies with many pebbles of andesite and basalt, representing an intervolcanic channel later than the Tertiary gravel channels.

A small patch of Tertiary gravel occurs at American House, in the Bidwell Bar quadrangle. This deposit, lying in a sag 800' above Salt Creek, probably represents a tributary of the main La Porte channel. A capping of basalt covers the Calaveras bedrock east of the gravel patch. The bedrock to the west is amphibolite.

On both east and west the bedrock rises several hundred feet, showing the old river valley. A considerable body of white quartz gravel underlies the alluvium deposit in Little Grass Valley, two miles northwest of Bald Mountain. This has been much exploited by shallow shafts, but, being lower than the South Fork Feather River, because of excess water it can not be profitably mined. The gravel is not thoroughly rounded, thus resembling that at La Porte and Richmond Hill.

Above La Porte, the channel has been seriously disturbed by movements in a fault zone which is at least one mile wide and which has a general northwest direction. The total downthrow on the northeast side is probably 520'. The first fault is exposed in the bedrock at the upper end of the La Porte diggings; here the downthrow on the east side is 55', and the gravel beds are bent over the nearly perpendicular fault scarp.

Three-quarters of a mile southeast of La Porte on a bedrock of Calaveras formation a detached body of gravel lies abnormally depressed 200' below the level of the old channel. At this point the channel paralleled the fault lines, and several slices have been differentially dropped or elevated. The downthrow is 200' to the northeast, but there are several intermediate benches. The Clay Bank tunnel, portal elevation 4000', has been driven 3000' northwest to open a supposed channel, but no gravel of value had been found up to 1901. It is probable that only a fragment of the northeast rim, cut off by a fault, exists here.

At Dutch diggings, at the upper end of the La Porte gravels, the channel was drifted on northwestward for 500', and was then found to be cut off by a body of lava. The relations suggest that a downthrow on the northeast side of at least 130' had been encountered. This is no doubt the continuation of the fault zone that caused the depression in the vicinity of Spanish diggings.

LIGHT'S CAÑON MINING DISTRICT.

The mineral products of this district are gold and copper. Gold is obtained almost wholly by placering and hydraulicking the gravels of both recent and ancient streams. Copper is produced from the mines in the northwestern part of the Genesee mining belt. Some noteworthy deposits of iron ore in the district have not, as yet, been exploited.

Engels, about centrally located in Light's Cañon district, is at the terminus of the Indian Valley Railroad, twenty-two miles from Paxton, on the Western Pacific Railroad. The district as a whole is in the north central portion of Plumas County and Taylorsville is approximately seven miles, by stage, from Crescent Mills, a station on the Indian Valley Railroad. The climate in winter is cold and wet, and heavy rains and considerable snowfall renders travel by road very difficult. In summer it is warm and dry, and the roads are quite good.

Timber is plentiful throughout the district. The principal varieties are yellow and sugar pine, spruce, fir and tamarack. Manzanita and ceanothus brush cover the slopes.

The district is drained by Light's Creek and its tributaries. Sufficient water for mining is obtained in the lower parts of the district, but due to their altitude it is almost impossible to obtain enough water for even a few weeks of each year to work the gravels which rest upon the summits.

History of mining.

As early as 1850, the country about Indian Valley was prospected for gold. In 1851 the 'Bullion Ledge' was discovered a short distance northwest of Gibsonville, and many locations followed. Within ten years Greenville was an active mining camp. Copper ores were discovered in 1865, but their noteworthy development has taken place only within the last four or five years. No great mines had previously been developed around Indian Valley, but many small ones contributed to a total output up to 1914, of about $7,700,000. The ores carry values in gold, silver and copper. Iron ore, coal, building stone and mineral springs are present, but have not yet become sources of revenue. About the head of Light's Creek, Mountain Meadows and Moonlight, ancient gravels have been mined in a small way for over twenty years, and the total yield has been approximately $500,000. Placering of recent stream gravels has been carried on at a number of points, particularly in Cooks Cañon and on Light's Creek, where rather persistent efforts have been made. The entire yield of the placer mines within and bordering on the Indian Valley quadrangle is about $10,000 annually.

Bibliography.

Diller, J. S., Geology of the Taylorsville region, U. S. Geol. Survey Bull. 353, 1908. Lindgren, W., Tertiary Gravels of the Sierra Nevada, U. S. Geol. Survey Prof. Paper 73, pages 114–116. U. S. Geol. Survey Topo. sheets, Indian Valley, Genesee, Honey Lake.

Topography.

This district lies in the northwestern end of the Diamond Mountain block on the gently sloping southwest side. The block gradually narrows beyond Lone Rock, loses its relative elevation, and dies out in a plain before reaching the head of Susan River. The upper courses of the stream are in broad, shallow valleys, but as they approach the middle portion of the block they cut deeper and deeper until they flow in cañons. Light's Cañon and Cook's Cañon, opening into a broad alluvial valley below, are good examples. Running northeast, on the southwest side of the district is North Arm, a branch of Indian Valley, which extends up Light's and Cook's creeks for nearly five miles. Mountain Meadows, triangular in shape and from one-fourth to nearly one mile in width, lies to the northwest of the district. Widening to the northwest, it merges into the plains bordering the volcanoes about Lassen Peak. Along the eastern side, its margin is rather indefinite on the gentle slope of the Diamond Mountain block. It has a general elevation of 4800', and is about 1300' above the general level of Indian Valley and North Arm, from which it is separated by a low divide at the head of Cook's Cañon.

The drainage of this region goes into two separate systems, the Great Basin and the Sacramento River. The northwestern part of the district is drained by Willards, Williams and Cheney creeks into Susan River, and finally into Honey Lake, which has no outlet. The eastern and southeastern parts of the district are drained by the headwaters of Indian Creek and Lone Rock Creek, one of its tributaries. The southwestern portion is drained by Light's and Cook's creeks, thence into Indian Creek, which flows into North Fork Feather River.

Geology.

On the west of the district is an exposure of Foreman formation averaging about a mile and a half in width, trending northwesterly from North Arm to Mountain Meadows. The west side is in contact with meta-rhyolite, Robinson formation and Kettle meta-andesite, in the order of their occurrence. On the east it contacts with Kettle meta-andesite, Reeve meta-andesite and auriferous gravels. At the head of Cooks Cañon there is an exposure of Reeve meta-andesite overlain by auriferous gravels to the north. East of the Foreman formation is a broad area of Kettle meta-andesite, trending in a general northwesterly direction with an average width of about two miles. Two small areas of Foreman formation, entirely isolated from the main mass, are seen in the area of Kettle meta-andesite, one on Light's Creek and the other on Surprise Creek. Lying between the Kettle meta-andesite and the granodiorite is a long narrow strip of River meta-andesite running a little east of south from Moonlight to Light's

Creek, where it bends, running into the Kettle meta-andesite. The balance of the district is composed of granodiorite, except where overlain by andesite and auriferous gravels. Between Lucky S. mine and Lone Rock Creek is a mass of andesite, capping the granodiorite and the auriferous gravels. North of Moonlight there is a mass of auriferous gravels overlying Kettle meta-andesite and granodiorite; and between Diamond Mountain, Thompson Peak, Lone Rock Creek and Lights Creek is a large area of auriferous gravels overlying the granodiorite. Two large areas of andesite on the north, two small ones in the west and east central portions cap the gravels.

The oldest rock in the district, the Kettle meta-andesite of Carboniferous age, is decidedly porphyritic, with many small phenocrysts of feldspar and some of hornblende, and rarely a few round grains of quartz. These are embedded in a reddish brown or gray, partially crystalline groundmass, containing small grains of plagioclase and quartz. The Kettle meta-andesite is clearly of volcanic origin. Its mass is made up of an extended series of lava flows and products of volcanic explosions, the individual sheets of lava and tuff being locally visible. The Reeve meta-andesite, an igneous eruption of the late Carboniferous, is made up of white crystals of plagioclase plentifully scattered in a compact dark groundmass, giving the rock a porphyritic structure. No phenocrysts of augite are present, and the dense groundmass appears largely amorphous and full of feldspar microlites. The Reeve meta-andesite occurs as a definite flow and tuff forming a long narrow belt running northwest. The relation of the Reeve meta-andesite to the Kettle meta-andesite is not clear, though it appears that the Kettle meta-andesite is the older. The Foreman formation of Jurassic age, is a succession of shale, sandstone and conglomerate, in which the sediment is for the most part derived from rocks which are not clearly volcanic. In this district the Foreman beds come in direct contact with the meta-rhyolite and Robinson formation without any intervening Jurassic and Triassic strata. The rock included under the head of granodiorite, of late Jurassic or early Cretaceous, is a light-colored and for the most part medium grained rock which looks like granite. It is generally a quartz diorite, but locally the orthoclase may increase and the rock passes into granodiorite. Most of the granodiorite is rich in quartz and hornblende and is fine grained. The quartz diorite is clearly younger than the Kettle meta-andesite and the meta-rhyolite which it intersects.

The auriferous gravels of the district are patches of the main mass of Tertiary gravels spread over an area about twenty miles in length by nine miles in breadth. The Moonlight region, twelve miles north of Taylorsville at the head of Surprise Creek, shows a total thickness of gravels of over 1000'. The lower 400' is chiefly sand, and the upper 600' is gravel or conglomerate. The latter is sometimes so firmly cemented that when the rock is broken the fracture passes through instead of around the pebbles. The deposit at the southeast head of Mountain Meadows is a body of well-rounded gravel which covers the broad and low divide between Mountain Meadows and Cooks Cañon. It is underlain by sand, and the whole mass is not over 20' in thickness. On the Sierra crest, near Diamond Mountain, at an altitude of 7000', there is a deposit of gravel about 300' in thickness, resting on the granite. Southwest of Diamond Mountain, in the flat country drained by the headwaters of Indian Creek, the gravels are widely distributed in a heavy body. The andesite, of Pliocene age, is a lava usually light gray, which is more or less porphyritic in thin sections. Crystals of plagioclase are numerous, those of biotite, hornblende and pyroxene in various proportions are somewhat less abundant. The felty dark gray groundmass contains many minute microlites of feldspar and black grains of magnetite in a light brown glassy base. It occurs in sheets around the volcanic vent from which the flows and ejected material issued. The masses around Lone Rock and between Lone Rock and Indian Creek are of hornblende andesite, closely related to that north of Kettle Rock. The andesitic tuff and breccia which form Diamond Mountain are full of black bordered hornblende. It is evident that the eruptions of lava occurred within the gravel period, overflowing the earlier gravels and furnishing the material for the later ones.

Mineral deposits.

The auriferous gravels which have been mined in the district are of two kinds: (1) gravels of the present stream beds and terraces near them, and (2) the gravels of ancient streams, or high gravels on the mountain summits far above the streams of today. Placer mining has been carried on in the auriferous gravel of present streams in Cooks Cañon and several other small streams, but the most effective and persistent effort has been made on Light's Creek. Here work is carried on for several months every year with giants and water under 100' of pressure, but the amount of debris moved is small.

The gravels of ancient streams are mined near the border of Moonlight, at the southeastern head of Mountain Meadows, and in Cook's Cañon. Operations have been maintained for a month or more every year for twenty years, but the work is confined to the lower edges of the deposits. As the gravels rest upon summits, it is almost impossible to obtain water in quantities sufficient for ordinary mining even a few days or weeks each year. In the east branch of Light's Cañon the gravels have been prospected, and good values are said to have been found in bore holes which penetrate the andesite covering to a depth of 200′ to 300′.

Several mines in the southern portion of the Genesee mining belt are located in this district. In some deposits the ore is auriferous quartz and limonite; in others the ore is chiefly bornite, chalcopyrite, chalcocite and copper carbonates. Quartz is the most common gangue mineral, but in one case barite appears and in another a green mineral like actinolite. A small vein of barite in the altered andesites at the old Indian Valley silver mine locally contains traces of copper ore. Near the northwestern end of the Genesee belt in the Superior mine, the gangue of the bornite is a green fibrous mineral, like actinolite. A number of parallel vertical veins are well exposed in the open cut and contain disseminated particles and nodules of bornite. The larger ore bodies are free from gangue. The wall rock, a fine-grained granodiorite, is the same on both sides, and the veins are sharply defined.

A promising deposit of iron ore is located eleven miles north of Taylorsville at the southern border of Moonlight, in a broad valley at an elevation of 5600′, where an area of about two acres occurs having red soil strewn with black chunks of hematite with some magnetite. Some of the fragments are 2′ in diameter. No excavations have been made, but the ore on the surface and the color of the soil indicate a considerable body of iron ore beneath.

About one-third of a mile west of this locality a small opening exposes a mass of hematite, in part breccia, over 4′ thick. It strikes nearly east approximately in line with the area noted above, and dips about 45° S.

A few degrees west of south from the two-acre area there are a number of small pits and fragments of iron ore in line to an old opening made by Hulsman, which exposes a vein-like mass of magnetite and hematite. Some of the fragments have magnetic polarity, others are not magnetic at all. The opening is only about 10′ deep, and the ore is said to run out at that depth. It is possible that there are two lines of iron ore deposits, one nearly north and south, and the other approximately at right angles. The two lines appear to meet in the two-acre area.

QUINCY MINING DISTRICT.
Including the region about Quincy, Elizabethtown and Wilson Point.

Small amounts of gold have been produced from the alluvial deposits in American Valley and from a number of gold-bearing quartz veins located within this district.

Quincy, the county seat of Plumas County, is situated in the central part. By road it is sixty-one miles northeast from Oroville on the Western Pacific Railroad and Southern Pacific Railroad. The Quincy Western Railroad connects Quincy with Marston, now called Quincy Junction, on the Western Pacific Railroad about four and one-half miles northeast. Roads from Quincy run north to Crescent Mills, Taylorsville and Greenville, south through Gibsonville and La Porte, west through Spanish Ranch, and southeast to Cromberg and Mohawk. These roads are serviceable to ordinary traffic during the dry warm summer, but in the winter a heavy precipitation of rain and snow makes them often impassable. In the vicinity of American Valley, however, the snowfall is very light.

The mountainous part of the district is covered with timber, consisting generally of yellow pine, sugar pine, spruce, fir and tamarack. Manzanita brush covers many of the steeper slopes.

In American Valley the growing of alfalfa and dairy farming are profitable occupations.

Water is plentiful. Spanish Creek runs along the eastern edge of American Valley and Thompson and Spring Garden creeks are branches to the mountains in the south. The Middle Fork Feather River, with its many tributaries, runs through the southern part of the district.

History of mining.

Some years ago a shaft was sunk in the middle of American Valley to reach the gold in the gravel deposits there, but little if any gold was taken out.

Placer gold has been mined, however, along the Middle Fork Feather River, principally at English Bar, and at another bank further to the east, and hydraulic mining has been carried on in connection with a deposit of late Tertiary gravel three-fourths of a mile northwest of Spring Garden Ranch.

About half a mile west of Nelson Point a Tertiary gravel deposit has been hydraulicked, and three miles northeast at the New Nelson placer mine a channel has been followed under the volcanic capping by a tunnel.

Bibliography.

Lindgren, W., Tertiary Gravels of the Sierra Nevada, U. S. Geol. Survey, Prof. Paper 73, pages 111–113. U. S. Geol. Survey Topo. sheet, Downieville. U. S. Geol. Survey Folio 37, 1897.

Topography.

In general, the district consists of the broad, flat American Valley lying between mountains to the north and south.

American Valley is nearly two miles across at the widest point. At Quincy, on the south edge of the western part, its width is three-fourths of a mile. Spanish Creek flows northeast along the northern edge.

Quincy is at an elevation of 3407'. To the south a stream cañon divides a moderately sloping spur from Claremont Hill, three and three-fourths miles south of Quincy. This star-shaped hill is characterized by many spurs with moderate slopes along their axes, but whose sides drop steeply down to the intervening streams. Claremont Hill consists of several peaks, the highest of which has an elevation of 7014'. A level-topped spur extends southeasterly for one

Photo No. 5.   View looking west from Quincy toward Spanish Peak.

mile to Crescent Hill, 6600' in elevation. From this point the ground slopes down steeply, forming part of the north side of Middle Fork Feather River Cañon.

From Claremont Hill a broad, flat divide extends southwest. At the southern edge of this area is the steep Middle Fork Feather River Cañon. Several tributaries, about one mile long, run down the cañon sides to the river 1800' below.

East of Claremont Hill a spur extends out that is joined at a little distance by a ridge of peaks running south to Limestone Point, 5811' in elevation, and 1800' above the river.

The more gradual eastern slope of Limestone Point ridge is drained by Willow Creek, a tributary of the Middle Fork Feather River. Further north, in Thompson Valley, Thompson Creek flows north in the opposite direction and joins Spring Garden Creek, the eastern branch of Spanish Creek.

The streams forming Spanish Creek flow northeast through American Valley, and northwest from Thompson Valley at a nearly level grade. Uniting two and one-half miles northeast of Quincy, in Spanish Creek, the waters flow north into Honey Lake quadrangle where they join Indian Creek, which empties into the North Fork Feather River, and later into the Sacramento.

Northwest of American Valley, in the vicinity of Elizabethtown, the ground slopes irregularly to peaks of less than 5000′ elevation.

Geology.

The greater part of the Quincy district is composed of closely folded slate and quartzite of Calaveras formation. In the south-western portion a broad belt of serpentine continues up from the Sawpit district, and this is joined on the east by a body of amphibolite. The northwestern corner of the district is composed of a large mass of augite porphyrite. Claremont Hill and Crescent Hill are capped by basalt, and a large area of basalt occurs several miles east of Claremont Hill, covering andesite breccia, which runs eastward across the ridges.

Serpentine occurs as a belt three miles wide along the Middle Fork Feather River, but it narrows somewhat in the north.

West of Claremont and Crescent Hills the contact is with amphibolite schist. Further north the contact is with the Calaveras formation. The serpentine and amphibolite schist extend from the surface downward indefinitely, as they represent intrusions of basic igneous rocks which have been metamorphosed to their present forms. North of Claremont Hill the amphibole schist lens, in contact on both sides with the Calaveras formation, narrows to a point.

All the region from Claremont Hill to the northeast of Thompson Valley, including the rock under the alluvial deposit in American Valley, is composed of the Calaveras formation.

A recent fault occurs in the Calaveras formation a little southwest of Spring Garden Creek and parallel to it.

About one and one-half miles northwest of Spring Garden Ranch a body of quartz-porphyry is in contact with the Calaveras formation and the augite-porphyrite. This is schistose in the same direction and in the same degree as the augite-porphyrite.

American Valley and Thompson Valley are covered by recent Pleistocene alluvial deposits. American Valley represents a basin filled with gravel, sand and other sediments deposited by large creeks emptying into it. The valley may have been a shallow lake bed.

The Calaveras formation was deposited in Carboniferous time, and is the oldest formation in the district. These sediments were metamorphosed to partly micaceous slates and to quartzites by land movements at the end of the Paleozoic era and again at the end of the

Juratrias, the latter movement being the first great uplift of the Sierra Nevada. The rocks that later formed the serpentine and pyroxenite were intruded at about this time. Before this, during the Juratrias period, the rhyolitic lavas and the basic lavas and tuffs which were later compressed respectively to quartz porphyry and augite-porphyrite, were formed. The age of the gold-bearing quartz veins is probably early Cretaceous. During the later Neocene epoch of the Tertiary period of erosion, auriferous gravels accumulated in the Neocene rivers. Toward the end of the Neocene extensive mud flows of andesite breccia occurred following smaller flows of massive basalt. This was followed by an uplift which increased the rate of erosion. In early Pleistocene time scattered eruptions of massive basalt took place. No remains of the Pleistocene glacial period are found within the Quincy district.

The youngest formation is the alluvial deposit in American Valley, which was formed in recent Pleistocene time.

The rocks found within the district are: Calaveras slates and quartzites, serpentine, amphibolite schist, quartz-porphyry, augite-porphyrite, andesite-breccia and basalt.

Mineral deposits.

Gold forms the most important mineral deposit, occurring in both the Tertiary and present river gravels, in the Pleistocene gravels of American Valley, and in quartz veins. The only other mineral deposit is a lenticular mass of limestone at Limestone Point, two miles west of Nelson Point.

The auriferous gravels occurring three-fourths of a mile northwest of Spring Garden Ranch belong to the volcanic period. Deposits from Pleistocene lake beds cover the ground about the gravels, but to the east they are covered by andesite. The bedrock is Calaveras formation.

On the north side of the Middle Fork Feather River half a mile west of Nelson Point a gravel deposit now exposed was presumably at one time covered by the andesite breccia overlying the adjacent country to the north. The gravel rests on a bedrock of Calaveras formation and is only about 200' above the present river, at an elevation of 4000'.

Four miles northwest of Nelson Point on the south slope of Claremont Hill, at an elevation of 6400', there is a channel containing gravel composed chiefly of quartz and other siliceous rocks, largely subangular in character, thereby indicating a small watercourse. The gravel, which was covered by andesite breccia, contained a good deal of gold in spots.

The New Nelson placer mine is located three miles northeast of Nelson Point on the slope of the high ridge overlooking the Middle Fork Feather River. The channel is opened by a tunnel having an elevation of 4500', and has been followed under the volcanic cover toward the northeast; this channel may connect with the gravels at Spring Garden, three miles northeast, or with the channel found in a nearby tunnel of the Western Pacific Railroad.

The gravels at Spring Garden are, however, at least 500' lower than at the New Nelson mine, due to an intervening fault running parallel to Spring Garden Creek.

Auriferous Pleistocene gravel occurs at English Bar along the Middle Fork Feather River, a little over two miles east of Nelson Point. The deposit extends for a mile along the river. One mile east of English Bar there is a similar but less extensive gravel deposit.

About one mile north of Nelson Point, on the west side of Willow Creek, there is a considerable deposit of early Pleistocene gravel. The western border of this area is 400' higher than the eastern side on Willow Creek.

In American Valley Pleistocene gravels are found between Quincy and Meadow Valley, several hundred feet above the present cañon of Spanish Creek on the north side of the stream. American Valley was a lake for a short time after the dislocation at the close of the Neocene period. Gravels indicating an outlet are found two and one-fourth miles northwest of Quincy, near Elizabethtown. The elevation of the slate bedrock at this point is 3800', and at Quincy it is 3407'. The gravels correspond to some small remnants of bench gravel about 500' above the present bottom of lower Spanish Creek and East Branch. This outlet was later abandoned by the stream.

In the gulch from Elizabethtown to American Valley auriferous deposits of later channels are found draining toward American Valley.

These deposits, 50' to 100' below the present creek bottom, connect with the gravels buried below the alluvium of American Valley. No rich gravel was found in the latter.

Quartz veins are abundant in the slates along Willow Creek east of Claremont Hill. Others occur near the serpentine belt contact, on the south side of the Middle Fork Feather River Cañon, only a few hundred feet above the river, opposite Crescent Hill. The veins are part of the system which runs along the serpentine belt, similar to that about Onion Valley. They strike in a northwesterly direction.

SAWPIT FLAT MINING DISTRICT.
Including Sawpit, Onion Valley (Eclipse) and Last Chance.

In this extensive area gold is produced chiefly from gravels of the old Tertiary rivers. Gold quartz veins are known, but few are developed, and the district may be classed as one of the smaller producers.

The district occupies a portion of the southern part of Plumas County. Sawpit is sixty-six miles by road northeast of Oroville on the Southern Pacific Railroad and Western Pacific Railroad, and fifty miles, by road, west of Clio on the Western Pacific Railroad. It is one and one-half miles northwest of Onion Valley, also known as Eclipse. Roads connect with Gibsonville and La Porte to the south and with Nelson Point (nine miles) and Quincy (twenty miles) to the north. The roads are fair and serviceable to ordinary traffic during the summer, but in winter they are often impassable, the winter months being accompanied by heavy falls of rain and snow. The summers are generally warm and dry. Elevation of Onion Valley 6300′.

The district lies about five miles north of the northern boundary of the Tahoe National Forest, and the vegetation includes yellow pine, sugar pine, spruce, fir and tamarack, with the steeper slopes covered by manzanita brush.

Limestone deposits are known within the district, but none are utilized.

Water is plentiful. South Fork Feather River and Onion Valley Creek have their sources within the district, and Nelson Creek flows northwest to the Middle Fork Feather River, whose many tributaries run throughout the northern part.

History of mining.

At Richmond Hill one-half mile southwest of Sawpit, auriferous Tertiary gravels are exposed, and have been mined by hydraulic operations. The Union Hill gravel mine, two miles to the east, on the slope of the intervening andesite ridge, has also been worked by the hydraulic method, as well as a deposit two and one-half miles northwest of Onion Valley, at the base of an andesite capping.

Bibliography.
Lindgren, W., Tertiary Gravels of the Sierra Nevada, U. S. Geol. Survey, Prof. Paper 73, 1911, page 110. U. S. Geol. Survey Topo. sheet, Downieville. U. S. Geol. Survey Folio 37, 1897.

Topography.

The district as a whole is quite mountainous. A number of irregular ridges extend in various directions, some with steeply sloping sides, others, like the one extending down to Grass Valley

Hill, and the one on which Sawpit is located being more gradual. Sawpit, at an elevation of 6050', lies on an andesite-covered upland area trending in a northwest direction. On the north and west, where the area of low slope ends, the V-shaped Middle Fork Feather River Cañon slopes down 1500' in one mile. Many tributaries, one or two miles in length, run down the slope at right angles to the river, which here flows from east to west.

Onion Valley Creek drains the south slope of Sawpit Flat, and runs west and then north, joining with the Middle Feather River in the Bidwell Bar quadrangle.

This creek drains the northern slope of the ridge extending northeast from Grass Valley Hill in the La Porte District.

One and one-half miles south of Sawpit across the headwaters of Onion Valley Creek, the highest peak of the Grass Valley Hill ridge rises to an elevation of 6842'. The ridge continues eastward for a mile, to a saddle where the road crosses, and then the ground slopes first slightly and then much more steeply to the top of Pilot Peak, 7505' in elevation, and a mile and a quarter southeast of Onion Valley. From Pilot Peak ridges radiate irregularly in various directions. The Gibsonville ridge runs southwest, the Grass Valley Hill ridge west; the Sawpit Flat northwest, the Plumas-Sierra county boundary ridge southeast. North and east of Pilot Peak, several spurs extend for a mile or so, and then drop rather steeply to Nelson Creek. Poorman Creek, a branch of Nelson Creek, runs between two of these spurs, both of which have steep southern slopes. About four miles southeast of Pilot Peak, the steep Blue Nose Mountain ridge runs north from the Sierra-Plumas boundary ridge and forms the divide between the headwaters of Hopkins Creek and a branch of Nelson Creek. On the east side of Nelson Creek a long ridge with many spurs extends north from Eureka Peak in the south. To the north of the mouth of Poorman Creek, the slope from the ridge top down is quite moderate, being from 1 in 7 to 1 in 8.

The drainage of the district in general is to the west and north, to the Middle Fork Feather River, which flows west and south, finally emptying into the Sacramento River. In the southwest part of the district, the headwaters of the South Fork Feather River run southwest between Gibsonville and Grass Valley Hill ridges.

Geology.

The greater part of the district is composed of closely folded slates and quartzites of Calaveras formation and serpentine, both extending downward from the surface indefinitely. A body of amphibolite occurs in the region of Sawpit and to the south; this also has an indefinite downward extension. Andesite covers Sawpit Flat and

Grass Valley Hill ridge. Small areas of glacial detritus occur at Onion Valley and a mile and a half southwest of that town. At Onion Valley it is partially covered by alluvium.

In the extreme west, north of the andesite breccia and basalt capping about Fowler Peak, the Calaveras formation extends northward in contact with serpentine on the east. Several long lenses of limestone occur, one along Last Chance Creek and another farther south.

Photo No. 6. Looking across the South Fork Feather River. Dumps of the Tefft and Oddie mines in right center.

The serpentine is extensively developed in this district, the belt varying in width from three to four miles. The serpentine on the broad flat interstream area northwest of Sawpit is covered by andesite. At the upper end of Bird Cañon, about a half a mile north of Sawpit, a belt of amphibolite is seen in contact west and east with serpentine and covered by basalt and andesite in the north. This belt widens from one mile in the north to three in the south. The serpentine and amphibolite form part of the great serpentine belt which extends southward through the Downieville and Colfax quadrangles.

The eastern contact between the serpentine and Calaveras formation runs in a northwesterly direction through Onion Valley, and extends north under the andesite breccia cap, appearing again one and three-fourths miles north of Onion Valley. The Calaveras formation composes the remainder of the district from this contact eastward. About four and three-fourths miles northeast of Onion Valley the strata strike northwesterly and have a vertical dip; two and one-half miles further east, however, the strike is northeasterly and the dip 80° toward the southeast.

The Calaveras formation is the oldest in the district, being of the Carboniferous period. At the end of the Paleozoic era and at the end of the Juratrias period the sediments were folded and compressed in uplift movements. The later movement was the first great uplift of the Sierra Nevada range. Basic rocks, such as diabase and pyroxenite, which were later metamorphosed to amphibolite and serpentine, were intruded at this time. The age of the gold quartz veins is early Cretaceous. During the later part of the Tertiary period, known as the Neocene epoch, auriferous gravels accumulated, and these were covered in a few places by flows of massive basalt and everywhere by mud flows of andesite breccia. Blue Nose Mountain ridge is covered by massive andesite, and there is evidence that lava issued from this region.

The flows of volcanic material took place before the end of the Neocene. At the close of the epoch a movement, accompanied by some faulting, increased the grade of the western slope, and the rapid erosion which followed left the andesite only on the high interstream areas. During Pleistocene time a period of glaciation occurred, and glacial detritus remains in Onion Valley and in several patches to the south and southeast.

The rocks found within this district are: More or less micaceous slates of the Calaveras formation, quartzites of the same formation, serpentine, amphibolite, andesite and basalt.

Mineral deposits.

The only mineral of present economic importance is gold. The entire production comes from placer mines in the old auriferous Tertiary river gravels, but gold is known to occur in quartz veins in the neighborhood of Onion Valley. Deposits of light gray limestone containing from 10% to 19.5% MgO are found at Last Chance, four and one-half miles northwest of Onion Valley.

The Richmond Hill hydraulic gravel mine is located three-fourths of a mile southwest of Sawpit, on Onion Valley Creek, at an elevation of 5500'. Bedrock is serpentine on the west and amphibolite on the east. The white quartz gravel is well exposed and not covered by andesite breccia. It is not thoroughly rounded, thus resembling the gravel underlying Little Grass Valley and at La Porte. The channel may possibly run from Little Grass Valley to the Richmond Hill below the andesite capping on the intervening ridge.

From the Richmond Hill mine the deposit is exposed for about a mile northeasterly and is then covered by andesite. A gravel deposit occurs on the same channel at the Union Hill mine, three-fourths of a

4—46902

mile farther east, on the east side of the ridge. This mine has also been worked by hydraulic operations.

Less than one-half mile north of Sawpit white quartz gravel occurring under the black basalt has been drifted upon. The gravel at Sawpit is probably on the Richmond Hill-Union Hill channel.

North of Sawpit the ridge is covered by andesite breccia. On the northern border of this capping, two and one-half miles northwest of Onion Valley, a deposit of gravel rests on serpentine bedrock. Immediately to the west is an area of Neocene basalt, extending further down the slope than the gravel deposit.

Two masses of white quartz gravel also occur at the north and west base of Blue Nose Mountain, at the edge of the breccia capping, on bedrock of the Calaveras formation.

Both deposits are about 500′ below the Bunker Hill tunnel, a mile and a half northwest of Hepsidam, a drift mine in the Gibsonville District. At the Bunker Hill mine the last of the La Porte channel was seen. It is possible that the two deposits at the base of Blue Nose Mountain represent downthrow portions of the Hepsidam deposit. Extensive faulting has occurred in this region, which was formerly one of enormous volcanic activity. Lavas have issued here, much of which is massive andesite, in part dikes, occupying fissures in the bedrock.

On the ridge north of Poorman Creek two and one-half miles northeast of Pilot Peak, the Blue Lead gravel mine is located. The white quartz gravel has a rubble of andesitic boulders on top, resembling the massive andesite immediately to the west.

Gold-bearing quartz veins occur at Onion Valley near the contact between the serpentine and Calaveras formation. Veins also occur further east in fissures in the Calaveras. About three miles northwest of the town two or three veins occur in the Calaveras formation or near the contact. They have a northwesterly strike, and are part of a vein system that seems to run parallel or along the contact between the serpentine belt on the west and the Calaveras formation on the east.

SPANISH RANCH MINING DISTRICT.

This district, which includes most of Meadow Valley, is typified by deposits of both Pleistocene lake gravels and those of Neocene rivers. Some chromic iron is found in place and pebbles of chromic iron are common in the lake and river gravels.

The district is in approximately the west central portion of Plumas County, Spanish Ranch being seven miles by stage west of Quincy. Quincy is connected to Quincy Junction on the Western Pacific Railroad by the Quincy Western Railway.

The altitude of Spanish Ranch is about 3650', and the climate is warm and dry during the summer months, with much snow and rainfall in the winter. As may be expected, the condition of the roads in winter is not dependable, but in the summer they are quite good.

The district is part of the Plumas National Forest, and it contains fir, spruce, tamarack, yellow and sugar pine timber. The slopes are usually thickly covered with underbrush.

The chief mineral is gold, found in Neocene river gravels and in Pleistocene lake deposits. Two deposits of chromic iron are found in place in the district, one about two miles to the west of Spanish Ranch Post Office, and the other about three-fourths of a mile southwest of Meadow Valley.

Spanish Creek in the northwestern part of the district, Wapanse Creek in the northeastern part, Rock and Snake creeks in the southern part and several small lakes furnish a plentiful water supply throughout the year.

History of mining.

The Meadow Valley Pleistocene lake gravels have been very extensively mined by the hydraulic method at Gopher Hill, a mile and a quarter east of Spanish Ranch. A large area of the lower gravel beds at Grub Flat, a mile and a half southwest of Spanish Ranch, have been mined, as well as some of the gravels three and a quarter miles east of Meadow Valley post office, on a branch of Slate Creek. The old mines known as Shores Hill and Badger Hill on the ridges east and west of Whitlock Ravine have been mined by hydraulicking.

At the west edge of the lava area which caps Chaparral Hill is a deposit of Neocene river gravel which has been hydraulicked. There are several other patches of the same gravels, some of which have been worked to the east of Spanish Creek. The Bean Hill hydraulic mine is two miles northwest of Spanish Ranch. Two miles north of Spanish Ranch the Pine Leaf channel has been worked underneath a capping of andesitic tuff at the Pine Leaf and Knewil mines.

Bibliography.

Lindgren, W., Tertiary Gravels of the Sierra Nevada, U. S. Geol. Survey, Prof. Paper 73, pages 98–99, 1911. Turner, H. W., Further Contributions to the Geology of the Sierra Nevada, U. S. Geol. Survey, Seventeenth Annual Report, pt. I, page 557, 1896. U. S. Geol. Survey, Min. Res. pt. I, page 218, 1907. U. S. Geol. Survey, Min. Res. pt. I, page 768, 1908. U. S. Geol. Survey, Topo. sheet, Bidwell Bar. U. S. Geol. Survey, Folio 43, 1898.

Topography.

To the east of Spanish Creek, which flows in a general southeasterly direction until it reaches Spanish Ranch, where it changes to an easterly direction, there is a ridge extending from Chaparral Hill, elevation 5500', in a general easterly direction throughout the district.

The general slope of the ridge is slightly towards the east. It slopes gently to the south into Meadow Valley, the elevation of which is less than 4000′. Two small hills of 4200′ are seen in Meadow Valley east of Spanish Ranch. To the southeast of Meadow Valley the ground slopes in a gentle rise to another ridge extending in a general southeasterly direction.

The whole district is drained by Spanish Creek and tributaries to it, whose waters flow into Indian Creek, which in turn, flows into the North Fork Feather River. Wapanse Creek, with headwaters at Smith Lake in the north of the district, flows southerly into Spanish Creek, draining Snake Lake Valley. Snake Creek and Rock Creek drain the southern portion of the district.

Geology.

Spanish Creek, from its headwaters down to Meadow Valley, cuts through a large area of serpentine. Chaparral Hill in the northwest part of this section is capped with a deposit of andesite tuff. Meadow Valley, Snake Lake Valley and several small areas, one to the east of Badger Hill diggings and three on the sides of Rock Creek Cañon, are composed of Pleistocene lake beds. On the northern slope of the ridge north of Meadow Valley is an area of the Cedar formation, composed of little altered clay slates. This is in contact on the west with the serpentine forming the ridge, on the south with the andesitic tuff capping this ridge and on the east with the Calaveras formation. A small exposure of serpentine is seen in Meadow Valley just to the east of Spanish Peak. The ridge south of Meadow Valley is capped with andesitic tuff.

The Meadow Valley lake beds of Pleistocene age are composed mostly of gravel. Some time late in the Pleistocene the rocky barrier between Meadow Valley and American Valley was cut through by Spanish Creek, thus draining the lake.

The Cedar formation is of the Juratrias period, being the only area assigned to that period in this quadrangle.

Of the bedrock series, only the serpentine and the Calaveras formation are present in this district.

The andesitic capping, exposed on the ridges, is of the Neocene period and belongs to the superjacent series.

Mineral deposits.

Gold is found in auriferous gravels of two periods and of different modes of deposition.

Several exposures of Pleistocene lake gravels are seen in and around Spanish Ranch. At Gopher Hill, a mile and a quarter east of Spanish Ranch, the gravels have been mined extensively by the hydraulic method. On the exposed cliffs there are two layers of gravels, about 50′ apart, of a light buff color, and from 1′ to 5′ in thickness. The pebbles are usually small, from 1″ to 4″ in diameter. There is but little doubt that all the isolated gravel patches were originally connected with the large Meadow Valley area of lake gravel.

Of the Neocene auriferous gravels there is an exposure at the west edge of the lava cap which covers Chaparral Hill. This exposure was worked by the hydraulic method and was known as Fales Hill. To the southeast of this, on the same ridge, are other exposures of these same gravels, some of which have been worked.

Two miles northwest of Spanish Ranch, at an elevation of about 4600′, is the old hydraulic mine of Bean Hill, containing quartz gravels of the oldest prevolcanic epoch. The Pine Leaf channel, two miles north of Spanish Ranch, has been traced northwesterly for about a mile. The channel is 200′ wide, the gravel 4′ thick, and it yielded about $1.50 per yard.

TAYLORSVILLE MINING DISTRICT.

The most important mineral in this district is gold, but some copper is produced as a by-product. Nearly all the gold has come from veins containing auriferous pyrite, found in the southern portion of the district in what is known as the Crescent Mills belt of quartz mines.

Taylorsville is situated a little north of the central portion of Plumas County. It is about seven miles by stage northeast of Crescent Mills, a station on the Indian Valley Railroad, and about twenty-nine miles by stage southwest of Susanville, county seat of Lassen County.

Owing to heavy precipitation of rain and snow during the winter months the condition of the roads is poor, but during the warm dry summer the roads are quite good. Taylorsville has an elevation of 3550′.

The ridges surrounding it are well covered with timber, chiefly fir, spruce, tamarack, yellow and sugar pine, and a liberal supply of underbrush covers the slopes.

Gold is produced both from drift and placer mines. There is a deposit of pyrrhotite a mile and a half south of Taylorsville, but it has not been exploited.

Indian Creek, and Montgomery Creek, one of its tributaries, assure a plentiful water supply to the district.

History of mining.

As early as 1850 prospectors found their way into Indian Valley. Mining claims are more or less distinctly grouped in two belts, the Crescent Mills belt and the Genesee belt. The southern end of the Crescent Mills belt lies southwest of Taylorsville and practically all the mining in this district has been done there.

Bibliography.

Diller, J. S., Geology of the Taylorsville Region, California, U. S. Geol. Survey Bulletin 353, 1908. U. S. Geol. Survey, Min. Res., page 180, 1905. U. S. Geol. Survey, Min. Res., pt. I, page 215, 1907. U. S. Geol. Survey, Topo. sheets, Taylorsville, Indian Valley, Honey Lake.

Topography.

The district lies in the Grizzly Mountain section of the Grizzly Mountain block, the latter extending from the Diamond Mountain block to the main crest of the Sierras. The Grizzly Mountains have a well-marked crest line and escarpment, which presents a steep slope of over 3000' to the west end of Genesee Valley. The crest line sinks and curves toward the northwest, running to Taylorsville, where it disappears in Indian Valley. A small notch is cut by Montgomery Creek across the north end of Grizzly Mountains, where it flows into Indian Creek, about two miles southeast of Taylorsville. The latter borders the district on the northeast edge and with Montgomery Creek and Houghs Creek comprises the drainage system of the district.

Geology.

In the southeastern portion of the district is a large exposure of Hull meta-andesite, trending generally northwest, in which there is an exposure of Mormon sandstone about one-fourth mile wide by one-half mile long in the northern portion. West of this Hull meta-andesite is meta-rhyolite, trending generally northwest with a deposit of Grizzly formation in contact with it on the west. Two miles south of Taylorsville, a lens-shaped mass of serpentine has been intruded. Further south a larger mass of serpentine cuts through both the Taylorsville formation and the Grizzly formation and into the meta-rhyolite. On the west this serpentine is in contact with Taylor meta-andesite. Southwest of Taylorsville is a body of granodiorite, narrow at the ends and about one-half mile wide in the middle, trending in a northwest-southeast direction for nearly four miles in contact on the west with Arlington formation. There are three rhyolite dikes about two miles to the west of Taylorsville at the contact between Taylor meta-andesite and the Taylorsville formation, and three cutting the serpentine which lies about two miles to the south of Taylorsville. Two small exposures of Hosselkus limestone are seen west of Little Grizzly Creek, in the Hull meta-andesite. In the Tant meta-andesite there are two exposures of Hardgrave sandstone, one lying on the contact with the meta-rhyolite and the other just to the northeast of it. Three exposures of Thompson limestone are seen, two in the Mormon sandstone and one just to the south of the contact between the Mormon sandstone and the meta-rhyolite.

The pre-Silurian meta-rhyolite is the oldest formation in the district. It is a massive gray siliceous rock with occasional inconspicuous phenocrysts of quartz in a uniformly fine, compact ground-mass. On the lower slope of Grizzly Mountains it has a decided schistose structure, due to the compression and consequent shearing.

The Grizzly formation of Silurian age is a gray, well-defined but thin-bedded quartzite overlain by lentils of limestone and interstratified with shaley, often siliceous slate (argillite) having irregular cleavage. The coarser beds of quartzite contain small pebbles of rhyolite.

The Taylorsville formation of Devonian age is composed of fine sediments, chiefly slates and thin-bedded sandstones. Near the middle are well-defined beds of light-colored quartzite, and at the base is locally a fine conglomerate. The general dip of the formation is to the southwest.

The Arlington formation, belonging to the Calaveras group of Carboniferous age, is made up chiefly of fine, gray thin-bedded sandstone, with some shale in part silicified and a few beds of conglomerate. Along Houga Creek it is bounded by granodiorite. These bordering igneous rocks are younger and either penetrate or overflow it.

The Taylor meta-andesite, of the Calaveras group of Carboniferous age, is a decidedly green rock. Where not much altered it is porphyritic with crystals of augite. It is apparently an eruption interstratified with Carboniferous rocks.

The Hull meta-andesite varies from greenish to reddish. Much of it is in well-defined sheets representing lava flows. The fact that it penetrates the Mormon sandstone indicates that its eruptions took place near the close of the Jurassic.

The serpentine in this district is a typical green serpentine, varying greatly in composition. The most abundant form is composed almost wholly of a light-colored pyroxene with a small amount of dark green hornblende. The serpentine intersects the meta-rhyolite and all Paleozoic rocks, but does not come in contact with later sediments. In turn, it is cut by quartz diorite, and dikes of the later rhyolite, indicating that it belongs among the first eruptions of the late Jurassic or early Cretaceous.

The rock included under the head of granodiorite is a light-colored and for the most part medium-grained rock resembling granite, composed chiefly of plagioclase feldspar and quartz. It is of late Jurassic or early Cretaceous age.

The dike rocks of the late Jurassic or early Cretaceous vary in color from light gray to pale green and reddish-brown. Small phenocrysts of quartz are always present, but they are rarely porphyritic.

The Hosselkus limestone, two small exposures of which appear directly in contact with the Hull meta-andesite, is of Triassic age. It is a dark blue on fresh fracture, but weathers light gray, and contains a few veins of white calcite.

The Hardgrave sandstone is of Jurassic age and only two small exposures are seen in the district. It is red or gray in color, varying from a fine shaley sandstone to conglomerate, and is almost wholly of tuffaceous character.

The Fant meta-augite andesite is a greenish to reddish brown rock, more or less porphyritic, sometimes with augite, but often with plagioclase phenocrysts. The groundmass is made up of small crystals and grains of feldspar, augite and magnetite, generally with some amorphous matter. It is of Jurassic age. That portion lying on the lower slope of Grizzly Mountains includes fragments of Hardgrave sandstone, showing it to be a volcanic effusion in the interval between the deposition of the Hardgrave sandstone and the Thompson limestone.

The Thompson limestone, of Jurassic age, is gray and somewhat shaley. On the lower slope of Grizzly Mountains are three isolated ledges lying along a line extending nearly east and west. This is later than the Fant meta-andesite to the west and seems to conformably overlie the Mormon sandstone.

The Mormon sandstone, comprising a curved area on the lower slopes of Grizzly Mountains, is chiefly gray.

Mineral deposits.

The metalliferous deposits in this district are confined largely, through not wholly, to the igneous rocks, but they are not definite contact deposits. They are in more or less well-defined quartz veins, usually running parallel to the course of the belt, but in a few cases small veins run nearly at right angles to the others. The ore belt itself is in the narrow mass of granodiorite southwest of Taylorsville. The ore is auriferous pyrite, sometimes in small bodies, but generally disseminated in the narrow strip of sheared rock of the partially formed vein in which there is usually some quartz. The pyrite is nearly always changed to limonite, setting the gold free.

Two-thirds of a mile south of Taylorsville at the old Pettinger mine, a small imperfect vein in the Taylorsville slate is impregnated with carbonates of copper, generally green but sometimes blue.

A mass of pyrrhotite, one and one-half miles south of Taylorsville, lies in a narrow strip of sheared sandstone, running north and south near the horizon of the Montgomery limestone, but the largest body, about 10' in thickness, is at a point where the sheared sediments end against serpentine.

Plumas County—Table of Mineral Production, 1880–1918.

Year	Copper Pounds	Copper Value	Gold, value	Manganese Tons	Manganese Value	Silver, value	Stone, value	Misc. Amount	Misc. Kind	Misc. Value
1880			$857,121			$181				
1881			1,890,000			2,000				
1882			1,250,000							
1883			980,000							
1884			900,000							
1885			940,308							
1886			884,432			62				
1887			608,069			16				
1888			636,060			250				
1889			706,754			235				
1890			499,664			811				
1891			482,462							
1892			432,295			11,731				
1893			362,498			14				
1894			499,339							
1895			612,351			271				
1896			462,327			58				
1897			330,252			701				
1898			369,493							
1899			381,151			15				
1900			363,219	1	$10	4,159				
1901			401,237	2	40	2,508				
1902	1,500	$247	382,686			517				
1903			424,112	1	25	510				
1904	1,090	157	270,439			464				
1905			285,810			530			Platinum	$25
1906			229,350	1	30	1,065	$5,000			
1907			219,355	1	25	948				
1908			254,737	8	25	3,560				
1909			167,491	5	75	687	2,000		Unapportioned 1900–1909	$75,575
1910			187,207	2	40	1,038	12,500	1,115 lbs.	Lead	50
1911	6,963	1,149	228,785	2	40	1,125	1,350	1,329 lbs.	Lead	60
1912	17,274	2,678	163,237			957	1,700	5,856 lbs.	Lead	264
1913			138,368			705	1,879	5,621 lbs.	Lead	247
1914	150,000	19,960	140,000			2,900	5,431	2,058 lbs.	Lead	90
1915	3,164,456	568,787	167,440			19,025	1,988		Other minerals[1]	82
1916	4,032,928	1,213,500	133,383			46,542			Other minerals[2]	3,920
1917	7,462,870	2,087,364	131,955	1,540	39,680	74,461	1,822	478 tons	Chromite / Other minerals[2]	9,800 / 304
1918	11,098,016	2,741,210	125,207	1,544	61,754	126,750	7,750		Other minerals	23
Totals	26,835,453	$6,570,042	$17,081,526	2,108	$101,819	$334,711	$40,920			$90,880

[1] Includes chromite, granite, and molybdenum.
[2] Includes gems, granite, and silica.

MINES AND MINERALS.

CHROMITE.

In the **Quincy District** three prospects were noted which had not made any production up to the end of July, 1918.[1]

L. Eddelbuttel and **Thomas Hughs** of Quincy had two locations in the inaccessible cañon of Middle Fork of Feather River.

J. L. Foisie of Quincy had one undeveloped prospect three miles west of Spanish Peak Sawmill.

J. Gifford of Meadow Valley had two locations which were under lease to F. R. Young and A. L. Smith of Quincy. Two men had started prospecting late in July, 1918, and hoped to produce a carload of ore.

Jitney Chrome Mine.[2] Owners, McCarty and Hughs, Quincy. Located in a very inaccessible part of the Quincy District on the east bank of Middle Fork of Feather River, in Sec. 14, T. 23 N., R. 9 E., ten miles southwest of Quincy. The group comprises two claims which were operated under lease by the Union Chrome Company.

The principal orebody was a lens of solid chromite 6' wide in the center, and 80' long; the southern 20' of the orebody had been offset a distance of 5' by a fault. This lens had a northerly strike and pitched 80° W. It was said to carry 46% Cr_2O_3.

It was developed by an open cut. At the end of July, 1918, 175 tons had been mined and there was said to be no more in sight.

The trail from this property raises about 3000' in ascending the mountain to the end of a road which, in turn, drops 3000' to Quincy in a distance of about six miles.

Valley View[2] chrome property is near Greenville. It is owned by W. P. Boyden and Fred Koenig of Greenville and was leased on royalty to A. E. Vandercook of Oakland, who is reported to have transferred his lease to the Western Ores Company.

It is said that one car of ore was shipped in 1916 and two cars in 1917, averaging 32% Cr_2O_3. The property was idle in July, 1917.

COPPER.

Blue Bell Mining Company. (See under Gold.)

Bullion. (See under Gold.)

Copper King and Copper Queen Mines. Owners, Wm. H. Bacon, Lever M. Bacon, Eureka, Utah.

Location: Sec. 21, T. 26 N., R. 15 E., 13 miles northwest of Doyle (W. P. Ry.) on Doyle and Squaw Valley Road. Elevation 6300'.

This property contains four claims—the Copper King, Copper Queen, Easter, and Pioneer—a total area of 80 acres covering 3000'

[1]From field notes furnished by U. S. Bureau of Mines

along the lode. It is situated on the ridge northeast of Last Chance Creek and there is a good stand of pine timber on the property.

The claims are prospects, located in 1914, and only a limited amount of prospecting has been done.

Development work at time of visit in 1913 consisted of a tunnel, 40' long on the Copper Queen and a series of shafts 10' to 20' in depth.

The deposit consists of a quartz vein capped with iron gossan between walls of diorite. It averages 2' in width with a maximum of 4'; strikes northwest, dips vertically and has a proven length on the surface of 3000'. The ore contains chalcopyrite and bornite.

The Golden Horse Shoe group adjoins on the southwest.

Cosmopolitan. (See under Gold.)

El Dorado Group. Owners, Paul Sonognini and L. Dufay, Chilcoot.

Location: Sec. 25, T. 24 N., R. 16 E., 8 miles north of Chilcoot (W. P. Ry.) by road. Elevation 6100'.

This property consists of five claims: the El Dorado No. 1 and No. 2, Bear, Wild Cat and Napoleon, situated on the timbered ridge east of Last Chance Creek. It covers a length along the lode of 3000', and is 70 acres in area.

The property was discovered in 1909 and has been worked off and on since that date. One car of ore, assaying 56% copper, was shipped.

Development work consists of a crosscut tunnel 60' to the vein, cutting it 50' below the outcrop, and a drift easterly for 155'.

The deposit consists of a series of quartz fissure veins in granite. The ore is basic, containing chalcopyrite, bornite, malachite, and azurite. The main vein has a maximum width of 5' with an average of 3', strikes east, and dips 55° N., with a proven length on the surface of 3000'. There is an E.–W. vein 500' south of the main vein with a tunnel on it 25' long, which shows the vein to be 5' wide, and the ore to average 5% to 6% copper.

Equipped with a whim only.

Mohawk mines adjoin on the north.

Engels Mine. Owners, Engels Copper Mining Company, 393 Mills Building, San Francisco; Henry Engels, president; E. E. Paxton, general manager.

Location: Lights Cañon Mining District, Sec. 4 (and others), T. 27 N., R. 11 E., on Indian Valley Railway, 22 miles from Paxton, the junction with the Western Pacific Railway. Elevation 5263'.
Bibliography: U. S. Geol. Survey Bull. 260 and 353. Cal. State Min. Bur. Rept. XII, pages 68–69. Mining and Scientific Press, July 31, 1915. H. W. Turner and A. F. Rogers: A Geologic and Microscopic Study of a Magmatic Copper Sulphide Deposit in Plumas County, Economic Geology, Vol. IX, No. 4, 1914. L. C. Graton and D. H. McLaughlin: Ore Deposition and Enrichment at Engels, California, Economic Geology, Vol. XII, No. 1, January, 1917. Mines Hand Book, 1918.

The property contains 154 claims, of which 23 are patented. There are two groups, known as Engels and Superior mines, the latter being two and one-half miles south of the Engels mine. The lode is covered for about three miles; there are good outcrops on many of the claims, and the entire area is believed to be well mineralized. In 1917 the company claimed an ore reserve of not less than 3,000,000 tons of ore above the tunnel levels, and total probable reserves of not less than 10,000,000 tons of $2\frac{1}{2}\%$ copper ore.

Diller mapped the country rock in the vicinity as granodiorite. Rogers describes the rock in which the ore occurs as norite-diorite. He notes granodiorite, some of it rich in biotite, as a differentiation product of the diorite. Graton and McLaughlin describe it as "noritic in character, being composed of plagioclase and slightly subordinate amounts of orthorhombic and monoclinic pyroxenes, and biolite." They observe that it is "probably a basic differentiate of the great Sierra Nevada batholith of granodiorite."

Turner and Rogers described the Engels mine deposit as a magmatic segregation. According to Turner, the ore occurs disseminated through the fresh diorite, in which most of the fractures are post mineral. The metallic oxides and sulphides, as described in their article, appear to have crystallized out from the magma in the same way as the feldspar hornblende, pyroxene and biotite. Quoting Turner, "the ore minerals are largely interstitial between the silicate minerals, and thus later in crystallizing out." In the Superior deposit, on the other hand, the ore minerals are largely deposited along joint planes, and are clearly of secondary origin. These writers, particularly Professor Rogers, came to the conclusion that the development of chalcocite and some covellite by replacement of bornite is the work of ascending, heated alkaline waters.

Graton and McLaughlin, as the result of later studies of the deposit and of many thin sections of the ores, took issue with the above findings. They concluded that:

"1. The ores, instead of being magmatic in the sense that they were initial constituents of the dioritic rock in which they occur, were introduced after the rock had solidified and had suffered notable dynamic and chemical changes, and constitute replacements formed under pneumatolytic and hydrothermal conditions * * *.

"2. Although the possibility of formation of a small amount of chalcocite from ascending solutions can not be absolutely excluded, no satisfactory evidence of chalcocite of replacement origin formed in this way, i. e., by upward secondary enrichment, has come under our observation. Most of the chalcocite and all of the covellite at Engels unquestionably result from replacement of earlier sulphides through the agency of descending meteoric waters and a competent explanation for all of the chalcocite is to be found in normal downward enrichment.'' The question of the origin of the rich chalcocite ore is of the utmost importance, as when once determined, it will throw much light on the future of the mine.

The deposit was discovered in the middle '80's by Henry Engels. At that time it was so remote from the railroad that production was nearly out of the question. Nevertheless, some high grade ore is said to have been shipped from the Superior group to Swansea. Assessment work was intelligently done, so that known ore reserves grew larger each year. In 1894 the Engels group, according to the State Mineralogist's Report, comprised three claims, developed by three tunnels, the longest then reported 425' long. In 1912 the same group was proven to a depth of 250', and the copper belt was described as being 1800' wide with a gossan outcrop 300' wide and 2000' long. Over 4000' of development work had been done in five years past on the Engels group, but only about 500' on the Superior group.

In 1911 a 500-ton blast furnace was built, but was never operated on account of government objection to fumes. Early in 1914 the company was reorganized and a minerals separation flotation plant capable of treating a maximum of 225 tons daily, was built at a cost of $50,000. This plant was put in operation in February, 1915, and gave the mine the distinction of being the first to depend entirely on oil flotation for the recovery of copper sulphides. This process gives a much higher grade concentrate than ordinary water concentration, because of the presence of iron oxides in the ore. An extraction of 77.6% was obtained from an ore said to average 3.8% copper. The concentrate that year averaged 33.82% copper. In ten months, 8,724,494 pounds dry concentrate were made. Development cost 67¢ a ton, mining 40¢, treatment $1.20, marketing $1.14 and general expense 78¢. The capacity of the mill was doubled late in 1915.

An electric plant with a maximum capacity of 400 horsepower was built and electricity was brought in over a line two miles long. This proved inadequate and had to be supplemented at once by distillate engines. The property at this time was twenty-six miles from the railroad and there was a grade of 1800' in the last two and one-half miles to the mine. The concentrate, carrying 5% to 6% moisture, had to be sacked and lowered on the tramway to the lower terminal, where it was picked up by trailers drawn by a Holt caterpillar tractor. This delivered it over the worst of the road to trucks which hauled it to Keddie for shipment to the Garfield smelter.

During 1916 the Indian Valley Railway (broad guage) was built twenty-two miles from Paxton to the mine at a cost of $500,000.

This road is owned principally by the Engels Copper Mining Company. The same year the Great Western Power Company built at a cost of $150,000 an electric transmission line thirty-eight miles long from its Butte Valley plant to the mine.

Over 14,000' of development work had been done to the end of 1916 in the Engels group, and during that year the Superior group was also opened with very encouraging results. The ore bodies have been opened by tunnels and winzes, and further proven to a depth of 500' below the lowest working level by diamond drilling. The oxidized zone is covered in most places by 6' of soil, but where bare it shows a leached rock stained by malachite, limonite and chrysocolla. The oxidized zone is irregular in its lower limits, merging into mixed chalcocite and carbonates, the richer parts of which have been mined but are now inaccessible. Below this, is the zone of sulphide enrichment which has yielded considerable chalcocite carrying 16% to 20% copper. This zone was 25' thick and dipped gently southwest. This ore gives place to bornite at depths of 100' to 130', with some stringers of chalcocite extending deeper. The ore body has an average width of 40' and maximum of 150'. It strikes N. 80° E. and dips 8° SW. Six tunnel levels have been opened. No. 1, the highest, was run 30' with a 50' raise; No. 2, 810' with 320' of crosscuts and a 75' raise; No. 3, 180' with 110' of crosscuts; No. 4, 1500' with 970' of crosscuts and 260' of raises and winzes, with a stope 400' long, 40' wide and 10' high in 1916; No. 5, drift 1110' with 650' of crosscuts, 200' of raises and a stope 300' by 40' by 70'; and No. 6 the lowest level. Recent work has been on levels 4, 5 and 6, but the extent to which these have been carried to date is not known. The ore body has been proven on the surface and in the upper levels for 1500' on the strike, and had been opened to a vertical depth of 700' at the beginning of 1919.

In the Superior group, developments have been equally gratifying. A main tunnel and shaft are being driven, and it is planned to sink the latter to a depth of 1000'. A stope 500' long was started early in 1919. The ore in the Superior occurs chiefly along joint planes and there are occasional small bodies of high grade.

Pyrite is notably absent from the Engels ore and has been mentioned as occurring at only one place in the Superior. This accounts in large measure for the high grade of copper concentrate obtained. The ore is now chiefly bornite averaging 2.3% copper as milled, giving a concentrate carrying about 25% copper. The total mill capacity of the two plants was said to be 1500 tons a day in April, 1919, and subsequently it was planned to increase the capitalization of the company and bring the mill capacity to 2000 tons a day. The production in 1918 was about 9,100,000 pounds of copper, costing 16.5¢ a pound to produce. This output made the Engels the largest single copper producing property in the state for the year.

Fordham Copper Property. Owner, Dr. Leonie H. Fordham, Hotel Stewart, San Francisco.

Location: ¼ mile northeast of Gibsonville on road to Hepsidam.

The property lies between the ridge which divides Plumas County from Sierra County and the high bedrock ridge which divides Slate Creek from Cañon Creek. It is the bedrock of the gravel which was hydraulicked off Gravel Hill years ago. The length of the 'copper outcrop' is 3000' and its width 600'. The country rock is described as amphibolite schist.

The following assays of samples from this property were made in June, 1917, by Walter L. Gibson (successor to Falkenau Assaying Company), Oakland, California:

	Ounces gold	Ounces silver	Percentage copper
'Oxidized'	.02	.30	3.26
'Chalcopyrite'	.04	.28	5.80
'Covellite'	.02	1.14	11.83
'Chlorite schist'	.02	.12	.31
'Chlorite schist'	.02	.10	.30

No work has been done to develop the prospect.

Folsom and Hunter Group. Owners, W. F. Folsom and Robt. L. Hunter, Indian Valley.

Location: Lights Cañon Mining District, 3 miles from Engels mine, thence 28 miles southerly to Keddie (W. P. Ry.).
Bibliography: Diller, J. S., U. S. Geol. Survey Bull. 263. U. S. Geol. Survey, Topo. sheets, Indian Valley, Genesee, Honey Lake.

This deposit of copper ore was located early in 1916 about three miles from the Engels mine by Folsom and Hunter. The vein has been tapped at a depth of 30' by a tunnel and shows a width of from 16' to 18'. Assays run as high as 14% copper, with a little gold and silver.

Golden Horseshoe Copper Mine. (Novak Copper Mine.) Owner, Jas. B. Novak, Eureka, Utah.

Location: Secs. 21 and 28, T. 26 N., R. 15 E., 13 miles northwest of Doyle (W. P. Ry.) on Doyle and Squaw Valley Road. Elevation 6150'.

This property embraces the Golden Horseshoe, Potosi, Mormon, French Cook, Despair, Incubus and Nightmare claims. There is an area of 140 acres, with a length along the lode of 3600'. It is situated on the slope of the ridge northeast of Last Chance Creek and contains a good supply of timber, mostly sugar pine, fir and spruce.

The property was discovered in 1905 and has been worked off and on since that time. In 1915 it was under bond and lease to J. F. Cutler and four men were working, two on top and two in the mine.

It is developed by a vertical shaft 120′ in depth, from the bottom of which drifts have been run 25′ south and 50′ north. There is also a crosscut tunnel 125′ long.

The deposit is a fissure vein filled with quartz and schist cutting the diorite, and containing bornite, chalcopyrite and some magnetite. The ore runs 3% to 5% copper with about $1.20 gold and some silver values. Wall rocks of the quartz vein are altered to actinolite schist. The vein has a maximum width of 15′, averages 4′, strikes N. 20° W., dips 85° W., and has a proven length on the surface of 3600′. The oxide zone has a depth of 35′ and is capped by an iron gossan.

Oil was being used for fuel in 1917, and a 25-horsepower steam hoist, a 40-horsepower boiler and a No. 5 Cameron pump are included in the equipment.

The Copper King and Copper Queen claims to the north adjoin.

Hinchman. (See under Gold.)

Hussleman and Shaw. (See under Gold.)

Iron Dike. (See under Gold.)

Little Gem. (See under Gold.)

Mohawk Copper Mines. (Last Chance Copper Mines.) Owners, Donberg, Reno, Nevada; Ludici, Vinta, California.

> Location: Sec. 25, T. 24 N., R. 16 E., 9 miles north of Chilcoot (W. P. Ry.) by Chilcoot and Last Chance road. Elevation 6250′.

This property consists of 160 acres of patented ground, covering a length along the lode of 3000′. The claims are the Mohawk, and Last Chance, both situated on the west slope of Adams Mountain, and carrying a plentiful stand of pine timber.

The deposit was discovered in 1905 and has been worked off and on since then. It is now under lease to F. J. Channing and C. N. Shaffer of Reno. In 1913 there was shipped to the Western Ore Purchasing Company a daily production of about eight tons, which runs 6% copper. The total production to date has been about 1000 tons.

The vein has been developed by a 180′ shaft inclined at 80°, on which there are three levels: the 50′, with a drift 125′ north, the 120′ with a drift 125′ north and the 180′ with a drift 65′ north, and about 240′ of crosscuts. The vein has been stoped from the 120′ level north to the tunnel level.

The deposit consists of a series of parallel veins cutting a granite formation. The main (Mohawk) vein, has a filling of quartz and granite, and granite walls. The maximum width is 10', average 4'. It strikes N. 20° E., dips 80° W., and has a proven length on the surface of 3000'. One ore shoot developed 30' long and averaged 4' in width. The ore goes 6% to 8% copper, 40¢ gold and 2 ounces silver. There is some molybdenite associated. A northwest-southeast vein, with a dip of 50° E., was cut on the tunnel level. It lies east of the main vein, but probably intersects it in depth. The oxidized zone has a depth of 50'.

Equipment comprises an 80-h.p. boiler, Ingersoll-Rand compressor, a 25-h.p. single-drum hoist and a Knowles pump. Fourteen men were employed in 1917.

Moonlight Copper Mine. Owners, E. C. Trask and Louis Coffer.
Location: In Indian Valley two miles from the Engel mine and one mile from the Indian Valley Railroad.

In June, 1918, a concentrating plant capable of 15 tons daily production was completed. In January, 1919, the company was employing about a dozen men and was said to be shipping high grade concentrate, which carries considerable silver. Ore of milling grade was reported to have been developed by a tunnel 500' long. Has been worked two years.

Steam is used for power, wood costing $2 per cord used for fuel. Freight from the mine to Chilcoot costs $3 per ton.

El Dorado group adjoins on the south.

Murdock Copper Mines. Owner, Andrew Murdock, Reno, Nevada.
Location: Sec. 25, T. 24 N., R. 16 E., 8 miles north of Chilcoot, 10 miles by wagon road north of Chilcoot station on W. P. Ry. Elevation 6500'.

This property consists of 8 claims—the Last Chance Nos. 1, 2, 3, 4 and 5, King George, King Edward and Copper King. There is a total of 160 acres, covering a length along the vein of 4500'. It is situated on the slope of the ridge northwest of Mt. Adams. Sugar pine and spruce are plentiful.

The property was discovered in 1909 and has been worked intermittently to date. Six men were working in 1917, three on top and three in the mine. It produced 90 tons of 6% to 8% copper ore.

Development work consists of a 104' shaft on Last Chance No. 1, from the bottom of which drifts run 38' southwest and 104' northeast. On No. 2 there is a shaft 42' deep, and on No. 3 a tunnel. There is a 125' incline tunnel on No. 4 and on No. 5 a 300' tunnel. Ore is being stoped on the 40' level on No. 2 from an orebody claimed to be 60' long, 6' high and 40' wide.

The deposit is a series of quartz fissure veins in granite formation. The average width is 4', strike N. 45° W., dip 15° W., and it has a proven length on the surface of 4500'. The ore is basic, containing malachite, azurite, chalcopyrite, bornite, chalcocite, and graphite.

5—46902

There are also lenses of molybdenite associated. It contains 6.66% copper, .03 ounces gold and .72 ounces silver.

Equipment consists of a whim, Keystone drill, compressor and gasoline engine.

Sorted ore is shipped. The haul from mine to Chilcoot costs $3 per ton, and from Chilcoot to Hazen, Nevada, by railroad $4.30.

Nevada-Douglas Copper Company. Owner, same.

Location: Lights Cañon Mining District.

Twenty-seven copper claims in Lights Cañon were filed for record at Quincy, in January, 1914.

Pilot Copper Mine. Owners, Joseph and Albert Goodhue.

Location: Near Indian Falls, between the Five Bears and Genesee mines.

Reported in October, 1918, to have struck a 2' ledge of copper ore carrying gold and silver. Preparations were being made at that time to ship high grade ore.

Peter. (See under Gold.)

Polar Star Claim. Owners, Cox, Keasy and Cooksey.

Location: Genesee Valley Mining District, Sec. 15, T. 25 N., R. 11 E., 6 miles southeast of Taylorsville, thence 12 miles southerly, by good automobile road, to Keddie (W. P. Ry.).
Bibliography: U. S. Geol. Survey Bull. 353, pages 111, 121. U. S. Geol. Survey Topo. sheets, Indian Valley, Genesee, Honey Lake. Cal. State Min. Bur. Bull. 50, page 180.

This property is opened by a tunnel and an open cut. The tunnel passes through the vein, which is 10' thick, and runs some distance ahead in the east wall. The open cut is in a body, or vein, of good peacock sulphide, and carbonate of copper ore, with considerable red oxide in seams and bunches. The mountain and adjacent country are heavily timbered with pine and fir. Water is plentiful.

Shoofly Group. Owner, G. H. Goodhue, Quincy.

Location: Crescent Mills Mining District, Secs. 32 and 33, T. 26 N., and Secs. 3, 4 and 10, T. 25 N., R. 9 E., 5 miles north of Keddie by good wagon road. Elevation 3000'–5000'.
Bibliography: Diller, J. S., U. S. Geol. Survey Bull. 353, pages 114–115. U. S. Geol. Survey Topo. sheets, Indian Valley, Taylorsville, Honey Lake. Cal. State Min. Bur. Bull. 50, page 182.

The 21 locations comprising the property, together with the Shoofly Ranch, patented, on which the first discovery of copper ore was made, extend in a general northeast direction, parallel with the strike of the underlying schists.

Besides numerous surface cuts, the principal development on the property is a tunnel 80' long crosscutting the strata. It enters on the bank of Indian Creek within the boundaries of the Shoofly Ranch.

The copper ore occurs disseminated in a quartz schist, with a nearly vertical dip; with clay slates to the west and a series of igneous rocks, chiefly porphyrites to the east. The copper-bearing vein belt is believed to follow the center line of the locations with an average width of 80′, and a copper content given as nearly 2%. The ores noted are generally bornite, with blue and green carbonates, the latter constantly forming at the surface from a leaching action. It occurs in minute sheets and lenses between the much contracted laminations of the schist, which everywhere exhibits the action of compressive force, and in general structure resembles strikingly the copper-bearing schists of Calaveras County.

Walker Brothers Mine. Owner, International Smelting Company, Utah. V. R. Hart, manager.

Location: Genesee Valley Mining District, Sec. 7, T. 24 N., R. 12 E., 22 miles northwest by wagon road, from Portola. Elevation 6500′–8000′.
Bibliography: Diller, J. S., U. S. Geol. Survey Bull. 260, pages 45-49. Diller, J. S., U. S. Geol. Survey Bull. 363, pages 111-121. U. S. Geol. Survey Topo. sheets, Indian Valley, Genesee, Honey Lake.

The property consists of 400 acres, 200 of which are patented. The patented claims are the Bullion, Bullion Extension, Copper Center, Copper Center Extension, Rob, Rob Extension, Walker, Walker Extension, Valley View and Valley View Extension. The holdings extend from the top of the mountain, south to Little Grizzly Creek, and the main workings are situated on top of the ridge about two miles south of Mt. Ingalls, at an elevation of 8000′. There is good timber on the property.

Walker Brothers have held the property for the last five or six years. The mine has been favorably reported on by numerous engineers and the controlling interest has been purchased for a large sum. The company was pushing development work late in 1918.

The vein has been developed by a 50′ shaft and two 75′ north and south drifts on the vein. A crosscut has also been driven 80′ through the vein from the bottom of the shaft, and there are 300′ of open cuts on the surface.

The vein is a quartz vein 6′ to 8′ in width in an altered zone of a maximum width of 80′ impregnated with sulphides containing copper, silver and gold. The ore of the quartz vein encountered in the shaft at a depth of 15′, contains basic sulphides, bornite, chalcopyrite and tetrahedrite (gray copper). This shaft was inaccessible at time of visit, but the vein walls are said to be diorite. The strike is northwest and the dip is 65° NE. Ore on the dump is reported to run 7% to 12% copper, with unknown amounts of gold and silver.

The mine is equipped with a sawmill, 7 thousand feet capacity, a 15-horsepower boiler and hoist. A new 60-horsepower boiler and engine and a compressor were installed in January, 1914. There are three houses, including a new bunkhouse.

The nearest mines are the Gruss and Mother Lode (Calman).

High grade ore assaying 12% copper was struck in October, 1915, in the 150' drift from the 125' level. Construction of a 4600' aerial tramway, a 100-ton flotation plant, and ore bins was progressing.

Prospecting with diamond drills has proven an ore body for a distance of 200' in the Walker mine. Assays average 7.20% copper, $1.11 gold and 2.7 ounces silver. This is an average of assays taken each five feet for 200' in a hole put down from the 65' level 250'. Further drilling is under way from the 125' level. Reserves are estimated at 20,000 tons. A crosscut at the 125' level averaged 6% to 8% copper and 3 to 4 ounces silver. A second crosscut now in 400' will open the ore 75' below the shaft bottom and 800' in. The Leschen aerial tram, under construction, operates by gravity, and will handle 250 tons in 16 hours.

A new flotation plant was completed in October, 1916. It had a capacity of 85 tons daily but was being enlarged to an ultimate capacity of 200 tons. The plant consists of Blake crusher, Marcy ball mill, Dorr classifier, Callow cells, Dorr thickener and Oliver filter. Daily output in summer of 1918 was said to be 18 tons of concentrate, and a recovery of 95% copper and 75% gold and silver was claimed. Electricity is used for power. Concentrate is shipped to Tooele. Cost per ton for milling during the first half of 1918 was said to be $2 a ton.

Williams Group. Owner, J. D. Williams.

Location: Genesee Valley Mining District, about 3 miles east of Genesee, thence 18 miles west by good automobile road to Keddie (W. P. Ry.).
Bibliography: Diller, J. S., U. S. Geol. Survey Bull. 260, pages 45–49. Diller, J. S., U. S. Geol. Survey Bull. 353, pages 111–121. U. S. Geol. Survey Topo. sheets, Indian Valley, Genesee, Honey Lake. Cal. State Min. Bur. Bull. 50, page 184.

About one-half mile west of Flournoy's the mountain is covered by mining locations, comprising the Williams group. On this mountain the whole outcrop appears to be heavily mineralized by iron and copper in the form of oxides, carbonates and sulphides. So little development work has been performed that no estimate of the worth of the claims can at the present time be made, but it is doubtless the outcrop of an immense mineralized dike.

GOLD—DRIFT MINES.

Antlered Crest Mine. (See Sierra County also.) Owner, Geo. Sanborn, La Porte.

Location: La Porte Mining District; Secs. 15, 14, 11, 12 and 3, T. 21 N., R. 8 E.; Secs. 7 and 6, T. 21 N., R. 9 E.; Sec. 31, T. 22 N., R. 9 E.; 3 miles northwest of La Porte. Elevation around 5000'.
Bibliography: Lindgren, W., U. S. Geol. Survey Prof. Paper 73, page 105. U. S. Geol. Survey, Folio 37, Downieville.

The property consists of the Sanborn, Hart No. 1 and No. 2, Antlered Crest, Fines No. 1 and No. 2, Thunderbolt, Socialist, Independent, Grizzly Bear, Chestnut, Grizzly, Lava Cap and Hardscrabble claims, situated on Moonville Ridge. Patents have been applied for. The total acreage is about 2000 and it covers a length along the channel of five to six miles.

The property was discovered about 1903 by Robinson & McIntosh.

Development work consists of a tunnel 500' long with 300' more to go to strike pay gravel. A lower adit was also being driven in 1913 to cut the lower portion of the Moonville channel.

The pay gravel in the old river channel at Coles is 100' to 300' wide and 3' deep. Bedrock is amphibolite schist and the gravel is 20' deep and capped by andesite. The course of the channel is southwest.

Equipment consists of a blacksmith shop and boarding house. Four men are employed in the mine. South Fork Feather River is available for power.

The same channel has been worked in the old Coles hydraulic mine adjoining.

Australia Mine. (Erickson.) Owner, Peter Erickson,* Spanish Ranch.

Location: Spanish Ranch Mining District; Sec. 1, T. 24 N., R. 8 E., 3 miles northeast of Spanish Ranch, 10 miles northwest of Quincy. Elevation 3800'.
Bibliography: Lindgren, W., U. S. Geol. Survey Prof. Paper 73, pages 98, 99. U. S. Geol. Survey Folio 43, Bidwell Bar.

This property consists of 80 acres, unpatented. It was worked in early days by the present owner, who still does assessment work.

Two tunnels have been driven through slate, one 200' and the other 500' in length.

The country rock is slate and serpentine and the deposit is old channel gravel, part cemented and part free, with some large boulders. There is from 2' to 3' of pay gravel on slate bedrock with an overburden of 80' of gravel; no lava. A little water is encountered.

Adjoining mines are the Bessie and Gopher Hill.

Barker Hill Claim. Owners, Savercool Brothers, Butte Valley; Mrs. C. Lazarovich, Seneca.

Location: Butte Valley Mining District, Sec. 8, T. 26 N., R. 8 E., 1 mile west of Seneca. Elevation 4600'.
Bibliography: U. S. Geol. Survey, Folio 15, Lassen Peak.

Beckwith Consolidated Mine. Owners, Beckwith Consolidated Mining Company; Ed. Kelsey, Beckwith; Wm. Smith, Jamison mine.

Location: Johnsville Mining District, Secs. 20 and 29, T. 22 N., R. 11 E., 9 miles west of Johnsville, 14 miles southwest of Blairsden by good wagon road. Elevation 6000' to 7000'.
Bibliography: Cal. State Min. Bur. Rpts. XII, page 213; XIII, page 288. Lindgren, W., U. S. Geol. Survey Prof. Paper 73, page 111. U. S. Geol. Survey Folio 37, Downieville.

*Since the above was written this property has been sold to the Australia Placer Mining Company, Quincy, California.

The property consists of 480 acres of placer locations, situated on the ridge dividing Jamison and Nelson creeks. It was discovered in 1884 by the Beckwith Company. Assessment work only was being done in 1913.

Development consists of a 400' tunnel, 200' in slate and 200' through lava. The country rock is slate and andesite and the deposit is gravel, of the old river channel on the east rim of Queen channel, which has a southerly course. The length along the channel is two miles, and the gravels are capped by 600' of lava.

Equipment consists of houses and a blacksmith shop.

Adjoining mines are the Queen, Continental Consolidated and Sunnyside.

Bellevue Mining Company. Formerly known as Bootjack, Volante, Edna and Bellevue Consolidation, Kenzie, Louise, Eureka Consolidated, and Last Chance. Owners, Bellevue Mining Company; Sir James Bell, Glasgow, Scotland, and Sir Henry Bell, London, England, partners; R. H. Kingdon, La Porte, staff.

Location: Gibsonville Mining District, Secs. 23, 24, 25, 26, 27, 34, 35 and 36, T. 22 N., R. 9 E., 4½ miles northeast of La Porte, 4½ miles south of Gibsonville and 54 miles from Oroville; all hauling from Oroville. Elevation 4784'.
Bibliography: Lindgren, W., U. S. Geol. Survey Prof. Paper 73, pages 106, 107. U. S. Geol. Survey Folio 37, Downieville.

The Bellevue Mining Company's holdings include the Louise, Feather Fork Gold mine, Chalcedonia, National, Eureka Consolidated, Blackie and Last Chance properties. The total area is 2000 acres with a length along the channel of three miles. It is located across a lava covered ridge on the steep west bank of Slate Creek.

Work was carried on through the 400' Thistle shaft from 1890 to 1896, but when the shaft was flooded in 1901 a lower tunnel was started.

Development work consists of a 5400' tunnel, 8' by 8' in the clear, costing $14.50 per foot, not including overhead charges. Working upstream from the end of tunnel, 3000' were explored, 1300' breasted, and downstream 900' explored and 600' breasted. A new tunnel will start 4811' from the portal of the main tunnel, running N. 27°, 16' W. 3060' to reopen the most northerly workings, which are about a mile south of Thistle shaft. Width of gravel deposit is 1400', prospected by tunnel in line with main tunnel. Area worked is 1700' by 120'. Tailings go into Slate Creek.

The deposit is free Neocene channel gravel, coursing southwest, containing large quartz boulders. Country rock is amphibolite and slate; the bedrock is slate. The gravel and sand is 150' deep, capped with andesite, the pay gravel being 120' wide and 4' deep, including 6" of bedrock. Several faults were encountered; 600' north of the tunnel a vertical fault had a downthrow of about 10'. At a point 1000' north of the first fault, a second occurred, the fault plane dipping northwest 30° with a downthrow of 30' to the north; and 600' further there is a fault striking northwest and dipping 45° SW.

The workings are timbered throughout with round timbers at 40¢, 7' caps 4½¢, lagging 3½¢. Forty men were employed in 1915, six outside; miners getting $3.50 per day, muckers $3.25. Two to six cars of one cubic yard capacity per man per day were produced; $4 to $10 a cubic yard is the total operating cost. Transportation charges are $1.25 per 100 pounds from Marysville. The mine is being worked at the present time, but with a small force only, on account of war conditions.

Bessie Mine. (Murdock or Mendota Hill.) Owner,* W. J. Clinch, Quincy.

> Location: Spanish Ranch Mining District, Sec. 1, T. 24 N., R. 8 E., 3 miles northeast of Spanish Ranch, 10 miles to the southeast by good automobile road to Quincy. Elevation 3800'.

The property contains 80 acres and has a length along the channel of one-fourth mile.

The mine was purchased by the present owner in 1900. Two men were working in 1912 and the spring of 1913.

It is developed by a 375' tunnel, but the area worked is very small, about 30' square, the only equipment being sluice boxes.

The country rock is slate and serpentine, the bedrock slate and the gravels are part cemented and part free with some boulders. The gravel has a depth of 80', of which 2' or 3' next to bedrock pays to drift. Not much water was encountered.

Adjoining mines are the Australia (Erickson) and Gopher Hill.

Blue Gravel Consolidated Mine. Owners, W. H. Spencer, Andrew Hewitt, Hector Forbes, Gibsonville; Lewis Hamm, Paterson, New Jersey.

> Location: La Porte Mining District, Secs. 21 and 22, T. 21 N., R. 8 E., 7 miles west of La Porte, thence 33 miles north to Quincy.
> Bibliography: Lindgren, W., U. S. Geol. Survey Prof. Paper 73, page 105, U. S. Geol. Survey Folio 37, Downieville.

This property, containing 230 acres, was discovered in early days.

The channel courses southwest and is capped with andesite, the gravel being from 12' to 16' in depth. A house and some mine cars are the only equipment.

The Coles hydraulic mine adjoining shows 16' of gravel, 100' of pipe clay, then lava capping. The Cole tunnel, 1500' long, was run 200' through bedrock, the balance through gravel and pipe clay, but it was too high; 15 acres were worked by hydraulicking.

The Antlered Crest mine also adjoins.

---

*Since the above was written this property has been sold to the Australia Placer Mining Company, Quincy, California.

Bull Claim.   Owner, Mrs. Reed, Berkeley.

> Location: Quincy Mining District, Sec. 25, T. 24 N., R. 9 E., 2 miles southeast
> of Quincy. Elevation 4500'.
> Bibliography: U. S. Geol. Survey Folio 37, Downieville.

Assessment work was being done when visited. A shaft 120' in lava and 25' in slate bedrock and a tunnel 140' in bedrock and gravel, striking the east rim of the channel, comprise the development on this property.

Bunker Hill Mine.   Owners, Wm. Metcalf, Jas. O'Brien, La Porte.

> Location: Sawpit Flat Mining District, Secs. 15 and 16, T. 22 N., R. 10 E.,
> Gibsonville is 6 miles southwest, Quincy 30 miles northwest via Nelson
> Point and Gibsonville by good road.
> Bibliography: U. S. Geol. Survey Folio 37, Downieville.

The Bunker Hill mine has worked the most northerly extension of the old Neocene channel that can be traced south from Bunker Hill through Gibsonville to La Porte. From 1875 to 1895 about a mile of this channel was worked under the lava-capped Bunker Hill ridge, the Niagara Consolidated Mining Company doing most of the work.

Bushman Mine.   Owner, Mrs. E. M. Hazzard, Quincy.

> Location: Quincy Mining District, Sec. 34, T. 25 N., R. 9 E., 5 miles north of
> Quincy by good wagon road. Elevation 3700'.
> Bibliography: Cal. State Min. Bur. Reports, XI, page 328; XII, page 214;
> XIII, page 288. U. S. Geol. Survey Folio 37, Downieville.

This property consists of 120 acres of patented ground, characterized by broad ridges and a wide ravine at the head of the creek. It was originally located by Bushman in early days. In 1911 and 1912 it was under bond to Capt. Henry Adams, but it has been idle since March, 1912.

Development consists of a 1200' tunnel, 600' of which was run in early days. A vertical shaft 133' to bedrock was sunk by Adams, passing through alluvial wash composed of slate, decomposed clays, etc. The quantity of gravel worked in early days is not known, but the last company handled very little.

The so-called 'Old Channel' gravel is really an alluvial wash composed of angular fragments of slate and vein quartz that have been derived from the disintegration of the surrounding slates, which are cut by numerous stringers from a few inches up to veins 8' in width, with heavy gouge and well defined walls. The width of pay gravel is 40' with a depth of 18" to 3'. The deposit ranges from 30' to 100' in depth, is free and has no large boulders but contains fragments of slate 1' to 2' in length, lying on slate bedrock. A large amount of water is encountered, too much to handle by pumping, and all of the workings have to be timbered.

The equipment consists of a Fairbanks-Morse gasoline hoist and a gasoline driven American Well Works pump, good houses and barn.

Adjoining mines are the St. Nicolas quartz and the Missing Link and Newton Flat drift mines.

Cameron Mine. Owner, A. N. Cameron, Seneca; bonded to Mr. Gilmer, Utah, July, 1914.

> Location: Butte Valley Mining District, Sec. 16, T. 26 N., R. 8 E., ¼ mile northeast of Seneca, 33 miles from mine by good automobile road to Keddie. Elevation 3300'.
> Bibliography: U. S. Geol. Survey Folio 15, Lassen Peak.

The property consists of 160 acres of unpatented placer locations, covering the channel for one mile. It is situated on the west bank of the North Fork Feather River, on a steep slope.

The claims were located in 1890 by different people and consolidated by Cameron in 1892. The mine is idle at present, but has produced about $38,000.

The development work consists of an 800' main tunnel, which cuts the front rim and a 35' upraise to gravel. Cost per foot $6. The area worked is 1100' by 35' by 6'. The workings are timbered, the timber coming from the property. The gravel is washed, the tailings going into North Fork Feather River, with a loss of some values.

The deposit is of old river channel origin, following approximately the course of the present stream, in general southwest. The gravel contains 'iron stain' and marbles of sulphide carrying $11.30 per ton of gold and fine sulphides, running $900 per ton, and lies on slate bedrock. Pay gravel is 20' to 100' in width, 5' to 6' deep, and 1' of bedrock is mined. It is capped by 500' of lava.

Adjoining are the Scott and Glazier mines.

Carr or **Brown Bear Mine.** Owner, Brown Bear Mining Company, Santa Cruz, care Lawrence Carr.

> Location: Quincy Mining District, Sec. 11, T. 24 N., R. 11 E., 10 miles by trail south of Genesee, 22 miles to Portola by wagon road. Elevation 6000'.
> Bibliography: U. S. Geol. Survey Folio 37, Downieville.

This property is situated on Grizzly Creek, between Spring Garden and Genesee, near the Cascade mine. Drift mining is carried on in the supposed course of the Jura channel.

Cash Entry Group. Owner, H. J. Patterson, Oroville.

> Location: Secs. 23 and 24, T. 25 N., R. 5 E., 6 miles west of Belden. Elevation 5000'.
> Bibliography: U. S. Geol. Survey Folio 15, Lassen Peak.

Claims patented. Very little work has been done in the last few years. Edison mines adjoin.

Channel Peak Mining Company. Owner, Channel Peak Mining Company, 518 Grant Building, Los Angeles; A. J. Gootschalk, Los Angeles; P. E. Daniels.

> Location: Edmanton Mining District, Secs. 13 and 14, T. 24 N., R. 7 E., 5 miles west of Meadow Valley, thence 9 miles east to Quincy, by good automobile road. Elevation 7000'.
> Bibliography: Lindgren, W., U. S. Geol. Survey Prof. Paper 73, pages 98-99; U. S. Geol. Survey Folio 43, Bidwell Bar.

This property consists of 820 acres, part patented, and part locations, situated on the top of Spanish Peak. The company has been working for seven years and has driven 1500' of tunnels in lava and granite without developing any pay gravel.

According to Turner (Bidwell Bar Folio), the gravel is composed of pre-Cretaceous rocks with some pebbles of white quartz. Lindgren says that the extent of the gravels in Spanish Peak is not great. The deposit depression, which contains a little gravel, is covered with 40' of pipe clay, and capped by tuffaceous andesitic breccia.

Claybank Claim. Owners, J. H. Thomas, La Porte, et al.

Location: La Porte Mining District.

Development in the tunnel was progressing and a new shaft was to be sunk on Buckley Ranch channel, a southern extension of Bellevue channel.

Continental Mining Company. Owner, Continental Mining Company, Langdon, North Dakota; president, F. W. McLean, Langdon, North Dakota.

Location: Johnsville Mining District, Secs. 7, 17, 18, 19, 29, 30, 31 and 32, T. 22 N., R. 11 E., Johnsville 9 miles east, Blairsden 14 miles by good automobile road. Elevation 6000'–7000'.
Bibliography: Lindgren, W., U. S. Geol. Survey Prof. Paper 73, page 111; U. S. Geol. Survey Folio 37, Downieville.

The property comprises seven placer claims, namely, Anglo-Saxon Placer No. 1, 150 acres; Nos. 2 to 7, inclusive, 160 acres each. The total area is 1110 acres which cover a length along the channel of two miles, with the Queen property between.

These claims were located in 1903 at the head of the west branch of Nelson Creek by the Continental people, and have been held in conjunction with the Queen, which was under option. This option has now reverted to the original owner and assessment work has not been performed on the claims for 1913. Last work was done in 1904 under B. L. Jones.

The deposit is old river channel gravel, the same as the Queen channel, trending south. It is capped with 600' of lava and its depth is from 20' to 90'. The country rock is slate and andesite.

Adjoining mines are the Queen and Sunnyside.

Deadwood Mine. Owner, Walter Robinson, Meadow Valley.

Location: Edmanton Mining District, Sec. 29, T. 24 N., R. 8 E. Meadow Valley is nearest town, lying 2 miles northeast. Quincy is 12 miles east by good automobile road. Elevation 4700'.
Bibliography: Lindgren, W., U. S. Geol. Survey Prof. Paper 73, pages 98–99; U. S. Geol. Survey Folio 43, Bidwell Bar.

This property was formerly owned by A. Robinson. The ground is patented and no work has been done on the claim for the last five years or more. Deep ravines are characteristic of the surface.

The depth of gravel is 150′ and the country rock is slate and serpentine. It is developed by a 300′ tunnel.

The Edman quartz mine is the nearest adjoining mine.

Dominion Mine. (Salmon Falls.) Owner, A. McMillan, Greenville.

Location: Butte Valley Mining District, Sec. 4, T. 26 N., R. 8 E., 2 miles north of Seneca; Keddie 31 miles southeast, via Greenville, by automobile road. Elevation 4000′.
Bibliography: Cal. State Min. Bur. Reports, XII, page 220; XIII, page 305. U. S. Geol. Survey Folio 15, Lassen Peak.

This property comprises five claims, all placer locations, totaling 100 acres and covering the channel for three-fourths of a mile. It is on the east bank of the North Fork Feather River with a steep rise from the river to a 6000′ ridge.

The property was located by Jack Skinner in 1885 and relocated by McMillan in 1906. Work stopped in July, 1913, when the water gave out, but three men were working up to that time.

Developments consist of a 650′ tunnel, 475′ in bedrock and 175′ across the channel, costing $8.50 per foot. A 40′ shaft extends through sandstone, slate and shale to bedrock.

The country rock is slate and schist, the deposit being in the former old river channel of the North Fork. The course is north, with a depth of 40′ of quartz and greenstone gravel with large boulders. The bedrock is slate. This channel can be traced southward where it crossed the North Fork above Seneca and has been encountered and worked in the Glazier, Cameron, Scott, San Jose, Wisbein and Sunnyside mines. The pay gravel is about 6′ deep above bedrock. Above this occurs a false bedrock of cemented sand upon which is said to lie another 5′ of pay gravel. No large amount of water encountered.

Equipment consists of pumps, houses and blacksmith shop.

Power can be had from North Fork Feather River under a head of 400′, 20″ in season.

The Pliocene, on the same channel, is an adjoining mine.

Dutch Hill Mine. (Dutch Hill No. 11 and Barker Hill No. 10.) Owners, Savercool Brothers, Seneca or Butte Valley.

Location: Butte Valley Mining District, Secs. 8 and 17, T. 26 N., R. 8 E., 2 miles west of Seneca, thence 32 miles by good automobile road to Keddie. Elevation 4690′.
Bibliography: Cal. State Min. Bur. Reports, VIII, page 482; XII, page 215; XIII, page 292. U. S. Geol. Survey Folio 15, Lassen Peak.

This property includes five claims, namely, the Dutch Hill placer, the Barker Hill placer, the Banner placer, the Barker Hill quartz, and the Cummings Hill quartz claim. It is situated on top of a high ridge which lies west of the North Fork Feather River and covers 4400′ along the old channel.

The deposit was worked from the early '50's until 1873 as a drift mine. In that year the small claims were consolidated by C. W. Read of Sacramento and a thirty mile ditch was put in from Lassen Peak at a cost of $500,000. This company is supposed to have taken out about $200,000 from the hydraulic cuts. After hydraulic work was stopped, drifting was again taken up but after $175,000 had been taken from 24,000 cubic yards of gravel, the mine was closed down. A few years later the Savercool Brothers reopened the mine and worked it continuously for twenty years by drifting and hydraulicking, taking out about $200,000, $100,000 from the hydraulic pits and $100,000 by drifting, the gravel running about $10 per yard. It has now been idle for some years.

The deposit is composed of gravels of Neocene age cemented in places and containing some large boulders, on bedrock of slate, sandstone and quartzite, with a basalt capping. The total overburden is 325' of gravel and lava. The course of the channel is north, and the width of pay gravel is 1600'.

There are also two quartz veins on the property. The Barker Hill vein, opened by a tunnel 200' in length, is said to have averaged $4.50 per ton. It strikes northwest and dips 60° southwest. The Cummings Hill quartz vein, discovered in working the Cummings gravel deposit, was never assayed, but prospected well in the pan. It strikes northwest and dips southwest. Below these veins the gravel was very rich in rough quartz gold. The channel has been faulted at two points; the lower fault strikes north and the throw is said to have been 800' vertical, while the upper fault strikes east, with a throw of 200'. The channel between for 2500' is unbroken.

Thirty inches of water are obtained under a head of 90', but steam is used for power. The cost of mining is about 95¢ a cubic yard.

Adjoining properties are the San Jose and Sunnyside.

Edison Claim. Owners, McLaughlin and Enslow, Oroville.
Location: Secs. 23, 25 and 26, T. 25 N., R. 5 E., 6 miles west of Belden (W. P. Ry.). Elevation 5000'.
Bibliography: U. S. Geol. Survey Folio 15, Lassen Peak.

Claims patented.
Cash Entry mine adjoins.

Elizabethtown Flat Mine. Owner, A. E. Leavitt, Quincy.
Location: Quincy Mining District, Sec. 10, T. 24 N., R. 9 E., 2 miles north of Quincy by good automobile road. Elevation 3500'.
Bibliography: U. S. Geol. Survey Folio 37, Downieville.

The property consists of 53 acres, with a length along the channel of 4000'.

A main shaft was sunk 107' deep and from the bottom of it drifts were run north toward Emigrant Hill, a distance of 3000'. The channel was worked for a width of 40'. This gravel is said to have averaged $20 per day per man. The ground was heavy and had to be closely timbered, and a large amount of water was encountered.

The deposit is a free quartz gravel covered with an overburden of gravel, clay and wash, lying on slate bedrock. The depth of the gravel is 75', the pay gravel being 1' to 6' deep. The course of the channel is northwest.

Assessment work only has been done for many years.

Adjoining mines are the Newtown Flat and Bell mines.

Emigrant Hill Mine. Owner, Mrs. Whiteney, Quincy.

> Location: Quincy Mining District, Sec. 2, T. 24 N., R. 9 E., 2 miles north of Quincy by good automobile road. Elevation 3600'.
> Bibliography: Cal. State Min. Bur. Reports, X, page 479; XII, page 219; XIII, page 293. U. S. Geol. Survey Folio 37, Downieville.

This property includes two claims, with an area of 40 acres. It is situated on Besty Gulch, tributary to Spanish Creek.

The mine was worked in early days by hydraulicking, and the ground is said to have been entirely worked out.

The deposit was old channel gravel, some rounded gravel and local wash, on bedrock of slate. There is 180' of gravel to bedrock, free and with very few boulders. The width of pay varied from 20' to 50' and it had a depth of 3' above bedrock.

The deposit was breasted by an 800' tunnel through the hill and an area 800' by 50' worked.

Adjoining mines are the Newtown Flat and Elizabethtown Flat drift mines.

Fairfield Claim. Owner, L. B. Fairfield, Belden.

> Location: Butte Valley Mining District, Sec. 34, T. 26 N., R. 7 E., 8 miles northeast of Belden (W. P. Ry.).
> Bibliography: U. S. Geol. Survey Folio 15, Lassen Peak.

This property is situated on the North Fork Feather River, one mile above the mouth of Mosquito Creek, near Caribou bridge. Said to be old river channel 100' to 150' above the present stream. It is lava-capped and resembles the Seneca channel.

Fordham Drift Mines. Owner, Dr. Leonie H. Fordham, Hotel Stewart, San Francisco.

> Location: Sawpit Flat Mining District, Sec. __, T. __ __, R. __ E., 20 miles from Quincy on the stage road to La Porte.

There are eleven claims, total area 1186 acres. The channel on this property is in line with and said to be the continuation of, the La Porte channel, which was worked for twenty-five years up to 1914 on the south, in the famous Belleview drift mine. The latter property is reported to have made an annual average output of $750,000.

Both rims of the channel are well defined. The bedrock is slate and there is an overburden of from 150' to 1000' of andesitic material. The property has a good stand of timber on the higher ground and the water supply is said to be ample during the entire year. Exact data on the depth and width of channel are not available.

Development work done lately indicates the presence of two channels, one crossing Onion Valley Creek about one-fourth mile west of the mouth of Bird Creek, and the other at the mouth of Cement Creek; some think that the channel forks on this property, one fork continuing south to the Belleview and La Porte, while the other branch connects with the Grass Valley channel.

W. de Varilla, in a report made in January, 1914, advised running a tunnel to strike the pay gravel in the channel at the lower end of the property to take advantage of gravity. He estimated a tunnel 1000′ long costing about $9000, would be required, and that the total cost of opening the property would be about $15,000.

Glazier Mine. Owners, A. McMillan, J. D. Baker, D. McIntyre, Greenville, et al.

> Location: Butte Valley Mining District, Secs. 9 and 16, T. 26 N., R. 8 E., ¼ mile south of Seneca; Keddie is 31 miles southeast via Greenville, by automobile road. Elevation 3300′.
> Bibliography: Cal. State Min. Bur. Reports, VIII, page 482; X, page 495; XIII, page 295. U. S. Geol. Survey Folio 15, Lassen Peak.

The property consists of a patented placer claim, 160 acres in area, following the channel for three-fourths of a mile. It was located by McMillan in 1884, and is situated on the west bank of the North Fork Feather River, with a steep slope to the top of the ridge.

It is developed by a tunnel 1450′ long. There are 800′ of raises, four raises showing gravel lying on a steep rim. The tunnel is now in 125′ beyond the last raise, and is expected to reach the channel in a short time. It passes through Calaveras slates and costs about $10 per foot to drive.

The deposit is composed of old river channel gravels, quartz gravel, free 'ironstone' and boulders, following the course of the present river, 250′ above it. The depth of gravel varies from 18′ to 30′ between slate bedrock and a 500′ capping of gravel and lava.

The only equipment is a blacksmith shop.

Adjoining mines are the Sunnyside, San Jose, and Scott, all working.

Gloria Mundi Claim. Owner, J. Larison, Quincy.

> Location: Quincy Mining District, Sec. 26, T. 24 N., R. 9 E., 2 miles south of Quincy. Elevation 4500′.
> Bibliography: U. S. Geol. Survey Folio 37, Downieville.

Golden Ancient Channel Mining Company. Owner, same address, San Jose, care Mr. Smith.

> Location: Edmanton Mining District, Secs. 2, 3, 10, 11, 14, 15, 22 and 23, T. 23 N., R. 8 E., 15 miles southeast of Quincy; there is a good automobile road from Quincy to Meadow Valley, thence 4 miles south, by trail. Elevation 5000′.
> Bibliography: Lindgren, W., U. S. Geol. Survey Prof. Paper 73, pages 98-99. U. S. Geol. Survey Folio 43, Bidwell Bar.

This company claimed 1460 acres by location, but a good deal of it is vacant, little assessment work having been done. The character of the surface is lava-capped ridges with steep descent to creeks.

The deposit is auriferous gravel probably laid down by Pleistocene streams emptying into Meadow Valley.

The latest work has been done in a shaft which is about 300' deep. Three men were working in July, 1913.

Hope or Valentine Claim. Owner, A. H. Reese, Meadow Valley or Spanish Ranch.

Location: Spanish Ranch Mining District, Sec. 5, T. 24 N., R. 8 E., 5 miles northwest of Spanish Ranch, by trail and wagon road, thence 7 miles to Quincy, by good automobile road. Elevation 4500'.
Bibliography: Lindgren, W., U. S. Geol. Survey Prof. Paper 73, pages 98-99. U. S. Geol. Survey Folio 43, Bidwell Bar.

This property consists of one location. It was owned by Val Roberts until relocated by Reese, who works it alone by sluicing. The deposit is free quartz gravel on slate and serpentine bedrock. The depth of pay gravel is 5'.

Adjoining mines are the Mountain House and Chaparral Hill, both belonging to the Plumas Investment Company.

Indian Placer Mines. (Providence Hill and Miocene.) Owners, J. W. Adams, R. T. Adams, South Bethlehem, Pennsylvania; Jerry Curtiss, superintendent.

Location: Butte Valley Mining District, Sec. 2(?), T. 25 N., R. 8 E., 4 miles north of Twain, 6 miles by horse trail, thence 17 miles to Keddie by way of Greenville and Round Valley. Elevation 4800'.
Bibliography: U. S. Geol. Survey Folio 15, Lassen Peak.

The property consists of three association claims, known as Indian No. 1, No. 2 and No. 3. There are 450 acres covering the channel for a mile and a half. Narrow ridges and steep ravines are surface characteristics.

The placers were first worked in 1852. In 1883 the mine was worked by C. N. Reed. The present company began work in 1911, working with 12 men, 6 on day and 2 on night shift underground.

Development consists of a main (4' x 6') tunnel 1600' long, costing from $5 to $10 per foot, average $8. About 20 acres was hydraulicked. Gravel is now being worked from the main channel near the rim, using sluice boxes 18" square, 150' in length with Hungarian riffles. Sixteen cubic foot cars are used. Tailings are disposed of in Rush Creek. Workings are closely timbered with spruce from the property, costing 2¢ per foot.

The deposit is composed of well-rounded free gravel on bedrock of slates and schists. There is 500' of gravel, sand and pipe clay strata. Fairly large amounts of water are encountered in the channel, which trends east, changing to north. The pay gravel contains boulders of rose quartz, the gold being heavy and well rounded. It varies in width from 40' to 50', and from 6' to 7' in depth above bedrock in the center. In 1883, the gravel is said to have averaged $4.50 per square foot of bedrock.

A 100 acre reservoir and three ditches, namely Providence Hill, four miles, 500' head; Rush Creek, two and one-half miles, 250' head, and Bullfrog, two and one-half miles, 400' head, are owned by the company. Transportation charges are 1½¢ per pound from Keddie via Greenville. The property is just starting to produce.

No adjoining mines are working.

Jumbo Mine. (Little Jumbo.) Owner, Chris. Gunderson, Belden.
    Location: Butte Valley Mining District, Secs. 18 and 19, T. 25 N., R. 7 E., 2 miles north of Belden, by wagon road and trail. Elevation 3500'–4000'.
    Bibliography: U. S. Geol. Survey Folio 15, Lassen Peak.

This property contains 100 acres of placer locations on the ridge between Yellow Creek and North Fork Feather River, covering (supposedly) 2050' along a channel.

It was discovered in 1898 by J. Hall and purchased by the present owner. Total production to date about $1500. Assessment work only being done at present.

Development work consists of a 192' shaft, which has caved. There are two tunnels, 143' through serpentine and slate and 55' in loose gravel. A few years ago a small area of gravel was found that was considered pay for a depth of 6' on bedrock. Area worked was 40' x 40' x 6'.

The country rock is slate and peridotite (serpentine). Blue gravel, part cemented with 'porphyry' and 'serpentine wash,' make up the deposit, which lies on slate bedrock. It is supposed to be an old river channel coursing southwest 1300' above the present North Fork Feather River. It is capped by 150' of basalt. No water was encountered and spring is the only possible time for washing.

Kelly Mine. Owner, John Kelly.
    Location: Sawpit Flat Mining District, Sec. 30, T. 23 N., R. 10 E., 10 miles south of Quincy, in a direct line, but 20 miles by road via Nelson Point. Steep grades to within 1 mile of mine and then horse trail only. Elevation 5700'.
    Bibliography: U. S. Geol. Survey Folio 37, Downieville.

The property comprises four claims, with a total area of 80 acres. It is located at the head of Washington Creek, two miles from North Fork Feather River on a lava-capped ridge. Steep cañons are characteristic; Washington Creek falls 2500' in the two miles to the Feather River.

The property was located by Kelly. Five men were working at time of visit and two large log cabins were being built preparatory to starting extensive development.

The deposit consists of old channel gravel on bedrock of serpentine and is capped with basalt. It is probably an extension of the adjoining Golden Gate-Bainbridge deposit.

King Solomon Mines. Owner, Lucky Strike Mining Company, Bacon Building, Oakland; Joseph McArthur, Quincy, president; H. L. Ross, Bacon Building, Oakland, secretary.

Location: Sawpit Flat Mining District, Secs. 27 and 34, T. 23 N., R. 10 E, 17 miles southeast of Quincy, by good automobile road to Nelson Point, thence 3½ miles by trail on ridge between Dixon and Union creeks. Elevation 5500'.
Bibliography: U. S. Geol. Survey Folio 37, Downieville.

This property embraces six claims, the Lucky Strike, King Solomon, King Solomon No. 1, No. 2, Philadelphia and Philadelphia No. 1. There is a total of 120 acres covering the channel for 6000'. Ridges and steep cañons characterize the surface.

The mine was discovered in 1909 by P. J. Faulkner and purchased from him by the present owners. Three men were at work in 1913 except when stopped for lack of water.

Development consists of opening the rims by shafts and open cuts.

The deposit is supposed to be an extension of the Gibsonville-Hepsidam-Bunker Hill old river channel. It consists of free quartz gravel with few boulders on a bedrock of slate. The channel courses north and is capped by andesite.

There are three houses on the property.

The Bunker Hill mine adjoins.

Lafayette Drift Gravel Mining Company. Incorporated with a capital stock of $50,000. Directors, L. J. Williams, F. J. Shields, F. W. Loehne, Byron Jakes of Marysville and F. J. Savage of Vallejo.

This company was organized in June, 1915, to operate drift mines which have been worked for the last two years by Shields and Williams.

Lava Bed Claim. Owner, M. Light Estate, Quincy.

Location: Spanish Ranch Mining District, Sec. 2, T. 24 N., R. 8 E., 2 miles north of Spanish Ranch by trail, thence 7 miles by good automobile road to Quincy. Elevation 4400'.
Bibliography: Lindgren, W., U. S. Geol. Survey Prof. Paper 73, pages 98-99. U. S. Geol. Survey Folio 43, Bidwell Bar.

The property consists of one claim, not patented. No assessment work has been done for a number of years and the claim has practically been abandoned.

Adjoining mines are the Bean Hill and Pine Lead, owned by the Plumas Investment Company.

Malvern Hill Claim. Owner, Frank Soroti, Susanville.

Location: Butte Valley Mining District, Sec. 18, T. 26 N., R. 8 E., 2 miles west of Seneca, thence 31 miles southeast to Keddie, via Greenville, by good automobile road. Elevation 3550'.
Bibliography: Cal. State Min. Bur. Report XIII, page 300. U. S. Geol. Survey Folio 15, Lassen Peak.

6—46902

Manhattan Mine. (Last Resort.) Owners, Manhattan Gold Mining Company, C. E. Hegard, president; Geo. E. Bangle, Vallejo, secretary; R. V. Whiting. Monadnock Building, San Francisco, home office.

> Location: Quincy Mining District. Secs. 28 and 33, T. 24 N., R. 9 E., 5 miles southwest of Quincy by trail. Elevation 5000'–5500'.
> Bibliography: U. S. Geol. Survey Folio 37, Downieville.

This property comprises 100 acres of patented ground and 350 acres in the following locations: Grand Prize, 110 acres; Bryan and Jubilee, 40 acres each, and Pasadena, 160 acres. It is situated on the divide between Rock and Deer creeks.

The property was discovered by John Tucker in 1856 but was purchased by the present owners in 1890 from Bennett. Two men were working in 1913.

Mine development consists of three tunnels, No. 1, 450'; No. 2, 300', and No. 3 (main tunnel), 700'. There is an air shaft from the main tunnel through 48' of gravel and 40' of lava. Formations passed through are serpentine, slate and quartzite. Very little of the area has been worked.

The deposit is old channel gravels on bedrock of slate and serpentine. They are free, having very little cement, but a good many boulders. The gravel is about 5' in depth and capped by lava.

Equipment consists of a blacksmith shop, bunkhouse for twelve men, and a mile and a quarter of ditch and flume from Rock Creek.

The Gopher Hill mine lies four miles to the north.

Mayflower Mine. (Washington and Mountaineer.) Owners, I. J. Mullen and Brothers, Eclipse; J. M. and W. H. Smith.

> Location: Sawpit Flat Mining District, Secs. 31 and 32, T. 23 N., and Sec. 6. T. 22 N., R. 10 E., 1 mile north of Eclipse, Quincy 24 miles north by good automobile road, via Nelson Point. Elevation 6300'.
> Bibliography: Cal. State Min. Bur. Report XIII, page 301. U. S. Geol. Survey Folio 37, Downieville.

This property comprises two claims, the Mayflower and the Mayflower Extension, with an area of 40 acres. It is on the lava-capped ridge on the west branch of Nelson Creek, with a steep drop to the ravine.

The property was abandoned by the former owners and relocated by the Mullen Brothers. The channel was exposed on the east side of Union Hill by hydraulicking in early days. The four owners are working the property themselves.

Development consists of a 5' x 6' x 800' tunnel. A raise was being put up 35' to strike the channel. A former raise proved the existence of a channel of quartz gravel but cut the rim and the gravel yielded only a few colors.

The deposit is an old lava-capped river channel that has not been tapped. Bedrock is slate and serpentine.

Mill Creek Mine. Owners, Clark Lee, Quincy; W. J. Clinch, Quincy; W. J. Miller, Quincy; under bond in 1913 to J. G. Steel, Quincy.

> Location: Quincy Mining District, Sec. 25, T. 24 N., R. 9 E., 3 miles southeast of Quincy by good wagon road.
> Bibliography: U. S. Geol. Survey Folio 37, Downieville.

This mine contains six claims, a total of 120 acres, covering the channel for 5000'.

It was discovered in the early days and has been held by the present owners for seven years. A large area of the old channel has been worked.

Development consists of a 100' shaft through an overburden of soil and gravel to bedrock and a number of tunnels.

The deposit is old channel gravel, free, with some boulders, on slate bedrock. Considerable water was encountered. Pay gravel ranges from 30' to 40' in width and from 4' to 5' in depth.

There is a hoist and machinery on the property. Water is obtained under 160' head.

The Bull mine adjoins.

J. G. Steel, in extending a bedrock drift tunnel in February, 1916, to develop an ancient channel under Claremont Hill, has shown that there is a large amount of coarse gold on the bedrock.

Morning Star Consolidated Placer Mines Company. (Blue Nose.) Owner, Peter Spaich, Johnsville.

> Location: Sawpit Flat Mining District, Sec. 12, T. 22 N., R. 10 E., 12 miles west of Johnsville, 20 miles west of Blairsden, via Johnsville, by good wagon road; mine is 3 miles from Johnsville road by trail. Elevation 5500'.
> Bibliography: Lindgren, W., U. S. Geol. Survey Prof. Paper 73, page 111; U. S. Geol. Survey Folio 37, Downieville.

There are two groups of claims, the Morning Star and North Star, containing 760 acres, in this property. They lie on the north side of Blue Nose Peak, which rises to an elevation of 7300'.

Development work consists of two tunnels, a crosscut tunnel 250' long passing through 50' of slate and 200' of lava, and a main tunnel driven 1600' from the north end of the Morning Star claim. A winze put down 65' from the end of the crosscut was abandoned on account of water. The main tunnel follows the course of the old channel, 300' being driven through schist; 800' from the portal, a 30' raise encountered gravel and 15' x 12' x 6' was stoped. From this stope another 20' raise was put up and ground 40' x 40' x 60' was stoped, 1000 cars yielding $1300. From the top of the last stope a drift was run 250' to the east, the first 50' in gravel, the rest in country rock and 3600 cubic yards were worked. Another tunnel has been started, 200' below the crosscut tunnel.

The deposit is old river channel gravel, possibly a downthrown portion of Bunker Hill channel. The gravel is composed chiefly of quartz and andesitic tuff on slate bedrock. It is capped with andesite. The bedrock in all workings is said to be pitching west.

Houses and a blacksmith shop make up the equipment.

Assessment work only has been done in the past few years.

Nelson Creek Gravel Company. Owner, C. M. Root, Nelson Point.

Location: Sawpit Flat Mining District, Sec. 22, T. 23 N., R. 10 E., 1 mile south of Nelson Point, thence 11 miles northwest to Quincy by good automobile road. Elevation 4000'.
Bibliography: U. S. Geol. Survey Folio 37, Downieville.

Property consists of one claim of 20 acres. Two men were employed in 1913 drifting on bench gravels and on the high bars above the former workings.

Newtown Consolidated Placer Mines. (Fairstake, Keystone, Missing Link and Newtown Flat.) Owners, H. L., L. F. and D. R. Cate, Sam Leavitt, Quincy; bonded from A. E. Leavitt.

Location: Quincy Mining District, Sec. 34, T. 25 N. and Sec. 3, T. 24 N., R. 9 E., 4 miles north of Quincy by good automobile road. Elevation 3700'.
Bibliography: Lindgren, W., U. S. Geol. Survey Prof. Paper 73, page 111. U. S. Geol. Survey Folio 37, Downieville.

This property comprises 200 acres of locations, with an undetermined length along the channel of approximately 4000'. It is situated in a comparatively wide ravine at the head of several creeks.

All of these claims, worked in early days as hydraulic and drift mines, were consolidated in July, 1913. The new company planned to start a tunnel from Litle Black Hawk Creek, on the Keystone claim, which is expected to cut the Jackass channel 200' in. This tunnel can also be extended to drain the Newtown Flat channel.

Numerous old tunnels have been run, including the Jeffery tunnel, 700' long. There is a new shaft, 90' deep, on the Missing Link.

The deposit consists of water-worn gravel and a few large boulders under a capping of 75' of clay, gravel and debris. It lies on a bedrock of slate, and the channel is supposed to course southwest. A large amount of water was encountered. As exposed in the Emigrant Hill hydraulic workings, pay gravel was 60' to 70' wide and from 3' to 4' above bedrock. About 11½ acres on Fairstake has been worked by hydraulicking.

The Buchanan, Bell and St. Nicolas quartz mines adjoin.

Water is obtained from Plumas ditch.

Newtown Flat Mine. Owner, A. E. Leavitt; now under bond to Cabe Brothers, and consolidated as Newtown Consolidated Placer Mines.

Location: Quincy Mining District, Sec. 3, T. 24 N., R. 9 E., 4 miles north of Quincy by good automobile road. Elevation 3700'.
Bibliography: Lindgren, W., U. S. Geol. Survey Prof. Paper 73, page 111. U. S. Geol. Survey Folio 37, Downieville.

This property consists of one claim, with an area of 430 acres. It is situated on the flat near the heads of Little Black Hawk and Spanish creeks.

The mine has been worked since early days. It was purchased by Leavitt in 1878 and bonded to Cabe Brothers and consolidated under the Newtown Consolidated Placer Mines in July, 1913. Five acres were worked about thirty years ago.

Development consists of a number of shafts, averaging 70' to bedrock through an overburden of clay and gravel. There is also a 500' tunnel. This part of the Newtown channel will be drained, it is said, by the new Cabe tunnel from Little Black Hawk Creek.

The deposit is water-worn quartz gravel, free and with only a few boulders on a bedrock of slate. The course of the channel is northerly. Considerable water was encountered.

The Buchanan placer mine adjoins.

Oliver Claim. Owner, J. H. Thomas, 2610 E. 14th street, Oakland.

> Location: Sawpit Flat Mining District, Sec. 36, T. 23 N., R. 9 E., 4 miles northwest of Eclipse. Quincy is 22 miles north by good automobile road. Elevation 5500'.
> Bibliography: U. S. Geol. Survey Folio 37, Downieville.

Claims patented and no work has been done in the last ten years.

Peter Henry Claim.

> Location: Sawpit Flat Mining District, Sec. 8, T. 23 N., R. 10 E., 2½ miles northwest of Nelson Point. Elevation 4900'.
> Bibliography: U. S. Geol. Survey Folio 37, Downieville.

Formerly owned by E. Remington and Company of Quincy.

Pioneer Mine. Owners, A. McMillan, Greenville; W. P. Boyden.

> Location: Crescent Mills Mining District, Secs. 28 and 33, T. 26 N., R. 9 E., 1 mile northwest of Indian Falls; Keddie 6 miles south of Indian Falls by automobile road. Elevation 4500'.
> Bibliography: Diller, J. S., U. S. Geol. Survey Bull. 353, pages 114–115. Lindgren, W., U. S. Geol. Survey Prof. Paper 73, pages 114–116. U. S. Geol. Survey Topo. sheets, Indian Valley, Taylorsville, Honey Lake.

This property comprises 110 acres of placer locations with a length along the channel of 1000' or more. The channel is in V-shaped ravines 400' above the present creek bed.

The owner located the property in 1900. Assessment work only is being done and as yet not enough has been accomplished to prove the worth of the property.

A 150' tunnel has been driven through bedrock.

The deposit consists of old river channel gravel on bedrock of Calaveras slates and quartzite. The gravel is made up of quartz and greenstone pebbles with big soft boulders. The channel courses north, is 20' in depth and is capped with lava. The pay gravel is from 20' to 60' in width and has a depth of 3' on bedrock.

A cabin and tools make up the equipment.

The Kutzendorf quartz mine adjoins.

Pliocene Mine. Owner, J. S. Bransford, Salt Lake.

Location: Butte Valley Mining District, Secs. 4 and 9, T. 26 N., R. 8 E.,
1 mile north of Seneca; Keddie, 31 miles southeast of Seneca, via Greenville Ry. and automobile road. Elevation 4050'.
Bibliography: U. S. Geol. Survey Folio 15, Lassen Peak.

This property is composed of 120 acres of patented ground with a
length of three-fourths of a mile along the channel. It is situated on
the steep slope of the east bank of the North Fork Feather River.

Bransford has owned the property for the last 20 years. It is
developed by a 1200' tunnel, but no work has been done lately.

The deposit is old river channel gravel of the same channel worked
in the Dominion and Sunnyside mines. The gravel is made of up of
quartz, 'ironstone' and greenstone boulders on a bedrock of slates
and schists. The channel courses north, following the course of the
present stream. It is capped by lava.

The Dominion and Glazier mines adjoin. The Glazier is working
at the present time, running a bedrock tunnel.

Plumas Development Company. (Chips Creek.) Owner, J. D.
Williams, Greenville.

Location: Butte Valley Mining District, Secs. 1, 2 and 12, T. 25 N., R. 5 E.,
8 miles northwest of Belden, by trail. Elevation 6000'.
Bibliography: U. S. Geol. Survey Folio 15, Lassen Peak.

Five claims of 160 acres each make up this property, namely, the
Union, Plumas Union, Morning Star, Chips Creek, and Last Chance.
A length of three miles along the channel is covered.

The present owner located the property in 1893 and applied for
patent in 1906. Two men were doing assessment work in 1913.

Development consists of a tunnel 137' long in bench gravel, No. 2
tunnel, 312' long in lava, and a lower tunnel 180' in length, 230'
below No. 2. There are some old shafts.

The deposit is old river channel gravel, the country rock being
diorite and slate. The channel courses west, and is capped by 800'
of lava.

Equipped with cabins, blacksmith shop and mine cars.

Adjoining mines are the Car, Lott, Motriss, Smith and Heller.

Plumas Investment Company. Owner, Plumas Investment Company, W. P. Hammon, 433 California St., San Francisco.

Location: Spanish Ranch Mining District, 3 to 4 miles by wagon road north of
Spanish Ranch. Elevation 4000'-5100'.

The holdings of the company comprise three groups:

Summit No. 61 claim contains a total area of 380 acres located in
Sec. 34, T. 25 N., R. 8 E. The ground is patented. No work has
been done on this claim in the last five years.

Bolyar No. 86 claim is located in Sec. 2, T. 24 N., R. 8 E. No work
has been done on this claim for a number of years.

Chaparral Hill No. 58, is an unpatented claim of 900 acres covering about 2000′ of channel. It is located mainly in Sec. 30, T. 25 N., R. 8 E. The width of pay channel is said to be 30′. The gravel is composed principally of rounded white quartz with a few larger boulders. Six men were at work in 1913 running a bedrock tunnel which was in 280′. Idle in 1918.

Plumas Klondike Claim.

Location: Sawpit Flat Mining District, Sec. 7, T. 23 N., R. 10 E., 3 miles northwest of Nelson Point. Elevation 4900′.
Bibliography: U. S. Geol. Survey Folio 37, Downieville.

Reported to have been abandoned, no assessment work having been done for a number of years.

Queen Group. (Centennial and Franklin Consolidated.) Owners, B. L. and Mrs. A. E. Jones, Quincy.

Location: Johnsville Mining District, Secs. 19, 20, 29 and 30, T. 22 N., R. 11 E., 9 miles west of Johnsville, 14 miles west of Blairsden, by good automobile road. Elevation 6000′–7000′.
Bibliography: Cal. State Min. Bur. Report XIII, page 295. Lindgren, W., U. S. Geol. Survey Prof. Paper 73, page 111. U. S. Geol. Survey Folio 37, Downieville.

This property embraces the following 670 acres of placer locations: Hampton Placer, 180 acres; Willow Placer, 90 acres; California Placer, 160 acres; Pacific Placer, 160 acres; and Alder Placer, 80 acres. The length of channel covered is said to be two miles. It is situated on the east side of Nelson Creek from the creek to the top of the ridge.

The present owner located the group in 1879. It was under bond to the Continental Mining Company at one time, but reverted to the original owner in 1912. Two men were working in 1913. The production to date has been about $3000.

Development work consists of a 180′ tunnel through gravel and pipe clay which cost about $10 per foot, a 260′ tunnel in slate costing about $5 per foot, and two shafts, 99′ and 80′, both through gravel and pipe clay. The tunnels are timbered. Twenty feet of gravel 600′ x 200′ has been hydraulicked.

The deposit is supposed to be on the old 'Blue Lead River Channel.' It is made up of free quartz gravel with medium-sized boulders on slate bedrock. The channel courses south and is capped with 600′ of lava. A good-sized flow of water was encountered. The pay gravel is 1000′ wide and has a depth of 90′ which it would pay to hydraulic.

There are several buildings and equipment for ground sluicing on the property.

Two ditches, the Porter Ravine ditch, one-half mile long, and the Frazier Creek ditch, one mile long, carry 800″ of water each under a head of 180′.

The Blue Nose mine adjoins.

Ray and Traynor Group. (Northern Placer Mining Company.) Owner, L. N. Prugh, Sacramento.

Location: Johnsville Mining District, Sec. 1, T. 23 N., R. 11 E., 3 miles northeast of Cromberg (W. P. Ry.). Elevation 5000'.
Bibliography: Cal. State Min. Bur. Report XIII, page 302. Lindgren, W., U. S. Geol. Survey Prof. Paper 73, page 111. U. S. Geol. Survey Folio 37, Downieville.

Assessment work done in 1913.

Red Ravine and **Red Rose Claims.** Owner, John Bevilauqua.

Location: Sawpit Flat Mining District, Sec. 25, T. 22 N., R. 10 E., about 10 miles by wagon road west of Johnsville.
Bibliography: U. S. Geol. Survey Folio, Downieville.

Red Slide Mine. Owners, Red Slide Mining Company; E. H. Hart, Penn Mutual Life Insurance Company, San Francisco; M. E. Sanborn, Yuba City.

Location: Sawpit Flat Mining District, Sec. 4, T. 22 N., R. 10 E., 1 mile east of Eclipse, 24 miles by automobile road southeast of Quincy via Nelson Point to Eclipse. Elevation 6500'.
Bibliography: U. S. Geol. Survey Folio 37, Downieville.

This property consists of 50 acres of locations. The surface is characterized by lava-capped ridges and steep cañons. Mine was idle in 1913, only assessment work having been done in the past five years.

Over 3300' of drifts were driven under the lava capping in search of old channels, but practically no gravel was found.

Rio Vista Mining Company. (Consolidation, X-Ray Mining Company.) Owner, Rio Vista Mining Company, 603 California Pacific Building, 105 Montgomery street, San Francisco; James De Fremery, president; H. S. Elliot, secretary.

Location: Sawpit Flat Mining District, Secs. 4, 5, 8, 9, 10, 15, 11 and 12, T. 23 N., R. 10 E. Nelson Point lies next to property, Quincy 11 miles northeast by good automobile road. Elevation 4100'.
Bibliography: U. S. Geol. Survey Folio 37, Downieville.

This property consists of 800 acres of patented ground and 1000 acres held by location. The claims are located for a distance of five miles along the supposed course of an old channel. The steep cañon of the Feather River and also low ridges and wide alluvial deposits along Willow Creek make up the surface.

The property is situated on a forest reserve, and a protest was filed on a portion of the ground which the company abandoned. The river bars and hydraulic mines were worked in early days. Nine men were employed at time of our visit.

Work on the five miles of channel has been almost entirely confined to the Blue Gravel claim, where an incline 250' long was put down and 500' of drifts were run from the bottom of the incline across the course of the channel and three raises were put up. No information is obtainable as to the amount or value of gravel developed. A 200' shaft, sunk through lava, is said to have reached the channel, but the present company has never had it unwatered. A small amount of gravel has been worked by hydraulicking.

The deposit is old river channel lying on a bedrock of slate, supposed to be the former course of the Middle Fork Feather River. The gravel is nearly all free. In places it is capped with andesite and older basalts. A large amount of water was encountered in the workings.

Equipment consists of houses and blacksmith shop.

There are two ditches of two miles each which supply a small amount of water under a head of 100'. Labor costs $3.50 per day and transportation $5 per ton.

English Bar mine adjoins.

Riverdale Mine. Owners, Riverdale Mining Company, A. S. MacDonald, Mills Building, San Francisco.

Location: Quincy Mining District, Sec. 10, T. 24 N., R. 9 E., Quincy is 1 mile south of mine by good automobile road. Elevation 3450'.
Bibliography: Cal. State Min. Bur. Reports, X, page 478; XII, page 215; XIII, page 292. Lindgren, W., U. S. Geol. Survey Prof. Paper 73, page 111. U. S. Geol. Survey Folio 37, Downieville.

This property consists of 119 acres of patented ground, covering a length along the channel of 2500'. It is situated in a flat arm of American Valley.

Discovered in 1852 and bought from W. W. Kellogg by the present owners in 1906.

A number of shafts have been sunk and the channel has been worked for a distance of 500'.

The mine consists of old channel gravels coursing southwest, said to be a continuation of the Emigrant Hill deposit. The gravel is free, being waterworn with angular local wash on bedrock of slate. There is about 140' overburden of sand and gravel. Large amounts of water were encountered, too much to handle, with a depth of pay of 4' above bedrock. It is estimated that there is still 2000' of virgin ground to be worked, the bedrock averaging $4 per square foot. The fact that the water can not be handled is a serious drawback.

The Newtown Flat and the Newtown Consolidated drift mines adjoin.

San Jose Mine. Owner, H. F. Kelly, Seneca.

Location: Butte Valley Mining District, Sec. 17, T. 26 N., R. 8 E., 2 miles south of Seneca. Keddie is 31 miles southeast of Seneca by automobile road via Greenville, daily stage Keddie to Seneca. Elevation 3500'.
Bibliography: U. S. Geol. Survey Folio 15, Lassen Peak.

This property consists of 10 claims, aggregating 200 acres which cover the channel for 2000'. It is situated on the west bank of a steep cañon of the North Fork Feather River, with a rise to the top of the ridge of 800', and there is good timber on the property.

Kelly has owned this ground for the last 20 years. It has been surveyed for patent and bonded to W. W. Robbins, 4115 Helena street, Spokane, Washington. Good pay was opened up in February, 1914, and four men were working then.

Development consists of a 5' x 6' tunnel, 1000' long, through quartzite and slate which cost $10 per foot. The last raise put up through 20' of slates struck a small amount of gravel and another raise to be put up is expected to encounter the center of the main channel. A small area of gravel has been worked by an old branch from the main tunnel. Hand drilling methods are used in working.

The deposit consists of old river channel gravel with a northerly course, composed of quartz, 'ironstone' and greenstone boulders. The bedrock is slate and quartzite. There is a gravel overburden and different flows of lava, totaling 600'. A quartz ledge was encountered in a former bedrock tunnel carrying gold and chalcopyrite and also some carbonates. No work was done on this vein. Quartz veins have also been encountered in the present tunnel, but no assays have been taken. A medium amount of water was encountered.

The Sunnyside and Western mines to the south and the Scott, Cameron and Glazier to the north are all on the same channel.

Fred Scott Mine. Owner, Chas. Emerson, Susanville. Leased to C. H. Grill, Seneca.

> Location: Butte Valley Mining District, Sec. 17, T. 26 N., R. 8 E., 1 mile west of Seneca; Keddie is 31 miles southeast of Seneca via Greenville, by automobile road.
> Bibliography: U. S. Geol. Survey Folio 15, Lassen Peak.

This property consists of 120 acres, unpatented, situated on the west bank of the North Fork Feather River, with a rise from the river to the top of the ridge of 600'. Good timber stands on the property.

The mine was under lease, when visited, to C. H. Grill of Seneca, and four men were working.

It is developed by an 800' tunnel passing through slates.

The deposit consists of old river channel gravel, trending northerly, a former course of the North Fork Feather River. The gravel is free and contains quartz, ironstone and greenstone on a bedrock of slates, with 600' of lava capping. Pay gravel runs about 100' in width and 3' to 4' in depth. Considerable water was encountered.

Equipment consists of a blacksmith shop.

The Cameron and San Jose mines adjoin.

Sunnyside Mine. Owner, Plumas Gold Mining Company, Boston, Massachusetts; R. N. Costar, lessee.

> Location: Butte Valley Mining District, Sec. 19, T. 26 N., R. 8 E., 3 miles south of Seneca by wagon road, thence 31 miles southeast via Greenville to Keddie by good automobile road. Elevation 3500'.
> Bibliography: Cal. State Min. Bur. Report XIII, page 306. U. S. Geol. Survey Folio 15, Lassen Peak.

This property consists of 160 acres of patented ground, covering a length along the channel of three-fourths of a mile. It is situated on the west bank of the North Fork Feather River. The tunnel and channel are 200' above the bed of the present river. Fair timber stands on the property.

The mine is developed by an 800' tunnel with a 30' to 45' raise at the end of the channel. A large but unknown amount of gravel has been worked from the east rim in old workings. In the old workings all of the tunnels were too high to bottom the channel, and drifts were run along the east rim only. From these drifts winzes were put down and the ground breasted regardless of the large amount of water that had to be pumped. The gravel stands fairly well. It is breasted and the large boulders separated by a grizzly in the chutes, then trammed 800' to the washhouse in one-ton cars. The old workings followed the east rim for half a mile, and the winzes that were sunk as deep as water would permit never reached the bottom of the channel. The Peterson crosscut 200' across the channel was 25' above the bottom, and a shaft put down 18' failed to reach bedrock. The center of the channel and the west rim are therefore supposed to be virgin ground. The present workings were also run too high. The main crosscut will have to be continued, and another raise put up to reach the bottom of the channel.

The deposit is made up of old river channel gravel on a bedrock of slate with stringers of quartz in it. The channel courses N. 17° E. and has an overburden of 600' of gravel and lava. A large amount of water was encountered. Width of pay gravel is 100', depth 3' to 4', above bedrock. Most of the gold occurs on bedrock. The production in the two years of 1913 and 1914 has been $20,000. The total production to 1913 is said to have been $150,000.

A small amount of water under 300' head is available. The cost of running the tunnel averaged $10 per foot, and the cost of working the gravel is about $1 per ton, assuming four cars are produced per man per day. Three men have been employed for the last three years during the summer season, and two men will work all winter doing development work.

There is a blacksmith shop and equipment on the property.

The Dutch Hill, Western and San Jose mines adjoin, the two former being idle.

Swiss Mine. Owner, B. Pizzoni, Seneca.

Location: Butte Valley Mining District, Sec. 18, T. 26 N., R. 8 E., 2 miles west of Seneca, thence 31 miles southeast by good automobile road via Greenville to Keddie. Elevation 4500'.
Bibliography: Cal. State Min. Bur. Report XIII, page 307. U. S. Geol. Survey Folio 15, Lassen Peak.

This property consists of 105 acres of placer ground and two quartz claims. There is a total area of 145 acres situated on the flat across the ridge that forms the west bank of the river back of Seneca, and it contains good timber.

The deposit consists of surface placers and old channel, supposed to be a southern extension of Dutch Hill. The bedrock is slate, and the gravel is lava-capped. A 30′ shaft was sunk in ore on a well-defined quartz vein in slates, developed on the property. A large dump from the shaft is said to average $8 per ton and is good-looking oxidized quartz. The vein strikes a little west of north and dips 60° W. The gulch in which the shaft is located cuts across the vein and is said to have been very rich below the vein. This ledge was cut 115′ below the outcrop by a bedrock tunnel and is reported to have been 12′ to 29′ in width, carrying a heavy percentage of auriferous pyrite and some free gold.

The ground has been owned by Pizzoni for the last 20 years. The surface placers are said to have been rich.

Assessment work only was being done in 1914. Tunnels aggregating 5000′ in length have been run, but all are believed to have been too high. A large amount of pay gravel was developed on a bench where breasts are said to have been 100′ in width, but no attempt is being made to open up the deep channel.

Adjoining mines are the Dutch Hill, to the north, and the Sunnyside to the south, the latter in operation.

West Elizabeth Mining Company. (Miller, Pittsburg, Pennsylvania, and Duquesne.) Owner, West Elizabeth Mining Company, Johnsville; R. R. Gumbert, Johnsville, manager.

> Location: Johnsville Mining District, Sec. 32, T. 22 N. and Sec. 5, T. 23 N., R. 11 E.; 6 miles northwest of Johnsville by trail, 5 miles southwest of Cromberg (W. P. Ry.) by trail. Elevation 5500′.
> Bibliography: Lindgren, W., U. S. Geol. Survey Prof. Paper 73, page 111. U. S. Geol. Survey Folio 37, Downieville.

This property contains 510 acres of placer locations, as follows: Pittsburg, 160 acres; Pennsylvania, 160 acres; Miller, 130 acres; Duquesne, 60 acres. It is situated on the divide between the east branch of Nelson Creek and Poplar Creek, and supports a good stand of timber.

The claims have been held by the present owners for over 15 years, but very little work has been done in that time.

The Bigelow quartz mine adjoins.

Western Mine. (Consolidation Alum Cove.) Owners, A. N. Cameron, Seneca; B. Pizzoni, Seneca.

> Location: Butte Valley Mining District, Sec. 17, T. 26 N., R. 8 E.; 1 mile south of Seneca, thence 31 miles southeast via Greenville to Keddie by good automobile road. Elevation 3300′.
> Bibliography: U. S. Geol. Survey Folio 15, Lassen Peak.

This property embraces 80 acres of placer locations covering from
3000′ to 4000′ of channel. It is situated on the west bank of North
Fork Feather River on a steep slope to the top of the ridge. The
timber on the property is good.

It is one of the oldest claims on the river, having been located by
Nick Meadows in 1884. Bought by the present owners in 1900. It
is idle, assessment work only being done.

The deposit is made up of old river channel gravels with about the
same southwest course as the present river. It contains ironstone
and fine gravel with large boulders, and lies on a soft slate bedrock.
Considerable water was encountered. There is 550′ of basalt capping.

The ground has been developed by a 200′ tunnel through slates into
rim gravel, but not reaching the main channel. The gravel worked
was about 15′ in width for 200′ to 300′ along the east rim.

One cabin on the property.

Adjoining mines are the Sunnyside to the south and the San Jose
to the north.

Wilson Claim. Owner, C. A. Wilson, Belden.

> Location: Butte Valley Mining District; mine is situated on North Fork
> Feather River, between Belden and Seneca, exact location not known.
> Bibliography: U. S. Geol. Survey Folio 15, Lassen Peak.

GOLD—HYDRAULIC MINES.

Blue Gravel Claim. Owner, Rio Vista Mining Company.

> Location: Sawpit Flat Mining District, Sec. 10, T. 23 N., R. 10 E., about 10
> miles by automobile road southeast of Quincy.
> Bibliography: U. S. Geol. Survey Folio 37, Downieville.

Bonnie. (See under Placer.)

Boycott. (See under Placer.)

Brown Bear Mine. (Jackson Mine.) Owners, C. W. Green, Cedarville, Modoc County; Jackson heirs, Cedarville, Modoc County.

> Location: Johnsville Mining District, Sec. 1, T. 21 N., R. 12 E., 2 miles south
> of Clio by wagon road. Elevation 5200′ to 5500′.
> Bibliography: Lindgren, W., U. S. Geol. Survey Prof. Paper 73, page 111.
> U. S. Geol. Survey Folio 37, Downieville.

The property consists of eight patented claims, with a length along
the channel of one mile. It is situated on a high ridge southeast of
Mohawk Valley, and contains 160 acres.

The mine was discovered by A. W. Jackson in 1872, and since that
time has been worked by the Jackson family. Developed by placering for a width of 40′ and a length of about a mile. Hydraulicking
had been done for a width of 300′, when stopped by the anti-
debris law.

The gravels are free and angular, lying on bedrock of slate,
quartzite, etc., near the southern border of Mohawk Lake beds. Gold

in the surface placers of the present creeks was probably derived from erosion of the Haskel Peak Neocene river gravels. The course of the channel is N. 20° E., and the width of pay gravel is 300', with a depth of 18'.

Eleven hundred inches of water under a head of 120' is obtained from Mohawk Creek.

The nearest adjoining mine is the Agate Hydraulic mine in Sierra County.

Cascade Mine. (Cascade Mining Company.) Owner, Mrs. Mary Turner, Vallejo, California.

> Location: Quincy Mining District, Secs. 11 and 14, T. 24 N., R. 11 E., 10 miles by trail south of Genesee; Portola 22 miles by wagon road. Elevation 6000'.
> Bibliography: Cal. State Min. Bur. Repts. XIII, page 290. U. S. Geol. Survey Folio 37, Downieville.

The Cascade consists of 800 acres of placer locations, developed by a 200' tunnel in the rim which has not struck pay gravel.

The country rock is slate and greenstone and the gravel is medium sized, round wash, with the bottom cemented, lying on granite bedrock. There is a capping of lava. Hydraulicking, when stopped by the debris law, left a bank of gravel 100' to 200' high.

Castle Rock Mine. Owner, Ed. Lindsay, Nelson Point.

> Location: Sawpit Flat Mining District, Sec. 10, T. 23 N., R. 10 E., 1 mile north of Nelson Point, about 10 miles southeast of Quincy by automobile road. Elevation 4800'.

Assessment work is being done by ground sluicing, the owner working alone.

Cleveland Claim. Owner, L. Soburo, Johnsville.

> Location: Johnsville Mining District, Sec. 3, T. 22 N., R. 11 E., 4 miles northeast of Johnsville. Elevation 6000'.
> Bibliography: Lindgren, W., U. S. Geol. Survey Prof. Paper 73, page 111. U. S. Geol. Survey Folio 37, Downieville.

This property consists of 120 acres of placer locations. Assessment work was done in 1913.

Emigrant Hill. (See under Drift Mines.)

Fordham Group. Owner, Dr. Leonie Fordham, Hotel Stewart, San Francisco.

> Location: Gibsonville District, at the head of Slate Creek, between Whiskey Creek diggings and North America mine, a mile and a half from Gibsonville by good road. Elevation 5000' to 6000'.

The property consists of Star and Vermont claims (once known as the New York and Ophir), the Hepsi tailing claim, P. S. damsite and New York damsite. All of the Star claim is on the northeast end of the Gibsonville channel, which is a branch of La Porte channel. Part of the channel on this claim is lava-capped and part can be hydraulicked. The Vermont claim is cut in two by Whiskey Creek.

It is hydraulic ground. The channel was 800' wide on the adjoining North America.

Application for permission to build a basket dam on the New York damsite has been made and the site approved. The site chosen is on the north branch of Slate Creek. About 1000 miner's inches of water are said to be available. There is a storage lake on top of the high crest, a large reservoir, and a complete system of ditches.

These claims were once held in common ownership with the higher ground on the North America. The tunnel driven to work the higher ground was too high to work these lower claims. It is said that ownership changed before the North America was worked out and the company had no occasion to undertake mining the lower ground. The new owners, known locally as the 'San Jose Company,' began hydraulicking the Vermont claim in violation of law, and were stopped by injunction. They failed to pay their men, who next year, through their foreman, jumped the claims when the company failed to do assessment work.

One rim of the channel has been reached by prospect shafts and an open cut which was driven from the northern branch of Slate Creek. The bedrock was found to be pitching away, dipping one foot in five, and the rim gravel was said to carry $1.80 a yard. It has been estimated that it will require 300' of drift to strike the bottom of the channel. The Hepsidam channel crosses the serpentine belt, which is held to make probable the occurrence of platinum.

There is a camp with accommodations for 20 men, at an elevation over 6000'.

Forest Grove. (See under Placer Mines.)

Golden Gate Mine. (Bainbridge.) Owner, A. W. Robinson, La Porte.

> Location: Sawpit Flat Mining District, Sec. 30, T. 23 N., R. 10 E. Quincy is 20 miles northwest of mine by good road via Nelson Point. Elevation 6000'.
> Bibliography: U. S. Geol. Survey Folio 37, Downieville.

This property is not patented, but assessment work is being done. It is situated on a lava-capped ridge, and after abandonment by the Bainbridge Company was relocated by Robinson.

The deposit consists of quartz gravel, lava-gravel and boulders, on a bedrock of slate and serpentine, capped with basalt.

The Kelly mine lies on the same channel to the west.

Gold Mountain Hydraulic and Dredging Company. (Hydraulic King.) Owner, same; G. W. Fagg, manager, 201 Grant Building, Los Angeles.

> Location: Edmanton Mining District, Secs. 14 and 15, T. 23 N., R. 7 E., 3 miles south of Bucks Ranch, thence 20 miles by good automobile road to Quincy. Elevation 5400'.
> Bibliography: Lindgren, W., U. S. Geol. Survey Prof. Paper 73, pages 98–99. U. S. Geol. Survey Folio 43, Bidwell Bar.

Holdings consist of 280 acres in section 14 and 160 acres in section 15, on the gentle east slope of Grizzly Hill.

The property was discovered by Lavasse in 1854 and is said to have been worked steadily on a small scale. The Hydraulic King Company worked it from 1907 to 1909, and the present company since that date.

The deposit consists of a large amount of silt and sand and a small amount of quartz on a slate and schist bedrock. The course of the channel is southeast, the depth of the gravel being from 6' to 24'. It is all said to carry gold.

Equipment consists of six houses, blacksmith shop, barns and a sawmill of 8000 feet capacity. The water installation consists of two giants working with 300" under a head of 120'. There are 7000' of 24" pipe and two ditches, three miles and one and a half miles in length.

The ground is worked by two giants, sluices 3' wide and 1500' in length and 1000' of tail races. Eight acres have been worked. Tailings are caught by a 20' concrete dam on Willow Creek.

There were 18 men (two shifts), employed at wages of from $2.25 to $3 per day and board, in 1914. Capacity is 1000 yards per day at a cost of 15¢ per yard. In 1912 the production was 7500 yards valued at $4800.

The New York, in section 15, is the nearest adjoining mine.

Lott Group. Owner, C. F. Lott, Oroville.

> Location: Sec. 20, T. 25 N., R. 6 E., 5 miles west of Belden. Elevation 5000'.
> Bibliography: U. S. Geol. Survey Folio 15, Lassen Peak.

Claims are patented. No work has been done for a number of years.

Maples Flat Consolidated Placer Mine. (Kanaka Flat Mine.) Owner, Parry R. Cole, Oxnard, Ventura County.

> Location: Spanish Ranch Mining District, Sec. 31, T. 25 N., R. 8 E., 6 miles northwest of Spanish Ranch, by trail and wagon road, 13 miles northwest of Quincy, via Spanish Ranch; good automobile road from Quincy to Spanish Ranch. Elevation 4800'.
> Bibliography: Cal. State Mining Rpt. XIII, page 298. U. S. Geol. Survey, W. Lindgren, Prof. Paper 73, pages 98–99. U. S. Geol. Survey Folio 43, Bidwell Bar.

This property consists of 1257 acres, for which patent has been asked. It was worked in early days by Wampler and Jack, and purchased in 1912 by the present owner. Some work was done in 1913.

The pay is in a shallow deposit of free gravel, 1' to 3' in depth. The country rock is slate, serpentine and schists.

Mountain House and Chapparal Hill are adjoining mines.

Plumas Imperial Group. (Including Hungarian Hill and Orr mines.) Owner, Towle Brothers Lumber Company.

Location: Spanish Ranch Mining District, Secs. 17, 18 and 19, T. 24 N., R. 9 E., 4 miles west of Quincy by good automobile road. Elevation 3800'–4700'.
Bibliography: Cal. State Min. Bur. Rpts. X, page 479; XII, page 219; XIII, pages 298–303. Lindgren, W., U. S. Geol. Survey Prof. Paper 73, pages 98–99. U. S. Geol. Survey Folio 43, Bidwell Bar.

This property was purchased by the present owners for the timber on the land and no attempt is being made to work the mines. Very little work has been done on it during the last ten years.

Plumas Investment Company. Owner, Plumas Investment Company, W. P. Hammon, 433 California Street, San Francisco.

Location: Spanish Ranch Mining District. Elevation 3800'–4700'.

The company's holdings comprise four groups: Gopher Hill No. 90 located one mile east of Spanish Ranch in Sec. 12, T. 24 N., R. 8 E.; Bean Hill No. 85 located five miles northwest of Spanish Ranch in Sec. 3, T. 24 N., R. 8 E.; Red Hill No. 60 containing forty acres located four miles northwest of Spanish Ranch in Sec. 33, T. 25 N., R. 8 E., and the Toland Langdon No. 253 situated two miles northwest of Spanish Ranch in Secs. 9 and 10, T. 24 N., R. 8 E. The gravel on the Toland Langdon No. 253 is said to be 20' thick. All four groups have been idle for a number of years.

Queen Group. (See under Drift.)

Scad Point Claim. Owner, Walter Robinson, Meadow Valley.

Location: Edmanton Mining District, Sec. 28, T. 24 N., R. 8 E., 4 miles southwest of Meadow Valley, Quincy 13 miles by good automobile road. Elevation 3550'.
Bibliography: Lindgren, W., U. S. Geol. Survey Prof. Paper 73, pages 98–99. U. S. Geol. Survey Folio 43, Bidwell Bar.

This property is patented and very little work has been done on it in the last fifteen years.

Edman quartz mine adjoins.

Smith Mine. (Holloway.) Owner, J. Smith, Eclipse, via Quincy.

Location: Sawpit Flat Mining District, Sec. 11, T. 22 N., R. 10 E., 3 miles southeast of Eclipse; Quincy 28 miles northwest by automobile road, steep grade to Eclipse. Elevation 5000'.
Bibliography: Cal. State Min. Bur. Rpt. XIII, page 297. U. S. Geol. Survey Folio 37, Downieville.

This mine was worked as a hydraulic mine on the west side of Blue Nose Peak where the channel appears to pass under the lava capping of Blue Nose. Steep cañons are characteristic. The deposit consists of white quartz gravel, and, while it lies at an elevation 500' below the channel at the Bunker Hill mine, Turner (Downieville Folio) considers that it may be a downthrown portion of the Gibsonville-Bunker Hill channel.

The Bunker Hill is the nearest placer and the Oro Fino the nearest quartz mine.

7—46902

Star of Plumas Group. Owner, Star of Plumas Mining Company, care Victor Craig, Berkeley, California.

> Location: Edmanton Mining District, Sec. 8, T. 23 N., R. 8 E., 4 miles east of Bucks Ranch by trail, thence 17 miles northeast to Quincy by good automobile road. Elevation 5000'.
> Bibliography: Lindgren, W., U. S. Geol. Survey Prof. Paper 73, pages 98-99. U. S. Geol. Survey Folio 43, Bidwell Bar.

Situated on the headwaters of Bear Creek. Assessment work is being done on the claims.

Taylor Diggins Group. Owner, California Gold Mining and Investment Company, Chicago, Illinois.

> Location: Genesee Valley Mining District, Sec. 29, T. 26 N., R. 11 E., 3 miles north of Genesee, thence 18 miles west, by good automobile road, to Keddie. Elevation 5500'.
> Bibliography: Cal. State Min. Bur. Rpts. XIII, page 289. Diller, J. S., U. S. Geol. Survey Bull. 260, pages 45-49. Diller, J. S., U. S. Geol. Survey Bull. 253, pages 111, 121. U. S. Geol. Survey Topo. sheets, Indian Valley, Genesee, Honey Lake.

This property embraces 200 acres of patented land containing good timber. It has not been worked for a number of years.

GOLD—LODE MINES.

Alhambra Mine. Owners, M. McIntosh, Quincy; Jerry Curtiss, Twain, care Indian Mining Company.

> Location: La Porte Mining District, Sec. 15, T. 22 N., R. 8 E., 8 miles northwest of La Porte. Elevation 5500'.
> Bibliography: U. S. Geol. Survey Folio 37, Downieville.

The Alhambra mine embraces the Alhambra and Alhambra Extension locations. Patents have been applied for and final papers were expected by January 1, 1914. The total area, which cover 3000' along the lode, is 40 acres.

The mine is situated near the headwaters of the South Branch of the Middle Fork Feather River on the southwest slope of Franklin Hill. Deep cañons are characteristic of the surface.

It was located in 1855, but assessment work only has been done in late years. The development work consists of an 85' vertical shaft in diorite, and a tunnel driven on the vein, whose length is unknown on account of caving. At the 60' level in the shaft a crosscut 12' long through diorite shows the vein to be 14' wide and at the 80' level another crosscut shows the vein to be 16' wide. There is one small stope on the latter level, and an open cut on the vein 100' long and 20' deep.

The strike of the Alhambra vein is east, and the dip vertical. The south wall is diorite, the north wall 'porphyry' and the filling is solid quartz, varying in width from 6' to 8', with gouge on both walls. This quartz carries free gold, galena, pyrite, and chalcopyrite in small amounts. On the 80' level three samples taken across 16' of quartz assayed $9, but the ore is said to average only $5.

The nearest mine is the Butte Bar, on the Middle Fork Feather River.

Altoona Mine. Owners, S. Firmstone, Greenville; J. Murray, J. Richards.

Location: Crescent Mills Mining District, Secs. 14 and 23, T. 26 N., R. 9 E., 20 miles via Greenville by good automobile road to Keddie, 2 miles southeast of Greenville. Elevation 5000'.
Bibliography: Cal. State Min. Bur. Reports, X, page 472; XII, page 213. Diller, J. S., U. S. Geol. Survey Bull. 353, pages 114, 115. Lindgren, W., U. S. Geol. Survey Prof. Paper 73, pages 114, 116. U. S. Geol. Survey Topo. sheets Indian Valley, Taylorsville, Honey Lake.

The mine contains one patented claim, the Altoona, extending 1500' along the vein and 500' wide. It is situated on the flat top of the ridge between Crescent Mills and North Cañon, near the Round Valley Reservoir, and is 16 acres in area.

The mine was discovered by F. Emmons in 1870 and was bought by the present owners from the Emmons Estate in 1906. In 1912 it was bonded to A. N. Fauntenack of Seattle, and 12 to 14 men were employed, but during 1913 it was idle.

The greatest depth reached on the vein is by a winze, 100' below the tunnel level, or 230' below the outcrop, and the length driven on the vein is 800'. There is also a crosscut 170' to the south. A stope 30' x 5' x 150' extends from the adit level to the surface.

The wall rock is 'porphyry,' probably decomposed meta-rhyolite or andesite, and the vein is a quartz-filled fissure and stringers, with an easterly strike and a dip of 45° to 60° S. Its average width is 5', the maximum 16', and the length of the pay shoot is 306', with a width of 5'. The vein filling is iron-stained quartz containing free gold. In the upper workings the ore is oxidized, but at the bottom of the winze sulphides are found in places. It is said to plate $5 to $7 per ton in free gold. Both the country rock and vein are faulted.

Equipment consists of one Fairbanks-Morse 32-horsepower crude oil engine, blacksmith shop, four new cabins and a Fairbanks 16-horsepower distillate hoist. The mill building is equipped with a Denver roller mill, patent electrical amalgamator, rock breaker and Card concentrating table.

Adjoining mines are the Cherokee and Green Mountain, both of which are idle.

Antelope Mine. Owner, C. M. Johnston, Mohawk.

Location: Johnsville Mining District. Sec. 28(?), T. 22 N., R. 13 E., 2 miles east of Clio. Elevation 4500'-5000'.
Bibliography: Lindgren, W., U. S. Geol. Survey Prof. Paper 73, page 111. U. S. Geol. Survey Folio 37, Downieville.

This property consists of eight claims, with a total area of 160 acres. It is situated in the low hills on the east side of Mohawk Valley.

The property was worked in early days, but was bought by the present owner in 1902.

There are three veins in the lode—the Poorman, 3000'; Antelope, 3000'; and Hawkeye, 6000'. The Poorman vein has been developed by a 140' tunnel with a winze from the tunnel 110' deep and a drift 20' in length along the vein on the tunnel level. The Antelope vein is developed by a 65' shaft, and short drifts. A crosscut now being driven will cut the vein 310' below the surface. The Hawkeye is opened by a 70' shaft and a 200' tunnel driven on the vein.

Wall rock is quartzite in the Poorman and Antelope and a limestone foot-wall and granodiorite hanging wall in the Hawkeye. The Poorman lode is composed of stringers of quartz and country rock containing free gold and no sulphides. The vein is 14' wide, with 2" stringers, and strikes north with a vertical dip. The Antelope vein is 5' wide and is composed of silicious oxidized ore containing free gold, malachite and azurite. It dips 30° E. with a northeast strike. The Hawkeye contains lenticular bodies of chalcopyrite and native copper in a zone 75' to 100' wide, striking northeast and dipping 50° E. The ore runs $14 to $21 in the Antelope, and $5 to $40 in copper, gold and silver in the Hawkeye. This mine is undoubtedly on the southern extension of the Genesee-Walker copper belt, which seems to follow along the contact of the granodiorite wherever the overlying basalt and andesite have been eroded.

Equipment consists of a cabin and blacksmith shop.

The Bullion is an adjoining mine on which assessment work was done in 1913.

Arcadian Mine. Owner, D. McIntyre, Greenville. Bonded to an English company in August, 1914.

> Location: Greenville Mining District. Secs. 10 and 15, T. 26 N., R. 9 E., 1 mile south of Greenville; Keddie 16 miles south by good automobile road. Elevation 3900'.
> Bibliography: Cal. State Min. Bur. Rept. XIII, page 305. Diller, J. S., U. S. Geol. Survey Bull. 353, pages 114, 115. Lindgren, W., U. S. Geol. Survey Prof. Paper 73, pages 114, 116. U. S. Geol. Survey Topo. sheets Indian Valley, Taylorsville, Honey Lake.

The property consists of five claims, including the Arcadian, Antelope, Hongkong, Sunset and Sunrise, the last three being fractions. It contains 80 acres with a length of 3000' along the lode, and is situated on the steep slope of the ridge south of Greenville.

The mine has been owned for over 20 years by the present owner.

There are three veins in the lode, the Phoenix, Antelope and Savage. Development work on the Phoenix consists of a 3000' crosscut tunnel. On the Antelope a depth of 75' has been reached on the vein, and on the Savage a depth of 300' has been reached and 300' driven on the vein. The Savage vein has been stoped from

Taylor tunnel for a length of 600′ from tunnel to surface, a distance of 60′.

The country rock is granodiorite and meta-rhyolite, and the hanging and foot-walls are granite and porphry. The ore is free milling and oxidized in the upper level; concentrates, 1½% sulphides, are worth $185 per ton. The Phoenix vein is quartz and porphyry, with quartz stringers with a northeast strike and 40° S. dip. The Antelope and Savage veins are of quartz, the former striking east and dipping 75° S., the latter striking north and dipping 60° W.

Equipment consists of a 10-stamp mill, 750-pound stamps, in good condition, using water from Round Valley Reservoir under 325′ head.

Adjoining mines are the New York, which is idle, and the Droge, across North Cañon, which is working 25 men.

Austrian Syndicate Mine. Owners, J. S. Wardell, J. Barcel, San Francisco; Dr. Ivanovich, Petaluma, R.F.D. No. 3.

Location: Genesee Valley Mining District, Secs. 23 and 24, T. 25 N., R. 11 E., 3 miles southeast of Genesee and 21 miles via Genesee to Keddie by daily automobile stage. Elevation 5500′.
Bibliography: Diller, J. S., U. S. Geol. Survey Bull. 353, pages 111–121. U. S. Geol. Survey Topo. sheets Indian Valley, Genesee and Honey Lake.

The property consists of six claims, all said to be patented. It comprises 120 acres with a length along the lode of 5000′.

This mine has been worked at intervals for 16 years, but is idle at present. Fifty thousand dollars is said to have been taken from the shoot worked in early days in the Fissure vein (Queen of Genesee ledge), from ore reported to have averaged $20 in gold and to have carried a considerable amount of copper.

The old works, consisting of a 60′ shaft and numerous tunnels, 100′ to 300′ in length, are caved, but some work done by the Austrian Syndicate is in good condition. The property can be developed to a depth of 300′ to 800′ by tunnels from Robertson Ravine and to a depth of 1400′ by a proposed Cooper Mountain tunnel.

The country rock is meta-andesite and schists, in which there is a quartz fissure vein containing bornite and gold, 8′ wide, with andesite foot and hanging walls. It strikes northwest and dips 70° SW., and has a length proven on the surface of 5000′. There is also an ore-bearing zone in schists near their contact with porphyry. The ore contains bornite and carbonates and has schist hanging and foot-walls. An average width of about 2′, with a maximum of 8′, contains 2% copper and $3.10 gold. The strike is northwest and dip 50° SW. Length on surface, 2000′.

Adjoining mines are the Calnan and Five Bears mines, both idle at present.

Beetle Group. Owners, A. D. McMillan, W. P. Boyden, Greenville.

Location: Lights Cañon Mining District, Sec. 25, T. 27 N., R. 10 E., 7 miles north of Taylorsville, 20 miles by automobile stage to Keddie via Taylorsville; good automobile road to within 3 miles of mine. Elevation 4000'.
Bibliography: Diller, J. S., U. S. Geol. Survey Bull. 353. Lindgren, W., U. S. Geol. Survey Prof. Paper 73, pages 114–116. U. S. Geol. Survey Topo. sheets Indian Valley, Genesee and Honey Lake.

This property, consisting of the Beetle and Beetle Extension locations, is 40 acres in area and has a length of 3000' along the lode.

The mine was discovered in 1874, a shaft was sunk by J. Ford and ore was smelted in the old Genesee smelter. It was relocated in 1906 by the present owners, who shipped one and one-half tons of ore. Assessment work only is done now.

Workings consist of a 60' shaft, now inaccessible, and 50' drifted on the vein. The vein is proven on the surface for 50' only.

The deposit consists of a fissure vein of quartz and calcite containing copper and gold. It is 12" to 18" wide, with 6" of ore. Strike N. 60° E., dip nearly vertical, between a foot-wall of conglomerate, and hanging wall of porphyry.

Equipped with a blacksmith shop only.

Adjoining mines are the Hulsman and Engels.

Bell Quartz Mine. Owner, Professor C. Bayless, Dubuque, Iowa.

Location: Quincy Mining District, Sec. 3, T. 24 N., R. 9 E., 2 miles north of Quincy by good automobile road.
Bibliography: Cal. State Min. Bur. Reports, X, page 478; XIII, page 292. U. S. Geol. Survey Folio 37, Downieville.

The property consists of three claims in the Bell group, Bell, Iowa and Leavitt Extension, all of which are patented. The total area, about 60 acres, covers a length of 2000' along the lode. It is situated at the head of Elizabethtown Flat, where the ridge rises abruptly from the flat.

The mine was discovered in early days by hydraulicking and in 1879 the present owners erected a 10-stamp mill on the property. It is now idle. The ore is said to have averaged $15.

Development work consists of two tunnels, an upper tunnel 500' long, and the lower tunnel 50' below, 600' long. There are numerous crosscuts in the lower tunnel, and it has been stoped to the extent of 100' in length, 11' in width and 50' in height. On the north side of the hill, a tunnel has been run on the vein a distance of 75', then a winze sunk to a depth of 30' and a drift driven from the bottom, south, for a distance of 30'. Old workings have caved.

The deposit is characterized by quartz veins and stringers in a siliceous dike 60' wide, with both hanging and foot-walls of slate. The vein is said to have been worked for a width of 11' to 15', the ore being free milling, with a small amount of pyrite and manganese. The strike is N. 15° W., dip 80° E., and it has a proven length on the surface of 1000'.

Adjoining mines are, Newtown Flat and Elizabethtown Flat placer mines.

Big Cliff Mine. Owners, Genesee Valley Copper Company, Sioux City, Iowa; A. L. Beardsley, president; Melvin Smith, secretary.

Location: Genesee Mining District, Secs. 25, 26, 35 and 36, T. 26 N., R. 11 E., 4 miles northeast of Genesee. 22 miles by good automobile road via Genesee to Keddie. Elevation 4000' to 6000'.
Bibliography: Diller, J. S., U. S. Geol. Survey Bull. 260, pages 45–49. U. S. Geol. Survey Bull. 353, pages 111–121. U. S. Geol. Survey Topo. sheets Indian Valley, Genesee, Honey Lake.

The property consists of 12 claims, viz, Genesee No. 1 to No. 12. The length along the lode is 6000' and the area 240 acres. The surface is characterized by precipitous cliffs on the north side of Genesee Valley.

The mine was purchased in 1910 by its present owners, but the only work that has been done consists of cuts across the face of the cliff and two holes or tunnels 20' to 40' deep. Great masses of the cliff have been blown off and some of this rock shows small amounts of purple bornite.

The lode is altered meta-andesite, porphyritic and impregnated with finely disseminated bornite. Not enough work has been done to determine the character of the vein, but the ore-bearing zone is claimed to be 80' to 400' in width, and gold and silver as well as bornite are said to occur. The country rock is meta-andesite and sandstone.

Equipped with two cabins.

Adjoining is the Reward, idle for a number of years.

Bigelow Claim. Owner, John F. Bigelow, San Francisco.

Location: La Porte Mining District, Sec. 32, T. 23 N., R. 11 E., 3 miles southwest of Cromberg by trail. Elevation 6000'.
Bibliography: Lindgren, W., U. S. Geol. Survey Prof. Paper 73, pages 114–116. U. S. Geol. Survey Folio 37, Downieville.

The property comprises one patented claim, having an area of 20 acres and covering the lode for a length of 1500'. It is situated at the head of Poplar Creek, tributary to Middle Fork Feather River, and sharp V-shaped cañons mark the surface.

The claim has been held by the present owner since 1885. In 1913 a small amount of work was done in cleaning out the tunnels.

Development work consists of a 200' shaft, a tunnel of 300' crosscut to the bottom of the shaft, and a 300' crosscut adit. Fifty feet have been driven on the vein south from the shaft on the 200' level on stringers of quartz.

The country rock is slate, augite-porphyrite and andesite, the deposit being a quartz vein striking N. 25° W. in slate, and containing free gold. Quartz stringers are characteristic. The vein was followed by the shaft to a shallow depth and then lost, probably on account of a slide.

Adjoining mines are the Lincoln and Gold Leaf.

Black Bart Mine. (Frazier.) Owner, Joseph Peppin, Brush Creek post office.

> Location: Granite Basin Mining District, Sec. 30, T. 23 N., R. 7 E., 30 miles southwest of Quincy by good automobile road via Meadow Valley, Bucks Ranch and Letter Box; also automobile road from Oroville. Elevation 4775'.
> Bibliography: Cal. State Min. Bur. Report XIII, page 293. U. S. Geol. Survey Folio 43, Bidwell Bar.

The property comprises one claim, called the Black Bart, with an area of 20 acres. It covers the lode for 1500'.

The mine was located by Peppin in early days, bonded to the Frazier Company and now reverted to Peppin. Assessment work only was being done in 1913.

It is developed by a 600' crosscut adit which strikes the Black Bart No. 1 vein 200' from the portal on Frazier Creek, thence 300' is driven through granite to the Black Bart No. 2, thence 40' through granite to the Black Bart No. 3, and thence 30' to the Black Bart No. 4. The lengths driven on the veins are as follows: B. B. No. 1, 500' south and 50' north; B. B. No. 2, 300' south; and B. B. No. 3, 150' north and 150' south. All ground developed has been stoped to the surface, which was 50' to 90' above the tunnel level.

This deposit consists of fissure veins in country rock of granite and diorite. The foot and hanging walls are vein granite, the vein filling quartz and decomposed granite containing free gold and pyrite. The veins are parallel, striking northeast and dipping 75° E., with a proven length on the surface of 500'. Short pay shoots occur in the veins at intervals. The width of the veins and values are as follows: B. B. No. 1, 1' to 2', $12; B. B. No. 2, 1' to 2', $20; B. B. No. 3, 1' to 2', $8 to $10; B. B. No. 4, 1' to 2', values unknown.

Equipment consists of houses and a Huntington mill and Triumph concentrator, operated by a 15-h.p. steam engine.

Adjoining mines are the Robinson and Morning Star.

Blue Bell Mine. Owners, Blue Bell Mining Company.

> Location: Genesee Valley Mining District, Sec. 2, T. 25 N., R. 11 E., 2 miles northeast of Genesee by good automobile road, thence 18 miles west to Keddie by automobile road. Elevation 4200'.
> Bibliography: Diller, J. S., U. S. Geol. Survey Bull. 353, pages 111–121. U. S. Geol. Survey Topo. sheets Indian Valley, Genesee, Honey Lake. Cal. State Min. Bur. Bull. 50, page 180.

A limestone belt passes through the country in a northwest and southeast direction, and the ore forms in limestone and slates near the contact with granodiorite. At the apex of a hill on the belt are some heavy croppings, under which the Blue Bell Mining Company ran a tunnel that intersected seven important veins.

Boyd Mine. Owners, O. G. Boyd, Bucks Ranch; A. G. Boyd, 1235 Powell street, San Francisco.

> Location: Edmanton Mining District, Sec. 10, T. 23 N., R. 7 E., 20 miles southwest of Quincy by good automobile road via Bucks to within one mile of property. Elevation 5500'.
> Bibliography: Lindgren, W., U. S. Geol. Survey Prof. Paper 73, pages 98–99. U. S. Geol. Survey Folio 43, Bidwell Bar.

This property consists of four claims, the Mammoth, Whip-poorwill, Jumbo and Jumbo Extension, located July 12, 1913. It contains 80 acres, with 2580' along the lode, and is located on a high ridge of serpentine lying south of Haskins Valley.

Development work consists of shallow surface cuts across the lode, which show the deposit to be auriferous for a width of 120'. The property contains a decomposed body of iron-stained talc and serpentine material, which strikes northeast. The gold-bearing zone lies near the contact of the serpentine and the Calaveras slates, and the ore is said to average $4 and $5 per ton for a width of 120'. Some coarse gold has been taken from this ground by panning on the surface, and it may be the source of the gold of the Gold Mountain Hydraulic and Dredging Company, whose property lies on the slope southeast of Boyd's.

Water supply can be obtained from Haskins Creek, a tributary of Bucks Creek, also on the ridge at the headwaters of Willow Creek.

Bullion Mine. Owner, A. L. Beardsley, Genesee.

> Location: Genesee Valley Mining District, Sec. 14, T. 26 N., R. 11 E., 7 miles northeast of Genesee by trail, 12 miles from Keddie to Taylorsville, then by Lucky S. road to within a few miles of mine. Elevation 5300'.
> Bibliography: Diller, J. S., U. S. Geol. Survey Bull. 260, pages 45–49; Bull. 353, pages 111–121. U. S. Geol. Survey Topo. sheets Indian Valley, Genesee, Honey Lake.

The property consists of seven claims, located in 1913 by the present owner, containing 140 acres and having a length along the lode of 4500'.

The deposit is porphyry impregnated with chalcopyrite in a country rock of meta-andesite, the ore containing chalcopyrite, 6 to 8 ounces of silver and $1 gold. There is said to be 50' of ore, then a zone of leached material 200' in width, and then 50' more of ore, the lode striking N 70° E., and dipping 50° SE. The length proven on the surface is 150'. There are also three quartz veins in the porphyry 4' to 5' in width, reported to carry free gold.

Work consists only of open cuts.

The Lucky Strike, an adjoining mine, has been idle for many years.

Bullion Claim. Owner, Mrs. A. E. Hayden, Reno, Nevada.

> Location: Johnsville Mining District, Sec. 29, T. 22 N., R. 13 E., 2 miles east of Clio by good automobile road. Elevation 5000'.
> Bibliography: Lindgren, W., U. S. Geol. Survey Prof. Paper 73, page 111. U. S. Geol. Survey Folio 37, Downieville.

Buster Group. Owners, Sol. Camp, Downieville; B. H. and G. M. Smith, Quincy; Al. Dednon.

Location: Taylorsville Mining District, Sec. 24, T. 25 N., R. 10 E., and Sec. 19, T. 25 N., R. 11 E., 8 miles northeast of Marston (W. P. Ry.) by old toll road, now a trail. Elevation 7000'.
Bibliography: Diller, J. S., U. S. Geol. Survey Bull. 253, pages 111–121. U. S. Geol. Survey Topo. sheets Taylorsville, Indian Valley, Honey Lake.

The Buster group consists of eight claims, Buster No. 1 to No. 8, inclusive, a total of 160 acres, covering a length along the lode of 4500'. The claims were located May 1, 1914, on the divide between Genesee and Quincy Junction. Nos. 3, 4 and 7 are well timbered.

The vein has been developed by a 30' open cut and tunnel. It is a deposit in limestone, 100' wide, dipping 45° SW., the hanging wall being limestone, the foot-wall porphyry. The surface ore is all carbonate.

Butte Bar Mine. (Nelson.) Owners, E. L. Fensier, J. Guerbe, 11 College avenue, Santa Rosa.

Location: Quincy Mining District, Sec. 35, T. 23 N., R. 8 E., 17 miles southwest of Quincy by trail. Elevation 3000'.
Bibliography: U. S. Geol. Survey Folio 37, Downieville.

The property is situated in the steep cañon of Middle Fork Feather River and consists of two patented claims, the North Butte Bar and the South Butte Bar, extending 1500' north and 1500' south of the river. The total area is 40 acres with a length along the lode of 3000'.

The vein was discovered in 1893 and high grade ore was taken out. A five-stamp mill was installed but it was destroyed by a landslide. Total production to date about $3000.

Development consists of a 250' tunnel driven on the vein on the north side of the river and an 80' tunnel on the vein on the south side of the river. The greatest vertical depth reached below the outcrop is 300'.

The vein is a quartz-filled fissure varying in width from about 6' to 15' at the crossing of the river, carrying free gold, galena, copper sulphide, and possibly tellurides. The foot-wall is a fine-grained diorite porphyry, the hanging wall a mica schist. It has a strike of S. 20° E. and a dip of 75° E. on the south side of the river and a strike of N. 40° W. and a dip of 70° E. on the north side of the river. Galena ore on mill test ran $12. Transportation costs are 10¢ per pound.

Nearest adjoining mine is the Little Nell.

Butte and Iron Lily Mines. Owner, Mrs. J. D. Williams, 617 Lincoln street, Oroville.

Location: Lights Cañon Mining District, Secs. 1, 2, 3, 10, 11, 14, T. 27 N., R. 10 E., 14 miles north of Taylorsville, 25 miles northeast of Keddie, good automobile road from Keddie to Lights Cañon, then 6 miles by trail to mine. Elevation 6000'.
Bibliography: Diller, J. S., U. S. Geol. Survey Bull. 353. Lindgren, W., U. S. Geol. Survey Prof. Paper 73, pages 114–116. U. S. Geol. Survey Topo. sheets Indian Valley, Genesee, Honey Lake.

This property consists of 43 claims, none patented, the Iron Lily No. 1 to No. 29 and Butte No. 1 to No. 14. It contains 800 acres, covering the Butte lode system for 6000' in a northward direction, and the Iron Lily system for 12,000' in an eastward direction. Steep cañons are characteristic of the surface.

The claims were located by J. D. Williams in 1902. Two men were working in 1912 and one man in 1913.

Development consists of a shaft 22' deep and 250' of open cuts, on the Iron Lily system. On the Butte system there are three adits, No. 1, 60'; No. 2, 130'; No. 3, 50', and from the latter a 250' crosscut.

The deposit lies near the contact of granite and andesites, the country rock being slate and meta-andesite. The Butte system is composed of quartz and calcite veins, containing pyrite and chalcopyrite, assaying $2\frac{1}{2}\%$ copper, and gold as high as $14 per ton. The hanging wall is 'Birdseye' porphyry, and though the vein has been crosscut for 74' no foot-wall was encountered. The deposits in the Iron Lily system are lenticular. The ore is said to average $2\frac{1}{2}\%$ copper, gold $1.50 and to carry a maximum of 39 ounces of silver.

Wood fuel and steam power are used.

There is a cabin and a blacksmith shop.

The Engels copper mine is the nearest neighboring property.

Butterfly Group. Owners, Mrs. Mary Smith, Quincy; F. N. Smith, Belden.

Location: Quincy Mining District, Sec. 34, T. 25 N., R. 8 E., 4 miles north of Quincy by fair wagon road. Elevation 3500'-3900'.
Bibliography: Cal. State Min. Bur. Reports XII, page 214; XIII, page 288. U. S. Geol. Survey Folio 37, Downieville.

This property consists of five quartz claims, the Blue Point, and Blue Point Extension, Columbia, Hornet and Butterfly, totaling 92 acres, and two placer claims, the Columbus placer, 160 acres, and Columbus Extension, 20 acres. The claims are on the ridge between Blackhawk and Butterfly creeks and cover the lode for 6000'. The surface is cut by deep ravines.

The property was discovered by John Radley, but was purchased by A. Smith and has been held by the Smith family for over 20 years. Two men were working the mine in 1913.

There are four veins on the property developed as follows: Governor vein developed by a 70' vertical shaft, a 60' crosscut and then 40' drifted each way on the vein, and a drift from the bottom of the shaft 60' northwest. A 300' crosscut cuts the vein 100' below the outcrop, 15' was driven on the vein, and 5000 tons of ore stoped. The Mound vein has an 80' vertical shaft and a total length of 20' driven on the vein. The Blue Point vein has a 75' shaft (caved) and a 250' tunnel on the vein. Mining is by hand drilling, but the porphyry dike was hydraulicked 700' x 20' x 20'.

Country rock is Calaveras slate and quartzite, the veins being true
fissures.   There is also a porphyry dike, decomposed and oxidized,
with quartz stringers.   The Governor is a quartz vein, carrying free
gold and sulphides, with slate foot and hanging walls.   It varies from
8' to 20', strikes northwest and dips 45° SW., with a proven length of
1500' on the surface.   The Mound vein is of decomposed quartz and
gouge carrying free gold and sulphides, with slate hanging and foot
walls.   This vein varies from 2' to 8' in width with an average of 4',
strikes N. 45° W., and dips 70° SW.   It has a proven length of 300'
on the surface.   The Blue Point vein is quartz and heavy gouge,
carrying free gold and a little sulphides, with a foot-wall of quartzite
and a hanging wall of slate.   Its average width is 6', and it can be
traced for 1200' on the surface.   The strike is N. 28° W., the dip
80° SW.   The porphyry dike, 4' to 40' in width, contains quartz and
iron stringers carrying free gold.   The walls are slate.   It has a
proven length on the surface of 800', with a strike to the northwest.
The ore from the Governor is said to have averaged $20 but this is
questionable.   Assays from the surface of the Mound vein have been
as high as $12 and ore from the Blue Point vein $8 to $10.

Equipment consists of two dwelling houses and a blacksmith shop.
A tramway is being built to the St. Nicolas mill.

Steam is used for power, though water might be obtained from the
Plumas Investment Company.

Nearest adjoining mines are the Buchanan and the St. Nicolas.

Caldwell Mine.   Owners, G. M. Sparks, Oroville; Mrs. A. Parker.
  Location: Granite Basin Mining District, Secs. 25 and 30, T. 23 N., R. 6 and
7 E., 30 miles by good automobile road via Bucks Ranch and Letter Box
to Quincy; Oroville 50 miles by automobile road.   Elevation 4600'.
  Bibliography: U. S. Geol. Survey Folio 43, Bidwell Bar.

This property consists of one claim, patented by Caldwell.   It is
20 acres in area and covers the lode for 1500'.   Low ridges are
characteristic of the surface.

The claim has been worked at intervals since early days.   J. A. Hall
is said to have an option on this property and to have grouped it with
the New Century, Whidden, Jennie and Alameda claims.

The deposit is a fissure vein of quartz in granite, varying in width
from 1' to 3', striking N. 35° E. and dipping 80° E.   The vein has
been proven on the surface for 1000'.   Small shoots of rich ore, going
as high as $50, occur at intervals.   It is free milling, containing only
2% auriferous pyrites.

Development work consists of two tunnels, the Upper tunnel 80'
below the outcrop, and the Jupiter 40' below the upper one.   The
Jupiter tunnel is 170' long and 80' has been drifted on the vein.   Two
raises extend to the Upper tunnel, one on a 3' vein assaying $7, the

other on a 14″ vein assaying $10. A crosscut adit has been started 100′ vertically below the Jupiter tunnel. This crosscut is now in 500′ but lacks 130′ of cutting the vein. All of the ore has been stoped from the Upper tunnel to the surface and part of the ore between the Jupiter and Upper tunnels. About 450 tons of ore, which is said to average $8 in free gold and $2 in sulphides, remains between the two tunnels. Mining is done by hand drilling.

The nearest adjoining mine is the Morning Star.

California Group. Owner, C. H. Goodhue, Indian Falls, Plumas County.

> Location: Taylorsville Mining District, Sec. 33, T. 26 N., R. 10 E., 1 mile southwest of Taylorsville by good automobile road. Elevation 4200′–5000′.
> Bibliography: Cal. State Min. Bur. Report XIII, page 289. Diller, J. S., U. S. Geol. Survey Bull. 353. U. S. Geol. Survey Topo. sheet, Taylorsville.

The property consists of four claims, the California Nos. 1, 2, 3, 4, a total area of 80 acres, covering 3000′ of the main vein, and 3000′ along a cross vein. It is situated on a high ridge offering excellent tunnel sites.

The property was discovered by A. C. Light in 1872 and was bought by Goodhue from the Light Estate. Nos. 2 and 3 are known as a pocket mine. Only assessment work has been done for many years.

On the main vein a 500′ tunnel and a 215′ crosscut (now inaccessible) have been driven. There is no drifting on the vein more than 100′ below the surface. On the cross vein there are 12 tunnels, all at present inaccessible except the lower one, which is a crosscut tunnel 140′ long with 70′ farther to go to cut the vein. The cross vein has been stoped, all pockets being taken out.

The country rock is granodiorite. The main vein is mixed quartz and country rock, carrying free gold and ½% sulphides. It is 42′ between the walls, 6′ going $4.10 and the rest $1. The strike is N. 55° W. and the dip is 65° SW. It has a proven length on the surface of 1600′.

The only equipment is a blacksmith shop.

Cayot Mine. Owner, Frank Cayot, La Porte.

> Location: La Porte Mining District, Sec. 18, T. 21 N., R. 8 E., 10 miles northeast of Lampkin, fair road from Lampkin to Oroville. Elevation 4500′–5000′.
> Bibliography: Cal. State Min. Bur. Reports, XII, page 214; XIII, page 290. Lindgren, W., U. S. Geol. Survey Prof. Paper 73, page 105. U. S. Geol. Survey Folio 37, Downieville.

The property includes four claims, the Young America, America, America Extension and Union, situated on the steep slope of the west bank of Fall River.

It covers a distance along the lode of 6000′ and has an area of 80 acres.

Two tunnels, one 20′ above the other, the lower one running nearly west and the other southwest, are driven to the vein, the former being

80' in length, and the latter 30', with 260' drifted northeast and 56' southwest on the ledge. Some ore was worked in the Fall River Consolidated mill.

The vein is a quartz fissure vein carrying free gold (oxidized pyrite), pyrite and considerable chalcopyrite. The foot-wall is porphyry, well defined, with 1' of gouge, and the hanging wall is granite. The vein varies in width from 18'' to 5', the average being about 4'. It strikes N. 30° E. and dips 45° W.

It has a length proven at intervals on the surface of 4500'. Ore from the upper tunnel averages $12, assays running from $3 to $500.

Equipment consists of one cabin.

Cherokee Group. Owners, Mrs. U. S. Webb, Sacramento; Mrs. E. M. Cornell.

> Location: Crescent Mills Mining District, Secs. 14 and 23, T. 26 N., R. 9 E., 2 miles west of Crescent Mills by wagon road; Keddie is 11 miles south via Crescent Mills. Elevation 4500'–5000'.
> Bibliography: Diller, J. S., U. S. Geol. Survey Bull. 353, pages 114–115. Lindgren, W., U. S. Geol. Survey Prof. Paper 73, pages 114–116. U. S. Geol. Survey Topo. sheets Indian Valley, Taylorsville, Honey Lake.

This property embraces four claims, the Robinson, Valentine, Brewster, and Standard, for which patent applications are said to have been made. It is situated on the ridge west of Crescent Mills, near Round Valley Reservoir.

The mine has been worked at intervals since early days, the last time about 1900. Very rich bunches of ore are reported to have been taken out of various veins and stringers near the surface.

Development work consists of a 200' shaft, the bottom of which is stated to be in serpentine, a 400' drift on the vein from the 100' level in the shaft, and the Green Mountain tunnel from the Crescent Mills side. This tunnel, after a circuitous course, is said to have reached a point within 400' of the bottom of the Cherokee shaft, and 1000' below it. The last 400' of this tunnel is reported to have been run in serpentine. A large amount of work has been done on the surface on various veins and stringers.

The deposit is a quartz fissure vein carrying free gold and very little sulphide, and is supposed to be an extension of the Green Mountain fissure. It varies from 4' to 5' in width, strikes N. 50° W. and dips 45° SW. The country rock is slate, granodiorite, serpentine and meta-rhyolite.

Adjoining mines are the Green Mountain and Altoona.

Chicken Flat Mine. Owner, P. Hansen, Meadow Valley.

> Location: Edmanton Mining District, Sec. 33, T. 24 N., R. 8 E., 4 miles southwest of Meadow Valley; Quincy is 15 miles via Meadow Valley by good automobile road to within 2 miles of mine. Elevation 4450'.
> Bibliography: Lindgren, W., U. S. Geol. Survey Prof. Paper 73, pages 98–99. U. S. Geol. Survey Folio 43, Bidwell Bar.

The property comprises one claim, upon which very little work has been done in the last ten years. The mine was reported to have been sold to Edman in 1913, but the sale could not be confirmed.

There is one vein 40' in width striking N. 37° W. and dipping 60° NE. The deposit is a replacement of dolomite, consisting of quartz lenses, chalcedony and iron oxide with a siliceous foot-wall and a schist hanging wall. It is said to be rich in free gold 200' below the surface and chalcopyrite and selenides of gold and silver are reported in small amounts.

The Diadem mine adjoins.

Chico Star Mine. Owners, R. K. Dunn, Mrs. C. Lazarvitch, Seneca; J. P. James, Chico.

Location: Butte Valley Mining District, Sec. 9, T. 26 N., R. 8 E., 1 mile north of Seneca, 31 miles northwest of Keddie via Greenville by good automobile road. Elevation 3300'.
Bibliography: Cal. State Min. Bur. Report XIII, page 290. U. S. Geol. Survey Folio 15, Lassen Peak.

The property comprises two claims, the Chico Star No. 1 and No. 2, having an area of 40 acres and covering the vein for 3000'. It is on the east bank of the North Fork Feather River, on a steep rise toward the summit of the ridge.

The property has been in the possession of the present owners for many years. It is now idle, assessment work only being done.

There is one fissure vein of quartz and quartz-cemented breccia, in slate, carrying free gold in the oxidized zone, and pyrite and arseno-pyrite. The foot-wall is 'greenstone' meta-andesite, the hanging wall slate. It varies from 14' to 20' in width, strikes N. 44° W. and dips 25° SW., with a proven length on the surface of 600'.

Development work is confined to an 80' crosscut tunnel, which strikes the vein at a depth of 150'. No drifting has been done on the vein but $1800 is said to have been taken from a pocket.

Adjoining mines are the White Lily, Del Monte, and Savercool.

Clara Mine. Owners, Ernest Leske, Herman Leske.

Location: Granite Basin Mining District, Sec. 5 or 7, T. 22 N., R. 7 E., fair wagon road to Bucks, 10 miles, then 17 miles by good automobile road to Quincy. Elevation 5000'.
Bibliography: U. S. Geol. Survey Folio 43, Bidwell Bar.

The property consists of one claim, 20 acres in area and covering the lode for 1500'. It is situated on Cold Water Creek, steep ravines being distinctive features of the surface.

It was discovered by the owner in 1901, but not located until 1910. Assessment work, which consists only of open cuts and a 20' tunnel, comprises the development.

There is one vein, a brecciated and silicified dike with solid quartz on both walls. Free gold, galena and chalcopyrite are found in the stringers of quartz which have recemented the angular fragments of the dike; one was probably shattered and then recemented and altered by the siliceous solution carrying gold. The foot and hanging walls are said to be slate. Its width is about 15', the maximum being 25', and it strikes northeast and dips 45° NW.

No assays have been made but quartz near the wall pans well.

The Coquette adjoins this property.

Commercial Mine. Owner, W. Murphy, Brush Creek.

Location: Granite Basin Mining District, Sec. 30, T. 23 N., R. 7 E.; nearest post office is Brush Creek; Quincy is 30 miles northeast by automobile road. Elevation 4700'.
Bibliography: U. S. Geol. Survey Folio 43, Bidwell Bar.

The property consists of one claim, having an area of 20 acres. It was abandoned by J. Peppin in 1911 and relocated by W. Murphy. Assessment work only is being done.

Development consists of a 140' crosscut adit and two 400' drifts on the vein, one north and one south.

The vein is a quartz-filled fissure in decomposed granite and is from 1' to 2' in width. The strike is N. 35° E., and the dip is 70° E. This property is credited with the production of $75,000, from the tunnel level to the surface, a distance of 100'.

Copper King and **Copper Queen Mines.** (See under Copper.)

Coquette Mine. Owner, Frank Douglas, Merrimac, Butte County, California. Under option to C. M. Carter, Oakland.

Location: Granite Basin Mining District, Sec. 32, T. 23 N., R. 7 E., 8 miles south from Bucks Ranch, or 30 miles to Granite Basin, thence 2 miles by trail. Elevation 4700'.
Bibliography: Cal. State Min. Bur. Report XIII, page 291. U. S. Geol. Survey Folio 43, Bidwell Bar.

The Coquette mine comprises four claims, the Coquette placer location, Boulder placer location, Coquette lode location and the Quick Fortune lode location. The total area is 80 acres with a length along the lode of 1500'. Steep cañons are characteristic of the surface.

Development work consists of a 200' tunnel on the Coquette vein and a 20' shaft and open cuts in the Quick Fortune.

Both veins are quartz fissure veins in granite, carrying free gold and sulphides. The Coquette vein varies from 6" to 4' in width, strikes east, and dips 70° S. It has a proven length on the surface of 500'. The Quick Fortune vein varies in width from 6" to 3', strikes northeast, and dips 65° E. Equipment consists of an old 10-stamp mill.

Adjoining are the Morning Star and Coyote (Darty mine).

Cosmopolitan Mine. (Reward.) Owners, S. Emrich, Reno, Nevada; Rosenthal, Rosenthal Shoe Company, San Francisco.

Location: Genesee Valley Mining District, Sec. 3, T. 25 N., R. 11 E., 2 miles northeast of Genesee by good automobile road; Genesee is 18 miles east of Keddie by automobile road. Elevation 4200'.
Bibliography: Diller, J. S., U. S. Geol. Survey Bull. 353, pages 111–121. Diller, J. S., U. S. Geol. Survey Bull. 260, pages 45–49. U. S. Geol. Survey Topo. sheets Indian Valley, Genesee, Honey Lake.

This property consists of four claims, all patented, having an area of 76 acres. It is situated on the ridge on the north side of Genesee Valley.

The mine was discovered in 1860. In the early days the ore was smelted in the old Genesee smelter, or was shipped to Swansea, Wales. No work has been done for a number of years.

There are several tunnels on the property. The main one is 500' in length with a number of drifts run on stringers. It developed a 5' vein of gold ore assaying $3.40. This vein, it is said, will cut the copper vein within 100' at a depth of 240'. Some ore has been stoped in the upper levels. The lower tunnel is in 270' in granodiorite. The upper tunnel, 60' long, exposes 14' of chalcopyrite, and the middle tunnel, 120' long, shows 17' of ore averaging 6% copper.

The first working was from a shaft 65' deep, now inaccessible.

The country rock is slate, limestone and granodiorite. The ore forms in solid masses of bornite and chalcopyrite, in limestone and slates near the contact with granodiorite.

Near the surface there is malachite and azurite. It is said to carry gold and silver. The maximum width of the ore-bearing zone is 200', with 15' lenses. It strikes northwest and dips 70° E.

The Gruss mine lies to the south, across Genesee Valley.

Coyote Group. Owner, A. E. Darty, Buck's Ranch.

Location: Granite Basin Mining District, Sec. 32, T. 23 N., R. 7 E., 8 miles by horse trail south of Bucks Ranch, thence 18 miles to Quincy by good automobile road. Elevation 5000'.
Bibliography: U. S. Geol. Survey Folio 43, Bidwell Bar.

The property comprises two claims, the Coyote and Bald Eagle. It contains 40 acres and 3000' of the lode. Sharp V-shaped cañons are features of the surface.

Development consists of a tunnel on the vein 96' long, reaching a depth below the outcrop of 75' at the face.

The ore body is a quartz vein, in granite, carrying free gold and some chalcopyrite, said to average $14. It varies in width from 3' to 4'.

The nearest mine is the Coquette.

Crescent Mine. Owners, Crescent Mill and Mining Company, 556 Mills Building, San Francisco; Mrs. M. J. McDonald, home office, 556 Mills Building, San Francisco, care W. H. Hamilton.

Location: Crescent Mills Mining District, Sec. 24, T. 26 N., R. 9 E., 11.5 miles north of Keddie by good automobile road. Elevation 3500'-3700'.
Bibliography: Cal. State Min. Bur. Reports, VIII, page 481; X, page 469; XI, page 330; XII, page 214; XIII, page 291. Diller, J. S., U. S. Geol. Survey Bull. 353, pages 114-115. Lindgren, W., U. S. Geol. Survey Prof. Paper 73, pages 114-116. U. S. Geol. Survey Topo. sheets Indian Valley, Taylorsville, Honey Lake.

The property embraces two patented claims, the Crescent and Pet, and two locations, the Miller and the Cole Fraction. It also includes

160 acres of timber in sections 14 and 15. It is situated on Indian Creek on the west side of Indian Valley at the base of a ridge which rises 1000′ above the floor of the valley.

The deposit was discovered in 1864 and worked at intervals until 1894, since which time it has been idle. The surface workings are caved and inaccessible and the 400′ shaft is full of water. It would cost from $25,000 to $50,000 to reopen the mine.

The country rocks are meta-andesite, andesite and slate. Apparently there are a number of quartz veins and cross veins in the meta-andesite and meta-rhyolite. They carry free gold and a very small

Photo No. 7.   Surface workings of the Crescent Mine, Crescent Mills district.

amount of sulphides. The foot-walls are 'blue porphyry' and the hanging walls 'porphyry' (meta-rhyolite). The Horseshoe vein has a width of 17′ of hard quartz and is 86′ between the walls on the 400′ level. It strikes N. 70° W. and dips 72° S., with a proven length of 400′ on the surface. The Pet vein is 3′ wide, strikes east, and has a vertical dip. The Crescent vein varies from 5′ to 8′, strikes northwest and dips 45° to 70° N. The ore stoped from the Crescent ledge from the 200′ level to the surface is said to have averaged from $8 to $12 per ton for a width of 5′ to 12′. On the 200′ level at the junction of the Pet and Horseshoe veins, the ore body was 15′ wide and went from $4 to $5 per ton. On the 400′ level an orebody 17′ wide and 60′ in length is said to have averaged $5 per ton for the total width.

Development work consists of a 400′ vertical shaft, and two cross-cuts driven on the vein from the 400′ level, 150′ and 250′ to the north and south, respectively. In the crosscut to the south at a distance of 117' a vein was encountered which is said to have had 17' of quartz on the foot-wall and 76' of soft oxidized 'porphyry' between the walls. The body of quartz was 60' long and apexed 60' above the 400' level. Ore was stoped from the Crescent ledge from the 200' level to the surface.

The mine equipment is practically useless. The mill was torn down and sold for junk in May, 1918.

Water for power was obtained from the Round Valley Reservoir, but any power in the future will probably be electric from the Great Western Power Company's Big Meadows project. Work begun under the supervision of Albert Burch in the summer of 1918, was discontinued because of war conditions.

The Green Mountain, the nearest mine, was last reopened in 1901.

Crescent Hill Gold Mining Company. Owner, Crescent Hill Gold Mines Company, W. E. Oddie, president and manager.

> Location: Quincy Mining District, Secs. 13 and 14, T. 23 N., R. 9 E., 6 miles south of Quincy. Elevation 5500'.
> Bibliography: U. S. Geol. Survey Folio 37, Downieville.

The property is situated on the north slope of the Feather River Cañon, and lies at an angle of about 45°.

The vein being worked is evidently an east-west vein in schist, which runs towards the contact of the schist and serpentine.

Equipment consists of a rockbreaker, Lane mill, concentrating plant and a distillate engine.

Crown Point and Summit Group. Owner, W. H. Black, Greenville.

> Location: Crescent Mills Mining District, Sec. 11, T. 26 N., R. 9 E.; Greenville is 2 miles north of mine; Greenville to Keddie is 17 miles by good automobile road. Elevation 5000'.
> Bibliography: Diller, J. S., U. S. Geol. Survey Bull. 353, pages 114–115. Lindgren, W., U. S. Geol. Survey Prof. Paper 73, pages 114–116. U. S. Geol. Survey Topo. sheets Indian Valley, Taylorsville, Honey Lake.

This property comprises two patented claims, the Summit, 750' by 600', lying between the Indian Valley property and the Hibernia claim of Standart, and the Crown Point, 600' by 1500'. It contains 30 acres and is situated on the top of the ridge south of Greenville.

The holdings were purchased in 1876 from the Bank of California, but were not included in the sale of the Indian Valley mine.

The country rock is granodiorite and meta-rhyolite. The veins are quartz-filled fissures containing free gold and sulphides, said to run $16. It is now idle.

Development consists of a 600' tunnel driven on the Summit vein, which is also cut at the 1200' level by the Union tunnel from the Indian Valley mine. The vein strikes N. 40° W., has a vertical dip and a proven length of 1500' on the surface. Considerable ore has been stoped from the Crown Point vein by two tunnels, one 150' long and the other 350' long. The lower tunnel is 82' below the 600' crosscut and has 80' farther to go to cut the vein.

Adjoining mines are the Indian Valley and Southern Eureka.

Dabney Claim. Owner, D. G. Dabney, Belden.

Location: Butte Valley Mining District, Sec. 34, T. 26 N., R. 7 E., 8 miles northeast of Belden (W. P. Ry.).
Bibliography: U. S. Geol. Survey Folio 15, Lassen Peak.

This property is situated on the North Fork Feather River, above the mouth of Mosquito Creek near Caribou Bridge.

Pioneer Mining Company's property adjoins.

Dean and Yearin Mine. Owners, Col. J. Dean, J. Yearin, Nelson Point, via Quincy.

Location: Sawpit Flat Mining District, Sec. 25, T. 23 N., R. 9 E.; Quincy is 18 miles north by wagon road. Elevation 5000'.
Bibliography: U. S. Geol. Survey Folio 37, Downieville.

The property embraces four claims, namely, the Hill Top, Black Bear, Western Slope and Sunnyside, 80 acres in all. Steep cañons are characteristic of the surface.

The deposit was located in 1911 and prospecting work was being done.

A 40' shaft sunk on a vein is now inaccessible, and a crosscut tunnel has been started which is in 20'. It will have to be driven 100' to strike the vein 75' below the outcrop.

The veins are of quartz, occurring near the contact of serpentine and Calaveras slates. The 40' shaft showed a vein 21" on the footwall and 12' on the hanging wall with a 'porphyry' horse between. This is probably a southern extension of the belt in which the Oversight claims are located.

Dean Mine. Owners, Dean and Sons, Seneca; J. S. Williams, Greenville. Bonded to J. D. Wilson.

Location: Butte Valley Mining District, Sec. 21, T. 26 N, R. 8 E., 1½ miles south of Seneca. Keddie is 31 miles southeast of Seneca by automobile road via Greenville. Elevation 3500'.
Bibliography: U. S. Geol. Survey Folio 15, Lassen Peak.

This property is situated on the steep slope on the east side of North Fork Feather River, and contains a quartz fissure vein in slate, carrying free gold and sulphides, including some arsenopyrite.

A number of tunnels comprise the development. Two or three men were doing assessment work in 1914.

Adjoining mines are the Hazzard, Dunn and White Lily.

Del Monte Mine. Owner, company, represented by J. J. Riley, Reno, Nevada.

Location: Butte Valley Mining District, Sec. 9, T. 26 N., R. 8 E., Seneca is ½ mile south of mine, Keddie 31 miles southeast, via Greenville, by good automobile road. Elevation 3300'-5000'.
Bibliography: U. S. Geol. Survey Folio 15, Lassen Peak.

This mine is situated on the southern slope of the mountains on the east bank of the North Fork Feather River.

The Del Monte was in litigation with the adjoining White Lily mine, and no data could be obtained.

Diadem Mine. (Edman and Red Point.) Owners, Edman Estate, Quincy.

Location: Edmanton Mining District, Sec. 33, T. 24 N., R. 8 E. Quincy is 14 miles east by automobile road to point where Edman road leaves the main Buck's Ranch road. Good road to mine, but bridges gone. Elevation 4750'.
Bibliography: Cal. State Min. Bur. Reports, X, page 486; XI, page 323; XII, page 214; XIII, page 291. Lindgren, W., U. S. Geol. Survey Prof. Paper 73, pages 98–99. U. S. Geol. Survey Folio 43, Bidwell Bar.

This property comprises the Diadem and Red Point patented quartz claims and the Victor Fraction, 20(?) acres in all, with a length along the lode of 3000'. It is situated on the southeast slope of Spanish Ridge, and steep ravines are characteristic of the surface.

The property was located in 1865. It is now idle and very little work, development or otherwise, has been done in the last 10 years.

There are three tunnels, the lower tunnel 1000' long cutting the vein at a vertical depth of 300', the Arrastra tunnel 550' long, and No. 2 tunnel 300' long, together with numerous crosscuts and a shaft from the lower tunnel to the surface. Most of the ore taken from this mine was from a shoot 125' long which was worked from the Arrastra tunnel level to the surface, a distance of 250'. In early days the surface was worked as a placer mine.

The lode is 60' in width, being a replacement of dolomite by silica, quartz, chalcedony and in the lower levels large amounts of silicified and altered dolomite. There is one vein, the Diadem, the filling being quartz lenses, chalcedony, iron oxide, siliceous dolomite and manganese, very rich in free gold 200' below the surface, with chalcopyrite and selenides. The foot-wall is slate, the hanging wall schist. Its strike is N. 37° W., and the dip is 60° NE., with a proven length on the surface of 3000'. Owing to the altered condition of the vein near the surface and the presence of oxides of manganese, there has probably been a surface enrichment to a depth of 250', below which point very little rich ore has been found. Pyrite concentrates go $110 a ton and compose 1% to 2% of the ore.

Equipment consists of good buildings, shops, etc., and two old Huntington mills. Steam and water power were used.

Adjoining mine is the Honeycourt.

Dora Mine. Owner, Girard Piano Company, Oakland, California.

Location: Edmanton Mining District, Sec. 34, T. 24 N., R. 7 E., 2 miles north of Buck's Ranch, Quincy 20 miles east, automobile road to Buck's, wood road to mine, 2 miles. Elevation 5000'.
Bibliography: Lindgren, W., U. S. Geol. Survey Prof. Paper 73, pages 98–99. U. S. Geol. Survey Folio 43, Bidwell Bar.

This property consists of the P. P. claim, a location on a gentle slope on the north side of Buck's Valley.

It contains a flat quartz vein in granite, 4' to 6' in width, which has been exposed on the hillside for a considerable area by open cuts and shallow shafts. The strike is east and the dip 20° N.

Droege Mine. (Formerly known as Consolidation, Drury and Pacific, Standart and McGill, J. Bull, and East Phoenix.) Owner, O. E. Lindbloom, 611 Mills Building, San Francisco. Leased until May, 1919, to John W. Daley.

Location: Crescent Mills Mining District, Secs. 9, 10, 15 and 16, T. 26 N., R. 9 E., 1½ miles south of Greenville. Crescent Mills is 11½ miles south by good automobile road. Elevation 4200'.
Bibliography: Cal. State Min. Bur. Reports, VIII, page 480; X, page 473; XII, page 217; XIII, pages 298–301.

This property comprises nine claims, namely, the Summit, West Pacific, Bird, Pacific, Drury, Arctic, John Bull, Phoenix, and East Phoenix, the latter seven being patented. There are 180 acres covering a distance along the lode of 4000', and 320 acres of timber land included in the property. The surface is formed of high ridges and steep cañons.

The property was discovered in 1869. It was purchased by Droege in 1905, and has been worked by Lindbloom since August, 1911. The Droege mine includes the John Bull and Phoenix claims, on which a considerable amount of work was done in early days. All work at present (1918) is on the Drury or Ellis vein. There has been a total production to date of about $300,000.

Development consists of two adits, No. 2 adit being 2400' in length, and No. 3 adit 255' below No. 2, being 1900' in length. The latter cuts the vein at a vertical depth of 600'. A winze sunk from No. 3 adit 1400' from the mouth, was put down 100' on the vein and drifts driven west 150' and east 200', where a fault was encountered. The vein was again picked up by driving along the fault for a distance of 98', and the adit was continued on the vein beyond the fault for 200'. Most of the ore above No. 3 adit level has been stoped to the surface. In some places two veins have been stoped with a horse of about 30' of country rock between. Short shoots have been and are being stoped, both east and west of the winze on the 100' level. The ore is run from stope chutes in small buckets, trammed 400' to the shaft, hoisted by a small electric hoist to adit No. 3, and dumped into bin; cars (1 ton) are hauled to the mill by horse, five cars to a train. Very little ore is blocked out.

The deposit consists of lenticular fissure veins in country rock of meta-rhyolite, granodiorite and serpentine. The Standart-McGill vein is a crushed and oxidized quartz vein in 'porphyry' and greenstone, probably a diorite, containing free gold and black oxide of manganese on the walls. In the unoxidized portion of the vein the ore is said to carry from 2% to 5% of surphides. The foot-wall is heavy decomposed and altered rock, possibly meta-rhyolite. The hanging wall in some places is the same as the foot-wall and in other is greenstone (diorite). The vein varies from a seam to 12' in width, will probably average 4½', and strikes east with a dip of 70° N. There are numerous faults, some being post mineral.

The mine equipment consists of a 14" x 14" Rix compound compressor driven by a Pelton waterwheel; three 3" machine drills, and electric generator, 220 volts, 148 amperes, with direct connected Pelton enclosed wheel. The mill contains 25 Hendy stamps, weight 1150 pounds, five Pindar concentrators (Buddle type), and amalgamating plates. It is in good condition.

Water is obtained from Round Valley Reservoir under a 300' head at the mill and the same water is used again at the compressor plant, 300' below the mill. The number of men employed is 23 on top, 20 to 25 in the mine, and 4 (3 shifts) in the mill. Labor was paid $3.50; mill men $4.50. The per cent extraction is 75%. Tailings run 40¢ and are disposed of in North Cañon.

Adjoining mines are the New York and Indian Valley, both idle for a number of years.

[Ten stamps were in operation in June, 1918. The ore is said to average $5 with occasional rich shoots. Fifteen men were employed. Cost of mining and milling, which was $1.50 a ton in 1914, had increased to $2.25 in 1918.]

Duncan Mine. (Brooks.) Owner, W. C. Duncan, Oroville.

Location: Butte Valley Mining District, Secs. 17 and 18, T. 25 N., R. 8 E., 4 miles east of Twain; Virgilia is across the river, but no bridge. Elevation 2600'-3100'.
Bibliography: Cal. State Min. Bur. Report XIII, page 292. U. S. Geol. Survey Folio 15, Lassen Peak.

The property consists of three claims containing 50 acres and having a length along the lode of 3600'. They are probably patented as practically no work has been done since the XIII Report.

The property lies on the north side of the east branch of the North Fork Feather River, and has been held for many years by the present owner. The surface along the river was placered in early days.

The deposit consists of a quartz fissure vein in country rock of slate, serpentine and limestone, carrying free gold and small amounts of galena, pyrite and chalcopyrite. The foot and hanging walls are slate, and the strike is N. 45° W., and the dip 55° SW. The lode is shown to be 75' in width where the river cuts it, and there is a proven length of 700' on the surface.

Adjoining mines are the Halstead and Elizabeth Consolidated.

Duncan Mine. Owners, J. B. Duncan, C. H. Hook, Genesee; A. W. Whitney, Crescent Mills.

Location: Genesee Valley Mining District, Sec. 31, T. 26 N., R. 12 E., 6 miles east of Genesee by wagon road, thence 18 miles by good automobile road to Keddie. Elevation 4000' to 5000'.
Bibliography: Diller, J. S., U. S. Geol. Survey Bull. 260, pages 45–49. Diller, J. S., U. S. Geol. Survey Bull. 253, pages 111–121. U. S. Geol. Survey Topo. sheets Indian Valley, Genesee, Honey Lake.

This property includes 12 claims, covering 240 acres and also a water right. It has been held by the present owners for a number of years, and developed by numerous tunnels aggregating 600' in length. A vertical depth of 150' on the vein has been reached by the lower tunnel and 150' has been driven on the vein. The contact can be developed to a depth of 1200' by a lower tunnel. Assessment work only is being done at present.

A mineralized zone 200' wide containing high grade kidneys forms a contact deposit in country rock of granodiorite and limestone. The ore carries bornite, chalcocite, $20 in gold, and 158 ounces of silver and is found in small bunches irregularly distributed. The orebody strikes east and dips 70° N.

Equipment consists of cabins and blacksmith shop. Water power can be developed from Indian Creek.

The Big Cliff is an adjoining mine.

Elizabeth Consolidated Gold Mines. (Formerly known as Thompson placer mine, Lewis quartz mine, Patten quartz mine, Scheiser Ravine quartz mine consolidation.) Owner, J. M. Little, Twain, Plumas County, or 3621 Broadway, Oakland.

Location: Butte Valley Mining District, Secs. 1 and 12, T. 25 N., R. 7 E., 4 miles northwest of Virgilia by good wagon road. Elevation 3900'.
Bibliography: Cal. State Min. Bureau Report XIII, pages 299–300. U. S. Geol. Survey Folio 15, Lassen Peak.

This property comprises the following claims: Thompson placer, Schafer quartz, Last Chance and Scheiser Ravine. Application for patent was made on the claims several years ago but the case was protested and afterward appealed by the Bureau of Forestry, but Little has won in both cases, and expects patents in the near future. There is a total area of 107 acres, 60 acres being placer. The length along the lode is 3600'. High ridges and deep ravines are surface features.

The property was worked as a placer in 1850, but all the workings do not cross the vein. It was first worked as a quartz mine by F. Lewis in 1880. Rich Gulch, when placered in early days, is said to have yielded $9,000,000, and the gold was undoubtedly derived, for the most part, from the erosion of the Halstead, Elizabeth, Cameron vein.

The deposit is a fissure vein in slate, with well-defined walls. There is one quartz fissure vein composed of quartz and slate with gouge on walls, containing free gold, small amounts of galena, chalcopyrite and arsenopyrite. It strikes N. 66° W. and dips 80° SW., with a proven length on the surface of 3600'. The vein is supposed to be faulted at the south end of the Scheiser claim.

Development work consists of three tunnels, the upper tunnel (elevation 3920'), 279' through slate; the middle tunnel (elevation 3750'), 530' through slate; and the lower tunnel (elevation 3620'), 150' through slate, but not yet to the vein. There are drifts, cross-cutting the middle tunnel as follows: 94', 38' and 60', and a raise of 30'. The middle tunnel cuts the vein at a vertical depth of 150'. There has been a total of 166' driven on the vein from the upper tunnel and 391' from the middle tunnel. All the ground has been stoped from the upper tunnel to the surface. The 391' of drifts, from the middle tunnel, on the vein are all in ore varying from 1' to 5' in width, which is said to have an average value of $10 per ton.

There were two men employed in 1914.

The Halstead mine adjoins the Elizabeth on the southeast and the veins are supposed to be the same, a fault having thrown the vein a distance of 600' northeast at a point where Scheiser Ravine cuts across the strike of the lode. The country to the northwest, which comprises the Elizabeth mine, is badly broken and Scheiser Ravine may be the result of the dislocation. This lode can be traced from the East Branch North Fork Feather River, which it crossed near Virgilia where the outcrop was extensively worked by hydraulicking, through the Duncan, Halstead, Elizabeth Consolidated and Cameron claims, a distance of twenty-five miles.

Fairplay Mine. Owner, F. E. Thomas, Quincy.

Location: Quincy Mining District, Secs. 3 and 10, T. 24 N., R. 9 E., 2 miles north of Quincy by good automobile road. Elevation 3600'.
Bibliography: U. S. Geol. Survey Folio 37, Downieville.

This property comprises two claims, the Fairplay and Fairplay Extension, the latter being a fraction (500' x 600'). In all, there are 26 acres, having a length along the lode of 2000'.

This ground was located by the present owner in 1897, but assessment work only has been done. The property is held in hopes that the adjoining Bell mine will be worked.

Development consists of two tunnels, 90' and 50' in length, with a winze from the lower tunnel sunk 25' which reaches the vein 70' below the outcrop. Ore with an average width of 7' is said to average $10 per ton.

This deposit is supposed to be a south extension of the Bell lode. There is one quartz vein in slate, varying in thickness from 6' to 8', striking N. 15° W. and dipping 80° E., with stringers from a few inches up to 3' in width. It is free milling and contains some pyrite.

Five Bears. (Centennial.) Owner, Five Bears Mining Company; J. D. Meidenger, Chicago, Illinois, president; G. H. Goodhue, manager, Indian Falls via Paxton.

Location: Genesee Mining District, Secs. 23, 25 and 26, T. 25 N., R. 11 E., 3 miles southeast of Genesee, thence 18 miles by good automobile road to Keddie. Elevation 3900'–5600'.
Bibliography: Cal. State Min. Bur. Reports, XII, page 213; XIII, page 290. Diller, J. S., U. S. Geol. Survey Bull. 260, pages 45–129. Diller, J. S., U. S. Geol. Survey Bull. 353, pages 111–121. U. S. Geol. Survey Topo. sheets Indian Valley, Genesee, Honey Lake.

This property comprises 1 placer and 9 quartz claims, namely, the Centennial placer, Centennial quartz, South Extension, Black Bear, Brown Bear, Polar Bear, Grizzly Bear, and Cinnamon; the latter being the only one unpatented. There are 204 acres in the tract, 184 patented, and a length along the lode of 8100'. Deep gulches with steep slopes to the top of the ridge, affording fine tunnel sites, are characteristic of the surface.

The property was discovered in 1876 by Geo. Brandt, and was later purchased by the Five Bears Mining Company. At present it is idle. The mill closed in December, 1912, but four men worked underground until May, 1913. Gold production to date about $32,000.

The mine is developed by a tunnel, driven 1400' on the vein, its face being 900' below the outcrop. In the tunnel between stations 909 and 1080 the vein is 9' wide and said to average $5\frac{1}{2}\%$ copper, from stations 1127 to 1240 the vein is 13' with chalcopyrite averaging 2.3%. At one point 350' from the mouth the vein is stoped 50' above the tunnel level.

The deposit consists of orebodies irregularly distributed through a zone of slates and shales of Calaveras formation, following a narrow shear zone and forming imperfect veins. There are three veins but only the main vein (zone) is developed. The filling is a small amount of auriferous quartz, crushed slate and gouge. The oxidized ore contains limonite, manganese oxide and free gold (rusty); the sulphide ore, chalcopyrite and chalcocite with a very small amount of quartz. A zone of slate and shale 400' wide occurs with altered and metamorphosed andesite on both foot and hanging walls, the andesite sometimes being porphyritic. The strike is north, the dip varying between 20° and 70°.

Equipment consists of two Pelton waterwheels, one 18" and the other 48", a two-drill Giant air compressor, assay plant, blacksmith shop, five houses, stable, air pipes in tunnel, a 10-stamp mill, 700-pound stamps, feeders, and two Eccleston concentrators.

Water from Weed Creek, 200" under 109' head, is used for power, but under 1200' head 500" can be developed.

Cost of development work about $7 per foot, mining 60¢ per ton, treatment 80¢, timber (own) $2\frac{1}{2}$¢ per foot, transportation 45¢ per 100 pounds from Keddie. Extraction of gold about 60%.

The Gruss mine, to the north, is in the same zone. Mines of the Genesee district will probably not be large producers until a branch road is put through Indian and Genesee valleys.

[The property was idle in the summer of 1918. The ore yields principally copper in depth. When working, the output is about 1600 pounds of concentrate a day, and this is shipped to a smelter.]

Friendship Mine.

Location: Granite Basin District, T. 23 N., R. 6 E., within 35 miles of Quincy by automobile road via Buck's Ranch and Letter Box.
Bibliography: U. S. Geol. Survey Folio 43, Bidwell Bar.

This property consists of two locations. A 1' vein in granite is developed by a 30' shaft and a 100' tunnel on the vein. There are two men at work and a 3-stamp (200-pound) mill is to be installed. Ore is claimed to go $20 per ton.

Gold Leaf Mine. Owners, J. A. Grove, J. J. Lowry, Cromberg.

Location: Quincy Mining District, Sec. 5, T. 22 N., R. 11 E., 3 miles northwest of Cromberg by trail.
Bibliography: U. S. Geol. Survey Folio 37, Downieville.

This property consists of one claim of 20 acres, covering the lode for 1500'.

A 600' tunnel and a 150' winze comprise the development work.

There is one quartz fissure vein, called the Gold Leaf, carrying free gold and sulphides, with foot and hanging walls of slate. The width of the vein is 2' and it strikes northwest. Ore is said to average $20 with occasional assays as high as $1000.

Gold Leaf Consolidated Mines Company. (Argentine and Heath.) Owner, Gold Leaf Consolidated Mines Company; Dr. H. Look, 491 K street, Sacramento, president; J. Hammock, Thos. Sutton, W. V. Gross, Spring Garden.

Location: Quincy Mining District, Secs. 19, 20, 29 and 30, T. 24 N., R. 11 E., 3½ miles north of Spring Garden by trail, 5 miles by poor wagon road. Elevation 5045'.
Bibliography: U. S. Geol. Survey Folio 37, Downieville.

This property comprises six claims, having an area of 120 acres and a length along the lode of 1000'. The surface is characterized by steep ridges and V-shaped cañons near the headwaters of several creeks.

It was bonded to the present company in 1907.

The deposit occurs as quartz veins in country rock of Calaveras slates and porphyrite. There are two veins, the Gold Leaf and the Hobart, the former being a quartz fissure vein with small gouge on both walls; both contain free gold and small amount of pyrite and galena. The foot and hanging walls are porphyrite and schists. In width the Gold Leaf vein varies from 2' to 14', the strike is north, dip 70° W., and it has a proven length on the surface of 600'. The Hobart vein varies from 3' to 20', with an average width of 4', strikes

east and dips 35° N. It has a proven length on the surface of 300'.
The pay shoot is 200' long and averages 4' wide.

A crosscut tunnel has been run 200' to the Gold Leaf vein, on which
there is also a 35' shaft. Another crosscut tunnel has been run 650',
cutting the Hobart vein 125' below the outcrop, and there is an incline
shaft on the vein 100' in length. The Hobart vein has been stoped
from the surface to 25' above the main tunnel for a length of 50'.
The average value of the ore is $3 per ton, while that in the Gold
Leaf vein is said to assay $6 to $19.

Houses and a blacksmith shop comprise the mine equipment. The
reduction equipment consists of an old 5-stamp mill (850-lb. stamps)
in a new building.

Power is obtained from 40" of water under a head of 150'.

The Henri Gobert mine adjoins.

Gold Stripes Mine. (Wolf.) Owners, F. J. Standart, Greenville;
Mrs. C. Hamilton, Oroville. Under bond 1913 and was being worked
by the Cliff Mining Company, vice president, Grant Snyder, 414 Judge
Building, Salt Lake City.

Location: Crescent Mills Mining District, Sec. 36, T. 27 N., R. 8 E., and
Sec. 6, T. 26 N., R. 9 E., 5 miles northwest of Greenville; Keddie is 21
miles south of mine by good road. Elevation 5200'.
Bibliography: Diller, J. S., U. S. Geol. Survey Bull. 353, pages 114–115.
Lindgren, W., U. S. Geol. Survey Prof. Paper 73, pages 114–116. U. S.
Geol. Survey Topo. sheets Indian Valley, Taylorsville, Honey Lake.

This property consists of nine claims in all, three, the Jersey, Ever-
green, and Wolf Creek, being patented. There are 180 acres covering
a length along the lode of 3000'.

The property was purchased by G. Standart, father of the present
owners, in 1882. It was idle from 1911 to October, 1913, when it was
reopened with 10 men employed in cleaning out. The mine has produced to date about $750,000.

The deposit is a lenticular fissure vein near a contact of slate and
serpentine. The filling in both veins is quartz and slate, containing
free gold and very little sulphide. The foot-wall of the Gold Stripe
is serpentine, the hanging wall slate, but both the hanging and foot
wall of the Wolf Creek vein are schist. The veins are parallel, 500'
apart, and strike east, with a dip of 45° S., the lenses varying from
5' to 10' in width. The Gold Stripe has a proven length on the surface of 4000'; the Wolf Creek about 1000'.

Development work on the Gold Stripe vein consists of a 300'
crosscut adit which cuts the vein at a depth of 230', and 1000' driven
on the vein. The Wolf Creek vein is developed by a 600' tunnel
driven along the vein, 60' below the surface. In the Gold Stripe
three shoots were stoped, No. 1, 300' x 80' high; No. 2, 220' long
x 130'; No. 3, 200' x 230'; and in the Wolf Creek vein two shoots,
No. 1, 60' x 60', and No. 2, 100' x 60' have been stoped.

Steam is used for power, the fuel used being wood.

The nearest mine is the Droege, which is working 25 men.

Gold Run Mine. Owners, A. Hall, Quincy; Wm. Metcalf, Eclipse; H. D. Seman, Quincy.

> Location: Sawpit Flat Mining District, Secs. 10 and 15, T. 22 N., R. 10 E., 2 miles southeast of Eclipse; Quincy is 30 miles northwest, by fair road of 4 miles from mine to Eclipse, thence good automobile road to Quincy via Nelson Point. Elevation 6500'.
> Bibliography: U. S. Geol. Survey Folio 37, Downieville.

This property comprises seven claims, namely, the Quincy Nos. 1, 2, 3, Gold Rim, Gold Rim Extension, Spring Nos. 1 and 2; the Quincy No. 1 is 1300' x 600', all others 1500' x 600'. The total area is 138 acres, covering 4300' along the lode. Lava-covered ridges and deep cañons with steep grades to the Feather River mark the surface.

The ground was located by Hall in 1911, and assessment and development work consists of two open cuts 13' x 17' x 10' deep, also a 60' crosscut from Poorman's Creek, cutting the vein at a vertical depth of 30'. Some good assays have been reported but it is not known what the quartz will average.

The deposit consists of quartz veins and stringers in slate, but development has not been sufficient to prove whether or not they are associated with an igneous dike. One vein can be traced through the Gold Rim, Gold Rim Extension and Quincy No. 1. Its filling is iron-stained schist containing free gold and arsenical pyrite with a foot and hanging wall of slate. The width varies from 6" to 24". It strikes N. 55° W., dips 80° E. and has a proven length on the surface of 2500'.

Adjoining are the Rose Quartz and the Oro Fino mines.

Golden Gate Mine. Owners, W. Clinch, John Barker, Louis Smith, Quincy, California.

> Location: Quincy Mining District, Secs. 29 and 30, T. 25 N., R. 9 E., 7 miles northwest of Quincy, by good road. Elevation 4200'–4700'.
> Bibliography: U. S. Geol. Survey Folio 37, Downieville.

This property comprises two claims, the Golden Gate and the Golden Gate Extension. The area is 40 acres and it covers the lode for 3000'.

It was discovered by Wagner, but was relocated in 1912 by the present owners, who were doing assessment work in 1913.

It is a quartz vein, in slate, with gouge on both walls, containing free gold, and a small percentage of sulphides. The foot-wall is slate and quartzite, and the hanging wall slate. In width the vein is from 2' to 10', the average being about 4'. It strikes northwest, dips 25° NE., and has a proven length on the surface of 500'.

Development consists of a crosscut tunnel 400' long, cutting the vein 75' below its outcrop. A 30' drift has been driven from this on the vein and there is a shaft 90' in depth, from the bottom of which a drift was driven 200' west. The latter is supposed to have cut the vein 40' from the shaft, but the drift was continued, in country rock, 150' beyond. There is another shaft 50' in depth from which a drift has been driven on the vein for a distance of 30'. The vein was worked as an open cut 300' x 30' x 12' and the ore is said to have averaged $20.

The Butterfly group of claims adjoins the property.

Green Ledge Mine. Owners, J. C. Young, Taylorsville; G. F. Brown.

> Location: Genesee Valley Mining District, Sec. 23, T. 25 N., R. 11 E., 3 miles southeast of Genesee, 21 miles east of Keddie, via Genesee and Taylorsville, by good automobile road. Elevation 4100'.
> Bibliography: Cal. State Min. Bur. Report XIII, page 296. Diller, J. S., U. S. Geol. Survey Bull. 260, pages 45–49. Diller, J. S., U. S. Geol. Survey Bull. 353, pages 111–121. U. S. Geol. Survey Topo. sheets Indian Valley, Genesee, Honey Lake.

This property composes one claim, the Green Ledge, which is not patented. It is situated on the east bank of Ward Creek with a steep slope to the top of the ridge, and is 21 acres in area.

It was one of the first claims worked in the Genesee Valley district and has been held by the present owners for over 20 years. From one shoot 90' long, 3' to 8' wide and 90' high it is said that $25,000 was taken, with an estimated loss in the tailings of $75,000 in auriferous copper sulphides. Assessment work is being done in a tunnel from the bank of Ward Creek 400' below the old workings.

Mine development consists of a tunnel 340' long, a shaft 138' deep and a 24' crosscut at the bottom of the shaft. Eighteen feet of this crosscut averaged $2.80 gold and 1½% copper. The shaft is full of water and the north adit has caved.

There are two veins, the Green Ledge and the Pocket, parallel and distant from each other 240'. The country rock is slate, schist and meta-andesite. The Green Ledge vein is a quartz and porphyry fissure vein carrying free gold and copper sulphides. The foot-wall is andesite and the hanging wall schist. It varies from 3' to 8' in width, strikes N. 20° W., dips 80° NE., and has a proven length on the surface of 5000'. The Pocket vein is a quartz vein with hanging and foot-walls of schists, carrying chalcopyrite and chalcocite, which contain high values in gold and silver. It varies from narrow stringers to 4' in width, strikes N. 20° W. and dips 40° NE. Values are found in pockets.

The only equipment is a blacksmith shop.

The Five Bears and Colnan mines adjoin.

Green Mountain Mine. Owners, J. D. Goodman Estate, San Francisco; E. L. Cornell, Yankee Hill; C. E. McLaughlin, Sacramento.

Location: Crescent Mills Mining District, Sec. 24, T. 26 N., R. 9 E., Crescent Mills is on the property; Keddie is 11.5 miles south by good automobile road. Elevation 3700'–4700'.

Bibliography: Cal. State Min. Bur. Reports, VIII, page 479; X, page 471; XII, page 217; XIII, page 296. Diller, J. S., U. S. Geol. Survey Bull. 353, pages 114–115. Lindgren, W., U. S. Geol. Survey Prof. Paper 73, pages 114–116. U. Geol. Survey Topo. sheets Indian Valley, Taylorsville, Honey Lake.

This property consists of three patented claims, the Ruby, Brilliant and Emerald Fraction, and two locations, the North Star and Sarah Jane. The two latter were relocated in 1913 by G. A. Hall and others who claim that assessment work had not been done for a number of years. The mill and entrance of tunnels No. 5 and No. 6 are situated

Photo No. 8. View from the Crescent Mine, showing location of the Green Mountain Mine on left.

on the relocated claims. The total area is 50 acres, with a length along the lode of 4500'. The outcrop is on the ridge which rises to an elevation of 1000' above Indian Valley.

The mine was discovered in 1860 and worked at intervals until 1890 and is said to have produced to date $1,000,000 to $2,000,000. The tunnel was last reopened in 1901 and all workings are now caved and inaccessible. It is estimated that $50,000 would be required to reopen this property. Very little ore was developed on the No. 6 level, the orebodies having apparently been lost by faulting between No. 5 and No. 6 levels.

The deposit is a quartz vein near the contact of slate and altered igneous rocks, meta-rhyolite, slate and serpentine making up the country rock. The foot-wall is 'greenstone,' the hanging wall 'porphyry,' probably altered rhyolite. It strikes N. 40° W., and dips 45° to 50° SW., with a proven length on the surface of 3000'. Ore from the Blake shoot was oxidized and free milling; that from the Sulphide shoot was mostly auriferous pyrite.

There are six tunnels in all: No. 1 was 250' long; No. 2, 350' long; No. 3, 1500' long; No. 4, 520' below the apex, 3000' long; No. 5 was 360' below No. 4; and No. 6, 480' below No. 5, was 6075' long. The No. 6 tunnel was driven 1100' as a crosscut to the vein, then continued for a distance of 1000' along the vein and then the hanging wall west of the vein was crosscut for a distance of 4000'; the last 400' being in serpentine. The end of this tunnel, when discontinued, was about 600' east of the Cherokee shaft. The Blake shoot was stoped 200' above and 330' below No. 5 level and is said to have been cut off, both above and below, by faults. This shoot was 300' long, 8' in width and ran $10 to $12 per ton free milling. The sulphide shoot was stoped from the 500' level to the surface, a distance of 920', and is said to have been 8' to 40' in width.

There is no mine equipment at present. An old 60-stamp mill is in ruins and worthless.

Water under 800' head was obtained from Round Valley Reservoir.

Adjoining mines are the Crescent, Altoona and Cherokee.

Grubstake and **Juniata Mines.** Owner, Frank Tolands, Brush Creek.

> Location: Granite Basin Mining District, Sec. 26, T. 23 N., R. 6 E., 10 miles southwest of Buck's Ranch; Quincy is 28 miles northeast by good automobile road from Quincy to Letter Box, thence 4 miles, by good automobile road, to mine. Elevation 4500'.
> Bibliography: U. S. Geol. Survey Folio 43, Bidwell Bar.

Property was formerly owned by E. H. Benjamin. At present, assessment work only is being done.

The development on the Grubstake consists of 1000' of tunnels and 150' of drifting. On the Juniata there are 200' of tunnels and drifts, the greatest depth below the outcrop being 125'.

Quartz fissure veins in granite comprise the deposit. On the Grubstake property there are two veins, striking north, and dipping 70° E., varying in width from 1' to 3' with a foot-wall of granite and a hanging wall of 'porphyry.' The ore is quartz, carrying free gold and some chalcopyrite. On the Juniata there is one quartz vein averaging 15" in width. It strikes N. 22° E. and dips 50° E.

There is a small 5-stamp water power mill at the mine.

Gruss Mine. (Genesee.) Owners, Mrs. G. Gruss, San Francisco; G. H. Gruss, Genesee; Dr. F. Gruss, 12 Geary street, San Francisco.

> Location: Genesee Valley Mining District, Sec. 14, T. 25 N., R. 11 E., 2 miles southwest of Genesee, 22 miles east of Keddie, by good automobile road. Elevation 3800'.
> Bibliography: Cal. State Min. Bur. Reports, X, page 476; XIII, page 294. Diller, J. S., U. S. Geol. Survey Bull. 260, pages 45–49. Diller, J. S., U. S. Geol. Survey Bull. 353, pages 111–121. U. S. Geol. Survey Topo. sheets Indian Valley, Genesee, Honey Lake.

This property includes three claims, the Genesee or Gruss, and Genesee Extension, lode claims, and the Lebanon placer claim. It has an area of 60 acres with a length along the lode of 2700'. The vein occurs at the base of the ridge where Ward Creek enters Genesee Valley Flat.

The mine was discovered in 1856 by Ward and Davis. It was purchased by Gruss in 1881 and since that time has been worked by the Gruss family, being credited with a total production of $460,000, of which amount $185,000 went to Gruss.

The mine is developed by a 100' vertical shaft from which there are drifts 500' north and 300' south. The new 200' vertical shaft is connected by an incline raise on the vein of 183'. From the 200' level a crosscut runs 96' east from the shaft to the lode, then 150' is driven south but not on the vein, and from this two crosscuts are driven at 80' and 150', west 25' and 70', respectively, to the vein; and 30' is driven on the vein south from the latter crosscut. The ground has been stoped from the 100' level to the surface, a length of 800' and an average width of 5'. A cross vein in what is known as north hill has also been stoped for 150'. Ore was being broken in 1913, 50' below the 100' level, but very little ore has been stoped from the 300' to the 100' level. Ore then being broken near the top of the raise is drawn off at the 200' level, trammed 300' to the shaft, hoisted to the surface by a water-driven hoist, crushed in a Gates crusher in the head frame and fed directly into a 10-stamp Hendy mill. Tailings are dumped on the placer claim.

The character of the deposit is crushed and brecciated shear zones in slates and schists near the contact of the slates and meta-andesite. There are no well-defined veins, but parallel stringers of quartz and calcite occur. The decomposed and altered rocks are iron-stained and the gold occurs in narrow seams and pockets containing limonite and manganese oxide. The foot-wall is altered schist and, in some places, slate, the hanging wall is black slate, altered and iron-stained near the vein. There are two parallel zones 20' to 30' apart, with an average width of 5' and a maximum of 20' each, striking N. 20° W. and dipping 45' to 60' W., with a proven length of 800' on the surface. Most of the gold occurs in the oxidized veinlets in the shear zones, oxidized to a depth of 200'. On the 200' level sulphide ore-bodies have been encountered, containing bornite, tetrahedrite and chalcopyrite following calcite seams in the altered schists. The gold in the oxidized zone is generally fine and 'rusty' and difficulty has been experienced in the past in amalgamating. One per cent concentrate ranges from $150 to $350 per ton in value.

9—46902

Mine equipment consists of a 25-horsepower Hendy water power hoist, small Ingersoll Rand compressor (3 stope drills) driven by water power, water driven 10½" Cornish pump, making four strokes per minute, and a blacksmith shop. Reduction equipment consists of a 10-stamp Hendy mill, with amalgamating plates and home-made concentrator, also a No. 2 Gates crusher, all driven by water power.

Water is obtained under 100' head from Sobrero for $10 per month. There were four men working, one on top, two in mine and one in mill. In summer seven are employed. Transportation costs $10 per ton to Keddie.

The Five Bears and Calnan are adjoining mines.

Halstead Quartz Mine. Owners, A. Halstead, Meadow Valley; I. Halstead, Blanchester, Ohio; W. H. Halstead, Havana, Kansas; Julia Batey, Elizabeth Vance, Frank Hill, Estate of H. A. Halstead, Quincy.

Location: Butte Valley Mining District, Sec. 12, T. 25 N., R. 7 E. and Sec. 7, T. 25 N., R. 8 E., 1½ miles northwest of Virgilia, by good wagon road. Elevation 3700'.
Bibliography: Cal. State Min. Bur. Reports XI, page 326; XIII, page 297. U. S. Geol. Survey Folio 15, Lassen Peak.

The property consists of four claims, including the Rich Gulch, Byers and Halstead. There are 80 acres, with a length along the lode of 6000'. The surface is characterized by steep ridges, giving excellent opportunities for development by tunnels.

It was discovered in 1881 by Joe Halstead. Most of the development has been in the form of assessment work, and consists of two tunnels, the English, 200' long and cutting the vein 150' below the outcrop; and the Blacksmith tunnel, 350' in length with two crosscuts in it. At present the mine is idle.

The country rock is slate and serpentine. The deposit is quartz fissure veins following the general strike of the slates, associated with veins in a brecciated mass of altered and silicified rock which has been recemented by quartz carrying gold, galena, pyrite and small amounts of chalcopyrite. The walls are slate. Quartz veins are 3' and 4' in width, but the altered and silicified breccia is 20' to 30'. The strike is N. 43° to 53° W., the dip 65° to 75° NE., and it can be traced at intervals for 6000'. There is a 200' pay shoot in the English tunnel. The ore is free milling and is said to average $3 to $4.50, but probably not for the whole width of the vein.

Elizabeth Consolidated mines adjoin.

Hazzard Mine. Owner, C. D. Hazzard, Quincy.

Location: Butte Valley Mining District, Sec. 15, T. 26 N., R. 8 E., 1 mile east of Seneca, thence 31 miles via Greenville to Keddie, by good automobile road. Elevation 5000'.
Bibliography: U. S. Geol. Survey Folio 15, Lassen Peak.

This property consists of ten claims, namely, the North West Extension, Ridge, Imperial, Bear, Gulch, Junction, South East Extension, Plumas, Kesmett and Seneca Eureka. The total area of 200 acres is characterized by a steep ridge running east. The ridge is very narrow, showing quartz on the surface, and the vein probably follows the course of the ridge.

The original locators were Rickard and Mandeville. The property, then consisting of three claims, was purchased in 1893 by Hazzard. There is one man working.

It is developed by two tunnels, the Ridge tunnel of 580' and the Bear tunnel of 230', and two crosscut tunnels on the Bear vein, below Bear tunnel, of 95' and 300'. Neither of the two latter have encountered the vein, which is supposed to lie very flat.

The deposit is apparently a dike of fine grained rock brecciated and recemented by quartz carrying auriferous sulphides, pyrite and arsenopyrite. There is one main vein of quartz and dike rock, which has been folded into an anticline, the filling being quartz and cemented breccia with streaks of solid sulphides. Free gold occurs in the oxidized portions, but very little is found in the sulphide zone, which is near the surface. The foot-wall is composed of slate, the hanging wall of slate and schist. The width of vein is from 5' to 20' and strike east. It dips 40° S., the Bear vein on the other leg of the anticline, dipping 45° N. Values are very unevenly distributed in the sulphide ore, assays from the same sample varying by a wide margin. Partially oxidized arsenical ore assays from $6 to $25.

Adjoins the Dawn, White Lily and Del Monte mines on the south.

High Grade Claim. Owner, L. A. Lambert, Brush Creek.

Location: Granite Basin Mineral District, Sec. __, T. 23 N., R. 6 E., within 35 miles of Quincy, by automobile road, via Buck's Ranch and Letter Box.
Bibliography: U. S. Geol. Survey Folio 43, Bidwell Bar.

The deposit consists of a 3' quartz vein with a granite foot-wall and porphyry hanging wall. There is a 30' shaft and a 100' tunnel on the vein. Thirty tons of ore on the dump are said to average $10 per ton.

Hinchman Mine. (Polar or North Star.) Owner, Sierra Range Copper Company; A. L. Beardslee, president, Sioux City, Iowa; Melvin Smith, secretary.

Location: Genesee Valley Mining District, Sec. 6, T. 25 N., R. 11 E., 2 miles northwest of Genesee, thence 16 miles, by good automobile road, via Taylorsville, to Keddie. Elevation 3800'.
Bibliography: Diller, J. S., U. S. Geol. Survey Bull. 260, pages 45, 49. Diller, J. S., U. S. Geol. Survey Bull. 353, pages 111-121. U. S. Geol. Survey Topo. sheets Indian Valley, Genesee, Honey Lake.

This property consists of the Roosevelt No. 1, No. 2 and No. 3 claims. There are 60 acres in all with a length along the lode of 3000'.

It was discovered in 1860, and purchased in 1907 by the present owners. Ore was shipped from the surface in early days.

The mine has been developed by 600′ of open cuts and a shaft 20′ deep. A crosscut adit of 400′ will encounter the vein, within a short distance, 300′ below the outcrop. One hundred tons of ore of two grades are on the dump, the best averaging 10% copper, $3 gold and $3 silver.

The deposit consists of a fissure vein, near the contact of the sandstone and meta-andesite country rock, containing bornite ore. The average width of the vein is 2′, the strike N. 20° W. and the dip 70° SW.

Hobson Group. (Plumas National.) Owners, W. F. Roedde, Crescent Mills; Wm. Stampfle.

> Location: Crescent Mills Mining District, Secs. 29 and 30, T. 26 N., R. 9 E.. 8 miles southwest of Crescent Mills, thence 11 miles, by good automobile road, to Keddie. Elevation 4500′–5500′.
> Bibliography: Diller, J. S., U. S. Geol. Survey Bull. 353, pages 114–115. Lindgren, W., U. S. Geol. Survey Prof. Paper 73, pages 114–116. U. S. Geol. Survey Topo. sheets Indian Valley, Taylorsville, Honey Lake.

The Dewey, Hobson and Black Jack claims comprise this property. With an area of 60 acres, it covers a length along the lode of 4500′. The vein follows the course of a steep gulch from Soda Creek to the top of the ridge with a difference in elevation of 1000′.

The mine was worked by J. S. Hall in 1875 and was then known as the Plumas National. Relocated by the present owners in 1903, it is now under bond to G. H. Hall, son of the former owner. When the sulphide orebody in the lower tunnel was encountered, a roaster was erected, and attempts were made to treat the ore in this manner, but only $12 of the $32, which the ore is said to have averaged, was recovered. The shoot was 600′ in length and 6′ in width.

Development work consists of an upper and lower tunnel. The upper tunnel cuts a 6′ vein 400′ from the portal at a vertical depth of 400′. The lower tunnel, at a distance in of 1540′, cuts the vein at a depth of 1000′. There is no connection between the tunnels.

The deposit is a quartz vein in slate, the country rock being slate and meta-andesite. There is one vein consisting of quartz, black talc gouge and black slate, containing free gold with some sulphides. The foot-wall is meta-andesite (altered) and the hanging wall is black slate (altered). The vein varies from 6′ to 8′ between walls, but it is not all solid quartz. The strike is N. 40° W., the dip 45° S., and there is a proven length on the surface of 4500′.

The Plumas Amalgamated adjoins this property, and Hall has a theory that the Plumas Amalgamated vein is a faulted portion of this vein.

Homestake Mine. (Basin Beauty.) Owners, Horace Waldron, Brush Creek; J. Young and (?)Smith, 310 Thirteenth street, Oakland.

Location: Granite Basin Mining District, Sec. 25, T. 23 N., R. 6 E., 8 miles northeast of Merrimac, 24 miles southwest of Quincy, by automobile road, via Letter Box. Elevation 4875'.
Bibliography: Cal. State Min. Bur. Report XIII, page 297. U. S. Geol. Survey Folio 43, Bidwell Bar.

This property consists of four claims, the Basin Beauty, Homestake, Stevens and Happy Thought. Waldron also owns a half interest in the Snow Flower claims.

Two tunnels on the property develop a vein 12" to 12' wide for 600', of which both walls are granite. Most of the ore has been stoped. The Franklin ledge, 6' to 8' wide, containing 6% sulphides but no free gold, is opened by surface cuts.

A 5-stamp mill (259-pound stamps) was erected in 1912.

Homestake Mine. (Highland Cliff.) (Mountain Chief.) Owners, Jas. Lesky, R. J. McKewen, Quincy.

Location: Quincy Mining District, Secs. 25 and 26, T. 24 N., R. 9 E., 2 miles south of Quincy by trail. Elevation 4000'–4500'.
Bibliography: U. S. Geol. Survey Folio 37, Downieville.

This property embraces four claims, the Homestake No. 1, No. 2, No. 3 and No. 4, an area of 80 acres containing 6000' of the lode. It is on the north slope of Claremont Hill near the summit of the ridge south of Quincy.

The deposit was worked in the early days. After abandonment by the Colonial Mining Company, it was relocated by the present owners in 1910. Two men work during the summer.

Developed by a main tunnel driven in quartzite 280' before encountering the orebody, then a 10' raise in the main tunnel on the Sulphide vein at a depth of 300', after which it is driven 25' in the orebody and 100' in slate. The Homestake vein is exposed by surface cuts 15' deep.

The deposit includes the Homestake vein and the Sulphide lode. The country rock is Calaveras slate and basalt. The Homestake is a quartz vein containing free gold and a small amount of pyrite. The foot-wall is slate and the hanging wall is quartzite and lava. The vein is from 4' to 6' wide, strikes northwest, and dips 45° SW. It has a proven length on the surface of 4500'. The Sulphide lode is composed of quartz and slate containing free gold and sulphides, principally pyrite. The foot-wall is quartzite, and the hanging wall slate. It is 20' wide, strikes northwest and dips 45° SW. Concentrates vary from $17 to $140 per ton in value.

A minimum of 25" of water is obtained from Mill Creek under a head of 300'.

Equipment consists of a blacksmith shop, cabin, cars, tools, etc.

The Tefft and Oddie mines are two miles south.

Honeycomb Claim. Owner, Thos. Halstead, Meadow Valley.

Location: Edmanton Mining District, Sec. 29, T. 24 N., R. 8 E., 4 miles south-west of Meadow Valley, thence 10 miles, by good automobile road, to Quincy. Elevation 4500'.
Bibliography: Lindgren, W., U. S. Geol. Survey Prof. Paper 73, pages 98–99. U. S. Geol. Survey Folio 43, Bidwell Bar.

This property consists of one location on the southeast slope of Spanish Peak. The surface is characterized by steep ravines.

The claim was formerly owned by C. Tryborn, after whose death it was located by the present owner. Very little work has been done in the last ten years, assessment work only being done at present.

Development consists of 500' of tunnels.

The property contains a northern extension of the Edman lode, a vein 20' to 30' wide, which is a replacement of dolomite. It strikes N. 30° W. and dips 60° E.

The Edman mine adjoins.

Horseshoe Mine. Owners, R. D. Hann, Quincy; Jerry Curtis, Twain.

Location: Butte Valley Mining District, Sec. 16, T. 26 N., R. 8 E., in Seneca, 35 or 40 miles Seneca to Keddie, 15 miles to Belden, by trail.
Bibliography: U. S. Geol. Survey Folio 15, Lassen Peak.

The mine is situated on a steep point on North Fork Feather River, and is developed by shallow shafts, 10' deep, 300' along the vein. A crosscut tunnel run 100' struck clay gouge, and a new crosscut in 175' will have to be driven 20' more to strike the vein.

The deposit consists of a 10' vein with stringers in slate. It strikes northwest, dips southwest and can be traced for 1000' on the surface. There is a 100' pay shoot.

Equipment comprises a 3-stamp mill, 1250-pound Merrill stamps with individual mortars, driven by an 8' Pelton waterwheel. A 22" pipe line, ditch and water right supplying 500", are owned.

Adjoining mines are the Dunn and Del Monte Consolidated.

Hulsman Mine. Owners, Wm. Hulsman and Brothers, Susanville.

Location: Lights Cañon Mining District, Sec. 12, T. 27 N., R. 10 E., 17 miles north of Taylorsville, by good wagon road and trail, thence 12 miles, by good automobile road, to Keddie. Elevation 5000'.
Bibliography: Diller, J. S., U. S. Geol. Survey Bull. 353. Lindgren, W., U. S. Geol. Survey Prof. Paper 73, pages 114–116. U. S. Geol. Survey Topo. sheets Indian Valley, Genesee, Honey Lake.

Development work consists of a number of tunnels on a quartz vein, carrying gold, silver and copper sulphides, near the contact of granodiorite and meta-andesite.

Engels copper mine is the nearest adjoining mine.

Husslemen and Shaw Group. Owners, Husslemen and Shaw, Susanville.

Location: Lights Cañon Mining District, Secs. 1, 12 and 13, T. 27 N., R. 10 E and Secs. 6, 7 and 18, T. 27 N., R. 11 E., 10 miles north of Taylorsville, by wagon road and trail, thence 12 miles to Keddie (W. P. Ry.) by good automobile road. Elevation 5000'.
Bibliography: Diller, J. S., U. S. Geol. Survey Bull. 353, pages 111–121. Cal. State Min. Bur. Bull. 50, page 187. U. S. Geol. Survey Topo. sheets Indian Valley, Genesee, Honey Lake.

This group comprises thirty-one locations, on nearly all of which some development has been done. They are the Moonlight, Wasp, Grant, Hulsman, Sherman, Oregon, Olympia, Davenport, Edward, Sidehill, Sperm, Oak, Shough, Gentle Annie, Cabin Ridge, No Wonder, Dexter, Live Oak, Fair View, Stone Point, Fritz, Big Spring, Big Boo, Belmont, Claremont, Vermont, Pala Cedar, Orient, Mammoth and Crystal. The mountain side on which they lie is very abrupt.

A tunnel has been started well down, so as to obtain 800' to 1000' of depth under the heaviest croppings. This is a crosscut tunnel and is in 150'. On the Mammoth claim several open cuts show sulphide and carbonate ore, which can be traced northerly for 900'. On the Orient claim a tunnel has been driven 150'.

The Gentle Annie claim is prospected with open cuts. On the Oregon there is a 13' shaft at the east end, and on the west end a superficial cut. Down the hillside from an outcrop on the Olympia claim is an 85' tunnel. There is a 20' open cut along the outcrop of the vein on the No Wonder claim. On the south hillside is the Palisades tunnel, which was driven to cut a ledge which crops 12' in width above it. This tunnel has a length of 197', but has not reached the ledge aimed at, although it has cut several small veins.

The country rock is granodiorite and meta-andesite, the veins being quartz veins carrying gold and silver and copper sulphides. On the mountainside and following the course of a proposed tunnel are 12 ledges. The widest vein is found near the apex of the hill and is about 13' wide. The character of the ore is carbonate with some sulphide. On the Gentle Annie claim there is a vein varying from 6' to 8' in width. The ore is siliceous, carrying red oxide, carbonates and pyrites, and can be traced for over 800'. A 13' shaft on two of the claims shows peacock copper ore in the bottom. Their width is unknown. Assays are reported as showing from 10% to 60% copper. The shaft on the Oregon claim is in green and blue stained ore, said to contain 20% of copper and to be rich in gold. Some copper glance is visible in the ore. The vein strikes south of west and the north wall is diabase, the south diorite. On the west end of the Oregon claim, a cut discloses some good carbonate and siliceous ore reported to assay 48% copper, $14 gold and 15 ounces silver. A vein parallel with the main one just described also shows good ore. On the Olympia claim a vein of carbonate ore outcrops and is exposed 30' in width by an open cut. The tunnel lower down the hillside cuts 30' of gray carbonate ore. The inclosing rock is a diabase, spotted with coarse crystals of feldspar. A vein of green carbonate ore, 8′ wide, outcrops on the No Wonder claim. Some copper glance can be seen in this ore.

The Engels copper mine is near.

Imperator Mine. Owner, L. Hemsath, Brush Creek.
> Location: Granite Basin Mining District, Sec. 13, T. 23 N., R. 6 E., 1 mile southeast of Letter Box, thence 22 miles to Quincy, by good automobile road, via Meadow Valley and Buck's Ranch.
> Bibliography: U. S. Geol. Survey Folio 43, Bidwell Bar.

This property is a relocation of an old claim, name unknown.

Old workings consist of 1000′ driven on the vein, a crosscut tunnel of 200′ and further drifts on the vein of 300′.

The vein is in granite and varies from 3″ to 3′, averaging 18″.

Assessment work only being done at present.

Independence Mine. (Seymore.) Owner, A. R. Seymore, Quincy.
> Location: Sawpit Flat Mining District, Sec. 30, T. 23 N., R. 10 E., 7 miles south of Quincy but 20 miles distant by automobile road to within 1 mile of mine. Elevation 5500′.
> Bibliography: U. S. Geol. Survey Folio 37, Downieville.

This property comprises four claims, Independence No. 1, No. 2, Emancipation and Gem. There is a total of 80 acres, covering 3000′ along the lode. Lava-covered ridges and steep ravines are characteristic of the surface. Winters Creek flows north from Mt. Washington, where the lava-capped 'Old Channel' is located.

The property was located in 1911, and eight men were working until November, 1912. One hundred twenty tons of ore said to average $186 per ton were shipped to the Selby smelter.

Development work consists of two inclined shafts, 50′ apart, 30′ and 55′ deep. There is a 30′ drift connecting the two shafts 25′ below the surface, and two crosscuts 10′ below the surface on the Emancipation-Gem vein.

There are two veins, the Emancipation-Gem being 200′ west of the Independence. Both are quartz veins associated with 'porphyry' dikes near the contact of serpentine, slate and schist. The Independence vein is composed of quartz and altered porphyry containing free gold and arsenopyrite in various stages of oxidation. The footwall is 'diabase schist,' possibly amphibolite, and the hanging wall slate. It varies from 3′ to 10′ in width, strikes N. 45° W., dips 55° W. and has a proven length on the surface of 500′. The Emancipation-Gem vein is composed of quartz and altered porphyry containing free gold and pyrite. The character of the walls has not been determined. There is a zone 150′ wide, 6′ to 20′ of which is claimed to be mineralized, which strikes N. 26° W., dips 55° E. and has a proven length on the surface of 3000′. These are supposed to be the southern extension of the veins worked in the Plumas Bonanza mine.

Indian Falls Mines. Owner, Indian Falls Development Company; C. A. Darmer, president, 754 St. Helena avenue, Tacoma, Washington; H. W. Tyler, secretary; G. H. Goodhue, Indian Falls, in charge.

Location: Crescent Mills Mining District, Sec. 3, T. 25 N., R. 9 E., Indian Falls on property, 5½ miles north of Keddie, by good automobile road. Elevation 3000'–4600'.
Bibliography; Diller, J. S., U. S. Geol. Survey Bull. 353, pages 114–115. Lindgren, W., U. S. Geol. Survey Prof. Paper 73, pages 114–116. U. S. Geol. Survey Topo. sheets Indian Valley, Taylorsville, Honey Lake.

This property contains twenty-one claims, a total of 577 acres, of which 148 acres are patented (agricultural). It covers 12,000' along the lode. The property takes in the flat at the bend of Indian Creek and then rises rapidly.

It was discovered in 1905 by Goodhue and sold in 1908 to the present owners.

Photo No. 9. Outcrop of quartz vein near Shoofly Bridge, on property of Indian Falls Development Company. Outcrop is 25'–75' in width and 75' high.

Tunneling comprises the development work. The River tunnel, 70' long, cuts the Copper vein (No. 3) 300' below the surface. At a point 70' north and 30' above is a 40' tunnel cutting 6' of 5½% chalcopyrite ore, 2000' northwest on the vein, the 60' Rose tunnel cuts the top of a vein carrying ½% copper and $2.80 gold, and 2100' northwest the 587' Emerald tunnel, cuts vein No. 2, and at 376' cuts the foot-wall of a copper vein.

There are five veins in this property, the No. 1, Gold Contact vein; No. 2, Gold; No. 3, Copper; No. 4, Shoofly, and No. 5. The country rock is slate and 'greenstone' (meta-andesite). Vein No. 1 is stratified flint quartz carrying free gold and sulphides, striking northwest and dipping southwest. The No. 2 vein, 200' from No. 1

vein, is made up of hard flinty quartz carrying gold and pyrite. It is from 22' to 80' wide, strikes northwest, and runs $2.80 gold. No. 3 vein has slate hanging and foot walls. It outcrops as a cliff at the river, 250' x 100' high and 60' wide. The deposit ranges 60' to 100' in width, strikes N. 40° W. and dips 55° southwest, with a proven length of 10,000' on the surface. Near the foot-wall is 8' of quartz in silicified slate and slate bands. Open cuts show a pay streak 4½' wide, averaging 9% azurite and black oxides. A 70' tunnel crosscut from the river level shows 6' of quartz carrying $1.10 gold and a small amount of copper, with an 18" pay streak going 6.2% copper, $1 gold and 2 ounces silver; 40' in it cuts 5' of 3% copper ore. No. 4 vein is a solid quartz fissure containing free gold and sulphides with slate foot and hanging walls. It varies 14' to 60' in width, strikes N. 40° W., dips SW. and has a proven length of 8000' on the surface. No. 5 vein is made up of soft quartz and is 16' wide.

Equipment consists of cars, track and a blacksmith shop.

Power is obtained from 2500" of water under 249' head, to which the company has a right. There is a 6500' ditch.

Indian Valley Mine. Owner, S. R. Prentiss, Bangor, Maine.

Location: Crescent Mills Mining District, Secs. 10 and 11, T. 26 N., R. 9 E., 1 mile south of Greenville, thence 15 miles to Keddie, by good automobile road. Elevation 4000'.
Bibliography: State Min. Bur. Reports, X, page 473; XIII, page 298. Diller, J. S., U. S. Geol. Survey Bull. 353, pages 114–115. Lindgren, W., U. S. Geol. Survey Prof. Paper 73, pages 114–116. U. S. Geol. Survey Topo. sheets Indian Valley, Taylorsville, Honey Lake.

The property consists of the Comstock (fraction), Dominion, Union and Indian Valley, all patented claims, comprising about 100 acres, and having a length along the lode of 4500'. The ridge on which it is situated rises from Greenville (3580') to the top of Green Mountain (5250').

The mine was first operated by Blood, Drake and Applegarth, who sold the property to Corbin of the Yale Lock Company, who afterward sold it to Prentiss. It has not been worked for the last sixteen years. The total production to date is about $1,800,000. A consolidation of a number of the properties in the vicinity, which includes the Indian Valley mine, was said to be progressing favorably.

Development consists of a 700' vertical shaft and a total of 2300' driven on the vein.

The deposit is a quartz fissure vein in meta-rhyolite. The ore is free milling, but contains sulphides. It varies in width from 7' to 10', strikes N. 45° W. and dips nearly vertically.

Water, under 300' head from Round Valley Reservoir, is utilized for power.

Adjoining mines are the New York, idle, and the Droege, working.

Indian Valley Silver Mine. Owner, Roy Starks, Taylorsville and Williams.

Location: Lights Cañon Mining District, Sec. 32, T. 27 N., R. 11 E., 7 miles northeast of Taylorsville, by wagon road, thence 12 miles to Keddie, by good automobile road. Elevation 4000'.
Bibliography: Diller, J. S., U. S. Geol. Survey Bull. 353, pages 111-121. Lindgren, W., U. S. Geol. Survey Prof. Paper 73, pages 114-116. U. S. Geol. Survey Topo. sheets Indian Valley, Genesee, Honey Lake.

This property comprises four claims, having 80 acres area and a length along the lode of 6000'.

It was worked in the early days and relocated in 1910 by the present owner. Assessment work only being done at present.

Development consists of a 200' tunnel on the vein and 6000' of open cuts at intervals.

The vein is a quartz and barite fissure vein in meta-andesites. The ore contains malachite, azurite, galena and silver, the copper minerals being in small amount. The foot and hanging walls are of altered andesite. The vein is 2' in width, with a pay streak from 4' to 8'. It strikes northeast and dips 75° W.

Iron Dike Mine. (Montgomery and Copper Bull.) Owner, Sierra Range Copper Company, Sioux City, Iowa; Melvin Smith, secretary; A. L. Beardsley, president, Genesee.

Location: Taylorsville Mining District, Sec. 2, T. 25 N., R. 10 E., 1 mile south of Taylorsville, thence 12 miles to Keddie, by good automobile road. Elevation 3800'-5600'.
Bibliography: Diller, J. S., U. S. Geol. Survey Bull. 353, pages 111-121. U. S. Geol. Survey Topo. sheets Taylorsville, Indian Valley, Honey Lake.

This property embraces eight claims, including the Mountain View, Waverly, Long Point, Snowclad, and Sulphide No. 1 and No. 2. There is a total of 160 acres covering a length along the lode of 6000'.

It was operated in 1860 through the Pettinger shaft. Purchased by the present company in 1905. Idle at present, assessment work only being done.

The main tunnel, now in 300', is 200' below the surface in partially oxidized material, and will give 1200' of backs when it encounters the vein. Other tunnels on the property aggregate 2000'. There is a 60' shaft on the Pettinger vein.

The deposit consists of two veins, the Pettinger and the Iron Dike, in country rock of sandstone, slates and serpentine. The Pettinger vein is an imperfect quartz vein in slate. The ore is malachite and azurite, averaging 12% copper. It strikes N. 54° W. and dips 50° SW., with a length proven on the surface of 2500'. The Iron Dike vein is a vein of solid non-nickeliferous pyrrhotite in a sheared zone of sandstone near contact with serpentine, and Montgomery limestone of the Grizzly formation and Taylor conglomerate. The hanging (?) wall is limestone, the foot(?) wall sandstone and fine conglomerate. The vein varies from 10' to 50' in width, strikes N. 13° W., dips 50°

SW., and has a proven length on the surface of 2500'. The two veins intersect. Ore occurs on both veins at intervals, but not in well-defined shoots.

Jamison Mine. Owner, Jamison Mining Company, 237 First street, San Francisco; Frank B. Peterson, San Francisco, president; Sam Cheney, San Francisco, secretary; Geo. S. Redstreak, Johnsville, manager.

Location: Johnsville Mining District, Secs. 25, 26, 35 and 36, T. 22 N., R. 11 E., 1¼ miles south of Johnsville, 7 miles southwest of Blairsden, by automobile road. Elevation 5370'.
Bibliography: Cal. State Min. Bur. Reports, VIII, page 480; X, page 485; XI, page 330; XII, page 217; XIII, page 298. Lindgren, W., U. S. Geol. Survey Prof. Paper 73, page 111. U. S. Geol. Survey Folio 37, Downieville.

This property comprises in all 580.9 acres, two patented placer claims, 235 acres, one placer location, 160 acres, and nine quartz claims, all patented, 185 acres. Steep slopes are characteristic of the surface, but the veins are near the creek level and can not be developed by tunnels.

The property was discovered in 1888 and bought by the present owners in 1889. From 47 to 50 men are usually working. Shut down in September, 1913, for lack of water, but reopened in January, 1914. No dividends have been paid for the past three years, all money taken out being put in exploratory work which has so far developed little ore, and unless other orebodies are developed the mine will probably be shut down for good within a couple of years. It averaged a monthly production of 1900 tons worth $5500 to $7000. Bullion production to November 1, 1913, was $1,358,925, concentrates 14,511 tons at $5. Fifty men working in July, 1915, with good ore coming from new workings.

Development consists of the Haskins drain tunnel, 1800' long, driven S. 20° E., which strikes the shaft at the 165' level, then a crosscut driven southwest 1150' from the bottom of the shaft, where the new vein was encountered by a raise of 170' from the crosscut. A drift was driven south on this vein for 1400' and the vein was stoped 50' above this level, where it was cut off by a fault. The main crosscut was then driven west 200' at an angle from its former course, and another raise of 100' was put up to the vein and a drift driven south about 1500'. No. 2 level: The ground has been stoped between this and No. 3 level, above. The crosscut was continued 100' and another raise was put up to the vein 50' above the crosscut and a drift was run south on the vein for 1160'. Most of the ore was stoped between this level and No. 2 level above. The crosscut was continued beyond the raise for a distance of 120', where it intersected the vein on its dip. From No. 3 drift a crosscut was run west and at a distance of 190' intersected a vein dipping 70° W. and some specimen ore was taken out. The hanging wall of this vein is a fine-grained porphyry dike. The crosscut was continued through this porphyry dike, driven 450' in gabbro, and from the end a 490' raise at 45° was put up. The shaft is 225' deep.

The deposit consists of fissure veins in gabbro. There are two, the old vein and new vein. The former is quartz containing free milling oxidized ore, and 600' of pay shoot has been worked. It averages 10' in width and has no outcrop, having been discovered in placering. It strikes N. 20° W., and dips 25° E. The new vein is quartz carrying free milling gold and auriferous pyrite which contains a small amount of gold ($13). This vein averages 10' in width and has no outcrop, having been encountered in crosscutting. It strikes N. 15° W. and dips 30° W. There are four pay shoots, worked for 800'.

Mine equipment consists of a 14" x 16" duplex Giant compressor, double drum friction hoist, buildings, office, bunkhouses, cottages, barn, etc., with a full equipment of drills and tools. The mill is a Fulton mill, erected in 1896, containing ten 1000-pound stamps and ten 900-pound stamps using No. 0 punched screen.

Water is obtained from Jamison, Wade and Grass lakes, and is used at the hoist under a 400' head and at the mill under 480' head.

Costs per ton were as follows in 1915: development, 83¢; mining, $1.68; treatment, 30¢; general, 24¢. Average daily output, 70 tons. Tailings run from 50¢ to 80¢. Power costs 4¢. Labor from $2.50 to $3.25, and timber, 8¢ to 12½¢.

The Plumas Eureka mine adjoins.

Jennie Mine. (Senator Perkins Mine.) Owner, Senator Geo. Perkins, Oakland. (Grouped with the Caldwell and New Century by J. H. Hall, Brush Creek.)

> Location: Granite Basin Mining District, Sec. 25, T. 23 N., R. 6 E., 30 miles southwest of Quincy, by good automobile road; also good automobile road to Oroville, 50 miles. Elevation 4600'.
> Bibliography: Cal. State Min. Bur. Rept. XIII, page 305.

The property consists of one claim, the Jennie, which is patented. It is 200' x 1500', covering the lode for 1500'. Low ridges and creeks are characteristic of the surface.

Development consists of a 250' tunnel on the vein, from which ore has been stoped to the surface.

The deposit consists of a small quartz fissure vein in granite, containing free gold and from 1% to 2% of sulphide. It varies in width from 2' to 25', strikes northeast, dips 80° E., and is said to average $5.

Equipment consists of a blacksmith shop, houses and an 8-stamp mill erected in 1870.

Water from Frazier Creek through one-half mile of ditch and 300' of 10" pipe furnishes power for the mill. It can be run eight months out of the year.

This property adjoins and lies northwest of the Whidden fraction, which adjoins and lies northwest of the Caldwell mine. All of these properties have been grouped and are under the management of J. A. Hall.

Joshua Moss Mine. Owners, Joshua Moss and Horace Waldon, Brush Creek.

> Location: Granite Basin Mining District, Sec. 25, T. 23 N., R. 6 E., 10 miles northeast of Brush Creek, 31 miles southwest of Quincy, by good automobile road, via Buck's Ranch and Letter Box.
> Bibliography: U. S. Geol. Survey Folio 43, Bidwell Bar.

The property consists of the Black Prince and Narrow Gauge claims. The Black Prince is an old producer formerly known as the Mexican mine. A tunnel 500' in length developed a vein of quartz 1' in width-in which a number of small, rich shoots occurred. The vein strikes northeast and both walls are granite.

Justice Group. (Clear Creek.) Owner, Mrs. Isabel Williams, Oroville.

> Location: Butte Valley Mining District, Secs. 26 and 35, T. 27 N., R. 8 E., 10 miles northwest of Greenville, thence 18 miles to Keddie, by good automobile road. Elevation 5000'.
> Bibliography: U. S. Geol. Survey Folio 15, Lassen Peak.

This property comprises ten locations, the Justice No. 1 to No. 5, Clear Creek No. 1, No. 2, Langford, Lookout and Mattie, with patent applied for on three. There are 140 acres with a length along the lode of 7000'.

Development work consists of a 1000' tunnel driven on the Langford claim cutting the vein at a depth of 255', from which a small amount of ore has been stoped.

The deposit forms a zone 200' wide which is said to be a system of parallel veins. The country rock is quartz and iron gossan, generally oxidized but with some chalcopyrite and pyrite. The foot-wall is said to be serpentine, the hanging wall meta-andesite. It strikes N. 30° W., dips 35° SE., and has a proven length, by open cuts, of 7000'. The ore is reported to have a maximum value of $8 gold and $6 silver.

Mine equipment consists of a cabin, blacksmith shop and barn. Wood fuel and steam are used.

Work was stopped in April, 1913.

The Gold Strike mine, now being reopened, adjoins.

Kennebeck Mine. Owner, P. H. Bailey.

> Location: Crescent Mills Mining District, Sec. 10, T. 26 N., R. 9 E., 1½ miles south of Greenville, thence 15 miles, by good automobile road, to Keddie.
> Bibliography: Diller, J. S., U. S. Geol. Survey Bull. 353, pages 114–115. Lindgren, W., U. S. Geol. Survey Prof. Paper 73, pages 114–116. U. S. Geol. Survey Topo. sheets Indian Valley, Taylorsville, Honey Lake.

There are three veins, cut by a 600' tunnel run in early days, and by another tunnel 300' lower, driven a distance of 500'.

King Solomon Mine. Owners, Mrs. H. A. Cabe, H. L. Cabe, L. F. Cabe, and D. R. Cabe, all of Quincy.

Location: Quincy Mining District, Sec. 25, T. 25 N., R. 10 E., 12 miles northeast of Quincy, by good automobile road, 8 miles northeast of Marston, by good automobile road. Elevation 6500'–7000'.
Bibliography: Cal. State Min. Bur. Report XIII, page 299. U. S. Geol. Survey Folio 37, Downieville.

The holding consists of two claims, the Grand Prize and King Solomon. Patents applied for two years ago are as yet not granted. There are 40 acres situated on the ridge dividing the headwaters of Taylor and Squirrel creeks, with a length along the lode of 3000'.

The property was discovered in 1885 by Compton and Cabe.

Development consists of a 55' shaft with a 50' drift to the south, crosscutting the lode, also an inclined shaft 45' deep, 100' southwest of the vertical shaft. An 1100' tunnel cuts the shaft 10' above bottom.

There is a lode 50' wide of quartz and stringers, then a horse of country rock, then solid quartz, striking N. 71° E. and dipping 32° E. The vein filling is clear quartz, free milling and carrying pyrite and chalcopyrite. Foot and hanging walls are supposed to be meta-andesite, or augite-porphyrite. There is a small reserve of $4 ore. Water power can be developed three or four miles from the mine.

Laura Claim. Owners, Mrs. E. Blood, Berkeley; W. Blood, Greenville.

Location: Johnsville Mining District, Sec. 7, T. 22 N., R. 13 E., 2 miles north of Clio by good wagon road to within a short distance of property. Elevation 4500'.
Bibliography: Lindgren, W., U. S. Geol. Survey Prof. Paper 73, page 111. U. S. Geol. Survey Folio 37, Downieville.

This property comprises one claim, the Laura, which is patented. It has an area of 20 acres and a length along the lode of 1500'.

The property has been held by the present owners for the last 20 years, but no work has been done recently.

The nearest mine is the Bullion, three miles to the south.

Leete Mine. Owner, B. F. Leete, Reno.

Location: Crescent Mills Mining District, Sec. 14, T. 26 N., R. 9 E., 1 mile northwest of Crescent Mills, thence 8 miles, by good automobile road, to Keddie. Elevation 5000'.
Bibliography: Cal. State Min. Bur. Report XIII, page 299. Diller, J. S., U. S. Geol. Survey Bull. 353, pages 114–115. Lindgren, W., U. S. Geol. Survey Prof. Paper 73, pages 114–116. U. S. Geol. Survey Topo. sheets Indian Valley, Taylorsville, Honey Lake.

This holding consists of 160 acres of patented timber land. It is situated on the ridge lying between Crescent Mills and Greenville and contains 1500' of the lode.

The property has been held by the present owner for a number of years and several tunnels have been run, but no work has been done lately. It is included in a consolidation of mines now under consideration.

The deposit consists of fissure veins near the contact of meta-rhyolite and granodiorite, the southern extension of the Indian Valley, Southern Eureka and McLelland veins.

Adjoining mines are the Southern Eureka and Indian Valley to the north and the Green Mountain and Crescent mines to the south.

Lincoln Mine. Owners, W. W. and F. V. Gallagher, Johnsville.

Location: Johnsville Mining District, Sec. 32, T. 23 N., and Sec. 5, T. 22 N., R. 11 E., 4 miles northwest of Johnsville; Cromberg or Sloat (W. P. Ry.) is 6 miles northeast by trail. Elevation 5200'.
Bibliography; Lindgren, W., U. S. Geol. Survey Prof. Paper 73, page 111. U. S. Geol. Survey Folio 37, Downieville.

This property consists of two claims, the Lincoln and Little Lincoln, containing 40 acres and a length along the lode of 3000'.

It was discovered by W. O. Wall in 1910 and purchased in 1911 by Gallagher Brothers.

There is a crosscut tunnel driven 300' to the vein, which it cuts at a depth of 100', and a 50' drift.

The deposit consists of a quartz fissure vein near the contact of slate and augite porphyrite. It has an average width of 8', strikes north, and dips 45° W. The ore is oxidized, free milling, and said to run $30 per ton.

There is a blacksmith shop and cabin on the property, and a 5-stamp mill may be erected in the spring.

Adjoining mines are the West Elizabeth placer and the Plumas Mohawk quartz mines, both idle.

Little California Mine. Owners, Lawrence Kittrick, Oroville; J. H. Kittrick, Lumpkin; A. Moore, Oroville.

Location: Edmanton Mining District, Sec. 6, T. 22 N., R. 8 E., 15 miles, in direct line, southwest of Quincy. Quincy is 18 miles by good road from Buck's Ranch, thence 8 miles by trail to mine. Elevation 3000'.
Bibliography: Lindgren, W., U. S. Geol. Survey Prof. Paper 73, pages 98–99. U. S. Geol. Survey Folio 43, Bidwell Bar.

This property consists of one claim, 20 acres in area and covering a length of 1500' along the lode. Steep cañons are characteristic of the surface.

There is a small lenticular quartz vein, 2' wide, with granite foot-wall and greenstone hanging wall, developed by a 400' tunnel. It is low grade.

A 5-stamp mill stands on the property.

Little Gem Claim.

Location: Genesee Valley Mining District, a few miles southeast of Genesee, thence 18 miles west, by good automobile road, to Keddie (W. P. Ry.).
Bibliography: Diller, J. S., U. S. Geol. Survey Bull. 260, pages 45–49. U. S. Geol. Survey Bull. 353, pages 111–121. Cal. State Min. Bur. Bull. 50, page 184. U. S. Geol. Survey Topo. sheets Indian Valley, Genesee, Honey Lake.

The vein is from 6" to 18" in width, and carries reported values of $17.96 gold, 31 ounces silver and 12.66% copper. It has been opened by a shaft.

Little Nell Mine. Owners, Sutherlan Murray, 412 Crocker Building, San Francisco; Tyndale Phipps, Quincy.

Location: Sawpit Flat Mining District, Sec. 35, T. 23 N., R. 8 E., 18 miles southwest of Quincy, by horse trail, poor in places. Elevation 3000'.
Bibliography: U. S. Geol. Survey Folio 37, Downieville.

The property comprises nine claims, namely, Little Nell, Little Nell No. 1 and No. 2, Bluebird, Budweiser, Budweiser No. 1 and No. 2, Union, and Union No. 1. There are 180 acres covering a length along the lode of 2000'. It is situated on a steep cañon of the Feather River, rising 2500' in two miles.

Two of the claims were located in 1900 by Hughlett, but the work up to the time the present owners took the property consisted only of open cuts. Two men were working in 1915.

A crosscut adit is being run to cut the Little Nell vein 80' below the surface. No ore has been stoped but a number of rich pockets have been worked by open cuts.

The two veins, the Bluebird and Little Nell, are of quartz associated with siliceous porphyry dikes, which have been altered by hydrothermal agencies. They are solid quartz fissure veins, following dikes. The Bluebird vein contains free gold, varies from 6' to 8' in width, strikes east, dips 30° N., and has a proven length on the surface of 400'. The foot-wall is slate, the hanging wall diorite. The Little Nell vein contains free gold and a small amount of galena and pyrite. It lies 450' west of the Bluebird and has a foot-wall of hornblende schist and a hanging wall of amphibolite schist. It varies in width from 3' to 4', strikes S. 20° E., dips 61° E., and has a proven length of 200' on the surface. The Bluebird ore averages $6 to $8 per ton, the Little Nell $6.

There is a blacksmith shop and a cabin on the property.

The Butte Bar mine adjoins, having a vein parallel to and 300' west of the Bluebird vein. It is idle at present.

Lucky S. Group. Formerly owned by Mrs. S. Wagener, Livermore.

Location: Lights Cañon Mining District, Sec. 28, T. 27 N., R. 11 E., 10 miles northeast of Genesee or Taylorsville, 12 miles from Taylorsville to Keddie by good automobile road. Elevation 6478'.
Bibliography: Cal. State Min. Bur. Reports, X, page 467; XIII, page 300. Diller, J. S., U. S. Geol. Survey Bull. 353, pages 111–121. Lindgren, W., U. S. Geol. Survey Prof. Paper 73, pages 114–116. U. S. Geol. Survey Topo. sheets Indian Valley, Genesee, Honey Lake.

This property has been abandoned, it is claimed, as no assessment work has been done for a number of years.

Lucky Strike Mine. (Darby Mine.) Owners, A. E. Darby, Buck's Ranch; C. Crane, Oroville.

Location: Edmanton Mining District, Secs. 4 and 5, T. 23 N., R. 7 E., 2 miles west of Buck's Ranch, Quincy 17 miles east by good automobile road. Elevation 5500'.
Bibliography: Lindgren, W., U. S. Geol. Survey Prof. Paper 73, pages 98–99. U. S. Geol. Survey Folio 43, Bidwell Bar.

This property consists of one claim, namely, the Lucky Strike, 20 acres in area, and covering the vein for 1500'. Steep ravines are a feature of the surface.

There is a tunnel 312' long which it is estimated will cut the vein 40' farther at a depth of 75' below the outcrop. Surface cuts on the vein give a proven length of 1500'.

The deposit is a quartz vein containing very little free gold but from 3% to 4% of sulphides and some chalcopyrite. It is in granite and said to be 4' wide and to strike N. 10° E., and dip 37° E.

Assessment work only is being done.

Magee Claim. (Hughes Mine.) Owner, J. Magee, Oroville.
Location: Edmanton Mining District, Sec. 27, T. 24 N., R. 7 E.; Quincy. 20 miles northeast by good automobile road to Bucks and trail 2 miles to mine. Elevation 5500'.
Bibliography: Lindgren, W., U. S. Geol. Survey Prof. Paper 73, pages 98–99. U. S. Geol. Survey Folio 43, Bidwell Bar.

This property is composed of one claim, 20 acres in area and covering a length along the lode of 1500'.

A tunnel 200' in length has been driven on the vein.

It is a quartz vein in granite, varying in width from 1' to 2', striking northeast and dipping 80° E. Both walls are granite. The ore is said to run from $8 to $14 per ton.

Malloy's mine is the nearest property.

Magpie Group. Owner, A. L. Beardsley, Genesee.
Location: Genesee Valley Mining District, Sec. 24, T. 26 N., R. 11 E., 5 miles northeast of Genesee by trail, thence 15 miles by good automobile road to Keddie. Elevation 5500'–6500'.
Bibliography: Diller. J. S., U. S. Geol. Survey Bull. 260, pages 45–49. Diller. J. S., U. S. Geol. Survey Bull. 353, pages 111–121. U. S. Geol. Survey Topo. sheets Indian Valley, Genesee, Honey Lake.

The property comprises two claims, the Magpie No. 1 and No. 2, 40 acres in area and covering 3000' along the lode.

It was discovered in 1883 and has been held by the present owner since 1910. Assessment work only is being done.

The only development is a 45' shaft on the vein.

The latter is a fissure vein in meta-andesite, containing hematite with gold $2.50, silver 4 ounces and copper 4%. The meta-andesite walls are well defined. The width of the vein is 6', it strikes northwest, dips 45° NE., and has a proven length on the surface of 2500'.

The Reward, idle for a number of years, is an adjoining mine.

Main Spring Claim. Owner, T. B. Lofton, Buck's Ranch.
Location: Edmanton Mining District, Sec. 26, T. 24 N., R. 7 E., 2 miles north of Buck's Ranch, thence 18 miles to Quincy, by good automobile road.
Bibliography: Lindgren, W., U. S. Geol. Survey Prof. Paper 73, pages 98–99. U. S. Geol. Survey Folio 43, Bidwell Bar.

This property consists of one location, called the Main Spring, with an area of 20 acres. It covers a length along the lode of 1500'.

The deposit is a quartz fissure vein in granite, 4' wide, free milling, and said to average $6 per ton in gold. The strike of the vein is northeast and the dip is 70° E.

It has been developed by a 30' shaft and a 100' tunnel, 40' of which has been driven on the vein. The tunnel cuts the vein 40' below the outcrop.

Assessment work only was being done in 1915.

Malloy Mine. Owner, P. Malloy, Buck's Ranch.
> Location: Edmanton Mining District, Secs. 28 and 33, T. 24 N., R. 7 E.; Quincy 20 miles northeast by good automobile road to Buck's and trail to mine. Elevation 5000'.
> Bibliography: Lindgren, W., U. S. Geol. Survey Prof. Paper 73, pages 98–99. U. S. Geol. Survey Folio 43, Bidwell Bar.

This property consists of one claim (possibly other locations) of 20 acres, covering 1500' along the lode. Steep cañons to the west and low ridges to the northeast characterize the surface.

Very little work has been done in the last few years.

There is a fissure vein of white quartz, free milling and carrying from 2% to 3% sulphides. Value unknown. It strikes northeast in granite, and dips 75° E..

A small 4-stamp mill with boiler and engine is on the property, but the mill buildings are in poor shape.

Magee's mine is the nearest mine in the vicinity.

Megown Mine. Owner, H. B. Hardy, Meadow Valley.
> Location: Spanish Ranch Mining District, Secs. 31 and 32, T. 25 N., and Secs. 5 and 6, T. 24 N., R. 8 E., 5 miles northwest of Meadow Valley, 7 miles by fair wagon road to Spanish Ranch, thence 7 miles by good automobile road to Quincy. Elevation 5100'.
> Bibliography: Cal. State Min. Bur. Reports, X, page 484; XI, page 324; XIII, page 301. Lindgren, W., U. S. Geol. Survey Prof. Paper 73, pages 98–99. U. S. Geol. Survey Folio 43, Bidwell Bar.

This property consists of one claim, called the Megown. It is 20 acres in area and contains 1500' of the lode. Ridges are separated by comparatively wide ravines at the head of the creek.

The property was discovered in 1876, and the surface to a depth of 75' to 100' has been worked by hydraulicking. It was relocated by Hardy. Two men were working in 1912, but only assessment work was done in 1913.

Development consists of a main adit 300' long, cutting the vein 40' below the bottom of an open cut and 40' driven on the vein. In the tunnel a high grade stringer was encountered and some rich pockets were taken out.

There is a quartz vein and stringers in Calaveras slates which lie between schists on the west and serpentine on the east. The quartz carries free gold and sulphides with heavy gouge. The walls are slate. The main vein varies in width from 3' to 4'. It strikes northwest and dips 45° S., with a proven length of 150'. The ore ranges from $250 to $500 per ton.

The Mountain House drift mine owned by the Plumas Investment Company adjoins.

Moreno Randolph Claim. Owner, Barbee.

Morning Star Mine. (Robinson Mine.) Owner, E. C. Robinson, First National Bank Building, Oakland, California.

> Location: Granite Basin Mining District, Secs. 30 and 31, T. 23 N., R. 7 E.: Quincy is 30 miles northeast via Letter Box, Buck's Ranch and Meadow Valley; good automobile road to property.
> Bibliography: Cal. State Min. Bur. Report XIII, page 304. U. S. Geol. Survey Folio 43, Bidwell Bar.

This property comprises two patented claims, the Morning Star and Trenton. There is a total area of 40 acres with a length along the lode of 3000'. Frazier Creek divides the property, cutting across the strike of the vein. There is an easy slope from the creek to the top of the ridges.

The claims were located in 1876 by O'Brien and Sullivan. In 1890 the property was purchased by Robinson, bonded in 1905 by Trowbridge and in 1912 by Holbrooke and Cohn, San Francisco, who, it was reported, spent $10,000 and only succeeded in sinking the shaft 10' before work was abandoned. Chas. Lyser was superintendent. It has been idle since the summer of 1912.

Development work consists of a shaft 100' deep near the portal of the lower tunnel on the east side of Frazier Creek and a drift on the vein 150' to the northeast from the bottom of the shaft. There are also three tunnels on the vein—the upper tunnel, 75'; middle tunnel, 300'; and lower tunnel, 300', northeast of the creek and 300' southwest of the creek. All ground is stoped from the lower tunnel to the surface, and a small amount from the 100' level in the shaft.

The deposit consists of a fissure vein near the contact between granite and diorite. The vein filling is quartz and in some cases decomposed granite and glass quartz crystals. The vein varies from 2' to 4' in width, strikes N 41° E., and dips 80° E. The foot-wall is granite, the hanging wall diorite, and there is a proven length on the surface of 2000'. Several pay shoots 40' to 50' in length developed in the 600' opening. The ore is said to average $10 per ton, 2% sulphides being worth $60 to $75 per ton.

Water is obtained from Frazier Creek by a 1650' ditch under 94' head. Steam is also used.

Equipment consists of steam and water power hoist capable of sinking to a depth of 500' and a 35 year old 20-stamp mill.

Adjoining mines are the Frazier and Black Bart.

Mother Lode Group. Owner, M. J. Calnan, Genesee.

> Location: Genesee Valley Mining District, Secs. 14 and 15, T. 25 N., R. 11 E., 3 miles southeast of Genesee, thence 18 miles, by good wagon road, to Keddie. Elevation 4000'.
> Bibliography: Diller, J. S., U. S. Geol. Survey Bull. 353, pages 111–121. Diller, J. S., U. S. Geol. Survey Bull. 260, pages 45–49. U. S. Geol. Survey Topo. sheet Indian Valley, Genesee, Honey Lake.

This property embraces seven and a fraction claims, namely, the Baltimore, Little Joe, Mother Lode, Evening Star, Fine Friend, Keystone, Gold Fish, and Home Rule. There are 150 acres covering a length along the lode of 4500'. It is situated in the cañon and on the ridges on both sides of Ward Creek.

The property was discovered in 1902 by the present owner, who has been working it alone.

A copper-bearing zone has been developed by numerous shallow shafts and superficial open cuts. There are two shafts on the Little Joe claim, 80' and 24' deep, and a shaft on the Gold Fish 30' deep. A tunnel has been started on a narrow stringer called the Keystone vein which is said to be an extension of the Gold Fish vein. On the Mother Lode claim a tunnel has been driven 110' through the andesite porphyry, 250' south of the Little Joe shaft. This will have to be driven 50' further.

The deposit is composed of stringers and bunches of quartz and altered schist, the quartz carrying sulphides of copper and free gold in the oxidized portion of the different zones. The foot-wall and hanging walls are schist and andesite. There are a number of parallel shear zones, all of which show more or less indications of copper. The general strike is N. 30° to 40° W. All dip about 45° E. except the Gold Fish, which dips 45° W., nearly the dip of the slates which lie to the west of the Gold Fish claim. A lot of 13 tons of ore is said to have been shipped to Selby's which averaged $86 per ton (gold $6.36, silver 43 ounces, and the rest copper). This ore was taken from the Little Joe shaft and was hand sorted, ratio unknown. A lot of 300 tons on the dump is said to average $30 per ton.

Water power could be developed if necessary.

Adjoining mines are the Five Bears and the Gruss.

Mother Lode Mining and Reduction Company. (Cyanide Plant.) Owner, Mother Lode Mining and Reduction Company, 251 Russ Building, San Francisco; Geo. Newman, 251 Russ Building, San Francisco, president; A. Altshuler, 251 Russ Building, San Francisco, secretary; C. A. Boydston, 2534 Grant street, Berkeley, staff.

Location: Crescent Mills Mining District, Sec. 19, T. 26 N., R. 10 E., 11 miles north of Keddie by good automobile road; ¼ mile east of Crescent Mills. Elevation 3400'.

This cyanide plant of 200 tons capacity, was erected to treat the tailings from the Crescent and Green Mountain mines. Sampling showed that the tailings would average $1.50 per ton and that there were approximately 1,000,000 tons covering the flat.

The method of working is as follows: the top sod is removed and the tailings underneath hauled to the plant by horse scrapers, elevated to a mill, slimed and agitated by air in small cone-bottom tanks. The slimes were dewatered by an Oliver filter and the gold recovered by zinc precipitation.

The plant consisted of two galvanized iron buildings, one containing a 100-horsepower boiler and engine, and 50-h.p. compressor, the other the assay office, precipitation plant, storehouse, Dorr classifier, Oliver filter, tube mill (now removed) and agitation tanks. Wood was used for fuel.

The plant has been idle since 1913, but experiments are now being carried on to find some economical method of treatment. Boydston expected that the plant would be altered and ready to run by January, 1914.

The company operating this plant also owns the Plumas Amalgamated mines.

Mountain Lily Mine. (Mountain View.) Owners, N. Kertchendorf, Robert Martin, Indian Falls.

> Location: Crescent Mills Mining District, Secs. 32 and 33, T. 26 N., R. 9 E., 2 miles northwest of Indian Falls, thence 5 miles, by good automobile road, to Keddie; wagon road from mine to Keddie by way of Crescent Mills, 17 miles. Elevation 4000'.

This property consists of two claims, the Mountain Lily and Heatherbell. There are 40 acres with a length along the lode of 3000'. It is situated on top of the ridge northwest of Indian Falls.

The mine was discovered by the present owners in 1895. The Wheeler Lumber Company tried to patent the ground but the patent was protested by Kutchendorf. The two owners worked the property in 1913.

It is developed by a main tunnel driven at an angle from the footwall to the dike, across the dike to the hanging wall vein and a drift run 300' east on the vein. A winze is put down from the point where the tunnel cuts the ledge 45' on the vein, also a winze 275' from the crosscut is sunk 20' on the vein. Another tunnel started on the east end of the claim in the dike, if run 400' more will cut the vein 100' below the upper workings.

The deposit is a dike of 'porphyry' 70' in width with quartz veins on each wall. The dike is decomposed and full of small quartz stringers. The country is badly faulted. There are two veins, the hanging wall and the foot-wall vein. The former is characterized by quartz, with gouge on both walls, containing free gold and pyrite, partially oxidized. The foot-wall is the porphyry dike and the hanging wall slate. The vein varies from 4' to 11', strikes S. 87° W., dips 60° to 70° S., and has a proven length on the surface of 1500'. The ore assays $2 to $7 per ton. The foot-wall vein is made up of quartz and clay carrying free gold and no sulphides. Its foot-wall is slate and the hanging wall is the porphyry dike. It dips and strikes the same as the hanging wall vein.

Steam, or electric power from Indian Creek is used.

Adjoining properties are the Plumas National, Plumas Amalgamated and Indian Falls Development Company.

Mountain Lion Mine. Owner, Sierra Range Copper Company, Sioux City, Iowa; A. L. Beardsley, Genesee, president; Melvin Smith, Sioux City, secretary.

> Location: Genesee Valley Mining District, Secs. 15 and 22, T. 25 N., R. 11 E., 2 miles south of Genesee, thence 18 miles by good automobile road to Keddie. Elevation 5500'.
> Bibliography: Diller, J. S., U. S. Geol. Survey Bull. 260, pages 45–90. Diller, J. S., U. S. Geol. Survey Bull. 353, pages 111–121. U. S. Geol. Survey Topo. sheets Indian Valley, Genesee, Honey Lake.

The Mountain Lion Nos. 1, 2, 3 and 4 claims comprise this property. There is a total of 80 acres with a length along the lode of 6000'. It is situated on the steep slope from Ward Creek to Peele Ridge (4000' to 6000').

The property was discovered in 1902 and acquired by the present owners in 1905. It is idle at present, assessment work only being done.

It has been opened on the surface by numerous trenches. A crosscut tunnel 750' in length will have to be driven 50' farther to cut the vein.

There is one vein, the Mountain Lion, from which white quartz came from some of the surface cuts carrying bornite, 'gray copper' (tetrahedrite), free gold $400, silver as high as 20 ounces and 6% copper. Both walls are meta-andesite. The vein varies from 5' to 6' in width, strikes N. 20° W., dips 75° SW., and has a proven length on the surface of 1100'.

Adjoining mines are the Gruss and Five Bears.

Mudhen and **Minnie S. Group.** Owner, Joseph Peppin, Brush Creek.

> Location: Granite Basin Mining District, Sec. 30, T. 23 N., R. 7 E., 7 miles northeast of Brush Creek; Quincy is 30 miles northeast, by good automobile road, from Quincy to Buck's Ranch and Letter Box. Elevation 4700'.
> Bibliography: U. S. Geol. Survey Folio 43, Bidwell Bar.

This property is composed of four locations, namely, the Plumas, Oliver Quick, Mudhen and Minnie S. The Mudhen is a north extension of the Minnie S., which is a north extension of the Morning Star. There are 80 acres covering a length along the outcrop of 3000'.

The property was located in the early days by J. Peppin. Assessment work only was being done in 1914.

The Minnie S. vein has been developed by shallow shafts and open cuts. A crosscut tunnel has been driven 700' through granite in doing the assessment work for the past 12 years and it is believed that the vein will be cut 160' below the outcrop, within a few feet.

Shallow shafts and open cuts comprise all that has been done on the vein covered by the Plumas claim.

The Minnie S. vein strikes N. 37° E. and dips 80° E. Ore from this vein resembles the Morning Star ore and contains free gold, galena and chalcopyrite in small amounts. The ore from the surface is reported to have run as high as $90 per ton. The foot-wall is granite, the hanging wall diorite, and the vein is said to be 3' wide.

Native Son Mine. Owner, Genesee Valley Copper Company, Sioux City, Iowa; A. L. Beardsley, Genesee, president; Melvin Smith, secretary.

Location: Genesee Valley Mining District, Secs. 13 and 14, T. 25 N., R. 11 E., 3 miles east of Genesee by wagon road and trail, thence 18 miles by automobile road, to Keddie. Elevation 6000'.
Bibliography: Diller, J. S., U. S. Geol. Survey Bull. 260, pages 45–49. Diller, J. S., U. S. Geol. Survey Bull. 353, pages 111–121. U. S. Geol. Survey Topo. sheets Indian Valley, Genesee, Honey Lake.

This property contains five claims, known as the Native Son No. 1 to No. 5. It is situated on a high ridge south of Genesee Valley, and east of Ward Creek.

The holdings were discovered in 1907 and purchased by the present owners in 1910.

The mine has been developed by a 200' tunnel, a 45' shaft and open cuts, but assessment work only is now being done.

There is one vein, a quartz stringer vein carrying chalcopyrite, in a siliceous zone near the contact of slates and altered andesite. The foot-wall is slate and the hanging wall slate and andesite. The siliceous zone is said to be 100' in width. It strikes N. 30° W., dips 70° SW., and has a length proven at intervals on the surface of 4000'. It is said to be a continuation northward of the Walker Brothers deposit, but this is doubtful.

The Gruss mine adjoins.

New Century and **Whidden Group.** Owners, J. A. Hall, Brush Creek; M. A. Whelden, Elks Club, Oakland.

Location: Granite Basin Mining District. Sec. 25, T. 23 N., R. 6 E., 9 miles northeast of Brush Creek; Quincy is 30 miles northeast by automobile road from Quincy via Buck's Ranch and Letter Box; also automobile road from Oroville, 50 miles. Elevation 4500'.
Bibliography: U. S. Geol. Survey Folio 43, Bidwell Bar.

This property comprises 23 acres with a length along the New Century vein of 1500' and along the Whidden of 1200'. Not patented. The New Century location lies southwest of the Caldwell claim, and the Whidden Fraction location, 1200' x 100', lies northwest of the Caldwell, between it and the Jennie mine. Low ridges are characteristic of the surface.

J. A. Hall is doing assessment work on the claims.

The Whidden vein is developed by a 40' tunnel. The New Century has three adits, the upper adit 160' long, 25' below the outcrop, the middle adit 190' long, 60' below the upper tunnel, and the lower adit 280' long, 90' below the middle tunnel. There is a raise from the middle to the upper tunnel, in which is said to be 60' of ore averaging $12 per ton, the limits being $8 to $40. Ore from the Whidden vein is said to mill $14. Concentrate to the amount of 2% assays $100 per ton.

The deposit consists of two small quartz fissure veins in granite. The New Century vein is free milling and contains 2% sulphides. It averages 18" in width, strikes N. 35° E., dips 70° E., and has a proven length on the surface of 5000'. The Whidden vein contains 2% sulphides and is free milling. It averages 16" in width, strikes northeast, dips 70° E., and has a proven length on the surface of 200'.

The Caldwell and Morning Star mines adjoin.

New York Mine. Owners, J. D. Whitney, Greenville; Estate of L. M. McIntosh, care R. C. Harrison, 640 Mills Building, San Francisco.

Location: Crescent Mills Mining District, Secs. 10 and 15, T. 26 N., R. 9 E., 2 miles south of Greenville, thence 15 miles, by good automobile road, to Keddie. Elevation 3600'–5000'.
Bibliography: Diller, J. S., U. S. Geol. Survey Bull. 353, pages 114–115. Lindgren, W., U. S. Geol. Survey Prof. Paper 73, pages 114–116. U. S. Geol. Survey Topo. sheets Indian Valley, Taylorsville, Honey Lake.

This property embraces the following claims: New York placer, 40 acres (patented), Buena Vista, Prospect, Plowboy (patented), New York (patented), Brooklyn, Luson placer, and 80 acres of timber. There is a total of 230 acres covering a length along the lode of 6000'. It is situated on the steep slopes from the cañon to the top of the ridge, giving good tunnel sites.

This mine was operated from 1872 to 1883 by Troleaven and May. It was reopened in 1898–1902 by J. D. Whitney, but assessment work only has been done in the last few years. The mine is said to have produced to date about $400,000. During the Whitney regime 12,000 tons of an assay value of $70,000 yielded $43,000 bullion.

The property is developed by three tunnels. No. 2 tunnel, 1800' in length, is 90' below the outcrop. It is driven as a crosscut for 297' and then on the vein for 1350'. No. 3 tunnel, 190' below No. 2, has been driven 450' as a crosscut and will have to be driven 300' farther, to cut the first pay shoot. From 1872 to 1883, 600' along the vein from No. 2 tunnel to the surface was stoped. Under the Whitney management it was extended 700'. Stopes in that distance yielded 12,000 tons for a distance of 100' above No. 2 level, the average length of the shoots being 90' and width 12'. From No. 2 to the surface it is estimated that the ore resources are 75,000 tons, net value $261,000 (ore value per ton $7, working costs and metallurgical losses $3.50, net value per ton $3.50). It is also estimated that if

No. 2 tunnel is continued ahead for 800' and the lower tunnel is driven 1500' on the vein with the same results as in No. 2 tunnel, 400,000 tons of additional ore will be blocked out.

The deposit consists of the main New York vein, and two smaller veins, which have not been prospected. It is a quartz-filled fissure, the orebodies occurring as lenses in quartz and porphyry vein filling. Some of the ore is a recemented fault breccia. The ore is free milling, oxidized near the surface, pyritic below. Both walls are quartz porphyry. The deposits are lenticular shoots 150' to 250' in length, 40' to 50' apart and 8' to 18' in width. The strike is N. 21° W., dip 63° SW., and it has a proven length on the surface of 6000'. Seven pay shoots averaged 90' in length and 12' in width. Minor faults are common.

Equipment consists of blacksmith shop and tools, small hoist, sinking pumps, Giant air compressor (320 cubic feet free air per minute), belt driven from Pelton waterwheel, air drill, cars, houses, stable, messhouse, assay office, and an old 15-stamp mill built in 1871.

Water from Round Valley Reservoir under a head of 320', but with an 800' head possible, is available. The ditch carries 600" and water costs 10¢ per inch.

Costs for mining $1.30 per ton, treatment $1.83 per ton (old mill). Loss in treatment per ton 52%, extraction 48%. Tailings $3.20 to $4. Total operating cost per ton $3. Concentrates 3% run $50. Labor cost $3.50 per day. Transportation charges San Francisco to mine 1¢ per pound. Good ore was encountered in the upper workings in November, 1915, and driving on No. 3 tunnel was to be immediately resumed. The operators planned to build a 10-stamp mill in the spring.

Oro Fino Mine. Owners, H. W. Hewitt and Brothers, Eclipse.

Location: Sawpit Flat Mining District, Sec. 10, T. 22 N., R. 10 E.; 4 miles southeast of Eclipse by wagon road, Quincy 30 miles northwest by good automobile road and fair wagon road. Elevation 5525'.
Bibliography: U. S. Geol. Survey Folio 37, Downieville.

There are eight locations, covering discoveries by Hewitt Brown in 1907 and 1910 in this property, a total of 160 acres with a length along the lode of 7500'. It is situated in deep V-shaped cañons, one mile east of Pilot Peak, a lava-capped elevation 7500' high.

An adit, 500' long, cuts the vein 100' below its outcrop, and there are two 10' crosscuts to the west wall 450' and 500' from the mouth of adit, also one crosscut to the east in slate for 50' and a raise of 100' to the surface. One stope 50' north of the raise extends 60' above the tunnel level. This length may be the limit of the pay shoot; the owners, however, claim that there are no well-defined zones of enrichment. All drilling is done by hand, and very little blasting is necessary as the material can, in most cases, be worked by pick and shovel. Ore is loaded in the tunnel from chutes, trammed to the adit mouth and lowered by cars to the mill 200' below. Tailings are disposed of in Hopkins Creek.

The orebody consists of stringers of quartz in a decomposed dike, which is so altered in the present surface workings that it is impossible to determine its original character. There are two parallel veins 300' apart, of the same character, replacement and impregnation of dike by quartz, only one of which is developed. The ore is for the most part oxidized but some small bunches of partially oxidized arsenopyrite have been found. The walls are Calaveras slates, and the decomposed dike material ranges from 10' to 15' in width. It strikes N. 13° W. Near the surface the vein dips 80° W.; where cut by the tunnel 100' down it is nearly vertical, and it will probably dip east at depth. There is a proven length of 3000' on the surface. The ore is said to average $10 with assays as high as $100 probably from quartz stringers. As all of the workings are in the oxidized zone, it is impossible at present to tell the size and value of the orebody in the unaltered zone, but at depth the quartz veins will carry a large percentage of arsenopyrite. It is doubtful whether the unaltered dike rock will carry values throughout its entire width. The arsenopyrite concentrates vary from $15 to $25 per ton in value.

Water is used for power. Equipment consists of a blacksmith shop, good house and barn, and a 5-stamp mill (1059 pound stamps) with two Johnson concentrators. Transportation charges are 1¢ per pound from Quincy.

The Rose quartz is the nearest mine.

Oversight Mine. Owners, August Binner, J. E. Wilson, Quincy.

Location: Sawpit Flat Mining District, Sec. 24, T. 23 N., R. 9 E.; 8 miles south of Quincy, good automobile road to within 3 miles of the property, then poor wagon road to point above mine, then 1 mile by trail; total distance from Quincy, via Nelson Point, 20 miles. Elevation 4000'.
Bibliography: U. S. Geol. Survey Folio 37, Downieville.

There are two claims composing this property, the Oversight and the Oversight Extension, 40 acres in area and covering the lode for 3000'. Steep V-shaped cañons are distinctive features of the surface. The claims were located by the present owners in 1911. One man was working in 1914.

The mine is opened by two tunnels, No. 1, 70' long, driven on the Big vein, and No. 2, 130' long, driven on the Stringer vein. Two winzes, 15' and 10' and two raises 10' and 25' from No. 2 tunnel, follow rich bunches of partially oxidized ore.

The Big vein is a quartz vein in decomposed serpentine. The footwall is altered serpentine, the hanging wall schist. The ore is quartz with mariposite, and bright green chromiferous mica, probably resulting from alteration of serpentine. It averages 6′ in width, strikes north and dips 65° W. The gold is evenly distributed and the vein has a proven length on the surface of 200′. It is said to average $4.99 to $6 per ton. The Stringer vein is a 6″ quartz stringer at right angles to the cleavage of the slates, containing arsenopyrite. Both walls are schist and slate. It strikes N. 3° W., dips 40° W., and contains rich pockets of oxidized ore. There is a fair prospect of developing good ore in the Big vein. The Stringer vein does not amount to a great deal but may enrich the Big vein at the point of intersection, approximately 100′ below the present adit level. On the surface the Stringer vein lies about 200′ east of the Big vein.

Adjoining mines are the Crescent Hill Gold Mining Company, one mile north across Feather River Cañon, and Plumas Bonanza, one mile east across the ridge in Winters Creek basin.

Recent crushing (in 1916) showed an average of $15 per ton with some ore of higher grade.

Peter Mine. Owner, W. F. Peter, Taylorsville.

Location: Genesee Valley Mining District, Sec. 7, T. 26 N., R. 11 E., 17 miles northeast, by good automobile road, from Keddie (W. P. Ry.). Elevation 3600′.

Bibliography: Diller, J. S., U. S. Geol. Survey Bull. 260, pages 45–49. Diller, J. S., U. S. Geol. Survey Bull. 353, pages 111–121. Cal. State Min. Bur. Bull. 50, page 184. U. S. Geol. Survey Topo. sheets Indian Valley, Genesee, Honey Lake.

This mine is situated on the eastern border of the north arm of Indian Valley at the foot of Indian Range.

It has been worked intermittently as a gold mine ever since 1867, but the old mine openings have long since caved. Development during later years consists of two tunnels crosscutting the ledge, with various drifts, upraises and winzes totaling 1700′ in length.

The ledge runs from 5′ to 15′ in width, and has a well-defined hanging wall formed by a fault plane. It strikes N. 33° W., with a dip of 50° SW. The formation is chiefly felsite, and felsitic porphyry, occasionally becoming schistose; overlain to the east by a red metamorphic schist, probably of igneous origin. The ledge is evidently an impregnation deposit, with the strongest mineralization next to the hanging wall. Above the water level its original sulphides of iron and copper are largely oxidized and the copper leached out, while the manganese silicate which abounds has originated various oxides, chiefly pyrolusite. Gold forms the principal value above the water level, with from 2% to 3% of copper, as bornite, copper glance and some carbonates of copper. The gold alone has so far been the object of development.

Pilot Peak Mine. (Pilot Hill.) Owners, Pilot Peak Mining Company, P. F. Turner and McCall, Eclipse via Quincy.

> Location: Sawpit Flat Mining District, Sec. 9, T. 22 N., R. 10 E., 1 mile southeast of Eclipse, 25 miles southeast of Quincy; good automobile road Quincy to Eclipse, wagon road to mine. Elevation 6500'–7000'.
> Bibliography: Cal. State Min. Bur. Reports, XII, page 218; XIII, page 303. U. S. Geol. Survey Folio 37, Downieville.

This property contains six claims, a total of 120 acres covering a length along the lode of 3000'. Lava-capped peaks and deep V-shaped cañons mark the surface.

It has been owned by Turner since 1900. Three men were working in 1914.

A crosscut tunnel 500' in length was being driven which will intersect a vein and give 100' of backs.

There are two veins on the property, one of which is developed. Slate, capped by lava, forms the country rock. The developed vein is a quartz-filled fissure with a large percentage of arsenopyrite and some free gold. It lies between a foot-wall of black slate, and a hanging wall of schist or slate. The vein varies from 4' to 6' in width, strikes northwest and dips east. Ore from this vein is said to average $15 for the whole width. It is mined by hand drilling.

The Rose quartz mine adjoins.

Pioneer Mining Company. Owners, J. N. Henry, Belden; H. G. _____, Fair Oaks.

> Location: Butte Valley Mining District, Sec. 34, T. 26 N., R. 7 E., 8 miles northeast of Belden (W. P. Ry.).
> Bibliography: U. S. Geol. Survey Folio 15, Lassen Peak.

Dabney property adjoins.

Plumas Amalgamated Mines Company. (Monitor.) Owner, Plumas Amalgamated Mining Company; S. Altshuler, president; 251 Russ Building, San Francisco; C. E. Boydston, superintendent, 2534 Grant street, Berkeley.

> Location: Crescent Mills Mining District, Secs. 29 and 30, T. 26 N., R. 9 E., 7 miles southwest of Crescent Mills, by fair wagon road, thence 11 miles to Keddie by good automobile road. Elevation 5200'.
> Bibliography: Diller, J. S., U. S. Geol. Survey Bull. 353, pages 114–115. Lindgren, W., U. S. Geol. Survey Prof. Paper 73, pages 114–116. U. S. Geol. Survey Topo. sheets Indian Valley, Taylorsville, Honey Lake.

This company holds nineteen claims, maps and names of which are not available. There are 380 acres in all, situated on the top of a flat ridge with a rapid fall to Soda Creek.

The property was discovered in 1880 and was purchased in 1910 by the present owners. About 20 acres of the 'blanket' vein was stoped by former owners. Six men were working in 1917.

All of the development work has been done under the blanket vein by a tunnel 275' below the top of the hill. This tunnel appears to be lower than any portion of the blanket vein and all of the ore has been developed by raises from different branch drifts. The main tunnel was driven a distance of 500′ S. 10° W., at which point a drift was run 400′ to the west. It was then continued 100′ S. 10° W., and a drift was run 100′ in an easterly direction. It turned and was driven nearly west for a distance of 200′ and then in a southwesterly direction for 700′, making a total length of tunnel of about 1500′. From points 200′ and 500′ beyond the turn, drifts were run west for 100′ and 115′, respectively. The work so far accomplished by the present owners has been in the nature of exploratory work only and no estimate of the ore reserves can be made.

The deposit is characterized by quartz veins and stringers near the contact of slates and meta-andesite. The Monitor blanket vein lies nearly flat on the top of the hill and covers an area of about 60 acres. All of the ore is oxidized and free milling. The foot-wall is quartzite and greenstone, the hanging wall clay slates. It lies as a sort of synclinal fold, and dips both north and south with a maximum of 20°. The width of the stringers and slate varies 8′ to 20′ with the pay ore occurring in bunches. The Black Prince vein is a free milling quartz vein in greenstone. The foot-wall is greenstone (altered andesite), the hanging wall quartzite and greenstone. The vein is solid quartz 3′ wide, striking N. 10° W., and dipping 15° SW., with a proven length on the surface of 400′.

The geology of this property is complex and a detailed study of the deposit would have to be made to arrive at any definite conclusion regarding the origin and possibilities of the Plumas Amalgamated deposit.

The mine is equipped with a superintendent's house, bunkhouse and blacksmith shop.

The mine was equipped in 1914 with ten 225-pound Straub stamps, operated by steam and having a capacity of 12 tons in 24 hours. Amalgamation only is used and recovery is said to be about 70%. The property was idle in 1918.

Adjoining mines are the Plumas National, idle, and the Droege.

Plumas Bonanza Mine. Owners, Chas. W. Reed, Belmont; F. W. Jordan, Pilots' Office, San Francisco; F. Roeder, 834 Market street, San Francisco; W. A. Wall, Nelson Point via Quincy.

Location: Sawpit Flat Mining District, Sec. 20, T. 23 N., R. 10 E.; 6 miles, by road, to Nelson Point, thence 18 miles to Quincy, by good automobile road. Elevation 4200′.
Bibliography: U. S. Geol. Survey Folio 37, Downieville.

The property embraces ten claims, a total of 200 acres, covering a length along the main vein of 3000′. High ridges and V-shaped cañons are characteristic of the surface.

John Kelly located these claims in 1906 and the property was purchased by the present owners in June, 1913. A crew of five men were working in 1914.

The mine at that time was developed by a 50′ shaft and 60′ driven on the vein from the bottom of the shaft. No ore had been stoped, the mill being run on rock taken out in development work.

The deposit consists of quartz veins cutting across the strike of slates, probably following a siliceous dike. There are two veins, but practically no work has been done on the Creek vein. The vein filling is quartz, gouge and kaolin, the solid quartz outcrop showing 15′ wide in places. The quartz is free milling, with very little sulphide as the workings are in an oxidized zone. It varies from 6′ to 20′ in width, averaging 8′, strikes N. 85° W., and dips 30° to 45° N., with a proven length on the surface of 3000′. The Creek vein is proven for 1500′. The ore averages $10 per ton, with assays reported as high as $100.

The mine is equipped with log cabin, 2-stamp, triple discharge, Union Iron Works mill and concentration plant, the latter not being used at present, as the ore carries practically no sulphide. The mill is run by water power from Winters Creek.

Tailings are disposed of in Winters Creek and Middle Fork Feather River.

The nearest producing mine is the Crescent Hill, two miles northwest across Feather River.

Plumas Eureka Mine. Owner, Plumas Eureka Mining Company; Geo. Phillips, New York, controlling interest; D. J. Lawton, Napa, vice president; J. R. Stark, Jr., Johnsville, assistant superintendent.

Location: Johnsville Mining District, Secs. 23 and 26, T. 22 N., R. 11 E., ½ mile west of Johnsville, 8 miles west of Blairsden by good automobile road. Elevation 5500′–7400′.

Bibliography: Cal. State Min. Bur. Repts. VIII, page 476; X, page 382; XI, page 330; XII, page 219; XIII, page 303. Lindgren, W., U. S. Geol. Survey Prof. Paper 73, page 111. U. S. Geol. Survey Folio 37, Downieville.

Photo No. 10. Plumas Eureka Mill with Eureka Peak in the background. Tramway can be seen in center. Photograph taken from Johnsville.

There is a total area, including timber rights, of 2500 acres in this property. It is situated on the east slope of Eureka Peak from Jamison Creek to the summit.

The mine was located in 1850 and operations began in 1851, considerable work being done prior to 1875. It was closed down by the Sierra Buttes Company in 1897, then purchased by the Johnson Graham Mining Company and in 1909 by the present company. Only exploratory work was being done in 1915.

The different veins have been worked for lengths varying from 300' to 1000'. The Eureka vein was exploited by the 1500' Eureka tunnel and a 150' shaft, the '76' vein for 400', the North vein for 500'

Photo No. 11. View of Eureka Peak taken from the trail to the '76' tunnel of the
Plumas Eureka Mine.

and the Lawton has been stoped for 200' above the Eureka tunnel level. A very large area has been stoped on different veins, but it is impossible to describe the workings without maps.

The deposit is made up of a complex system of quartz veins with well defined walls. The main vein is at or near the contact of quartz porphyry and gabbro. At intervals flat floors of quartz are found lying nearly horizontal. All the veins are of white free milling quartz carrying varying percentages of sulphides, pyrite, chalcopyrite, arsenopyrite and galena. The Eureka vein varies from 1' to 6' in width, averaging 4', strikes southwest and dips 75° NW. The '76' vein varies from 1' to 4' in width, strikes southeast and dips 25° S. The North vein averages 8' in width, varying from 1' to 20', strikes north and dips 45° E. The Lawton vein varies from 1' to 8' in width, strikes south and dips 45° E.

Equipment consists of buildings and machinery. The mill building had 60 stamps. The present owners put in 20 new stamps, repaired the building and reconstructed 20 stamps of the old mill.

Water power is obtained from Jamison Creek and Eureka Lake.

The Jamison is an adjoining mine.

After a brief idleness, work was resumed in July, 1915. A small crew is placing the main workings in shape for mining, and a lower tunnel is being driven to open the property at a considerable depth below the present workings.

On August 28, 1915, a voluntary petition of bankruptcy was filed in the United States District Court. Liabilities $133,633, assets $41,515.

Plumas Jumbo and **Little Jumbo Mines.** Owner, A. E. Murdock, Reno, Nevada.

Location: Sec. 25, T. 24 N., R. 16 E., 8 miles north of Chilcoot, 9 miles north of Chilcoot station on W. P. Ry., by Chilcoot and Last Chance wagon road. Elevation 6200'.

The Little Jumbo and the Plumas Jumbo claims comprise this property. There is an area of 40 acres covering a length along the lode of 1500'. It is situated on the ridge southwest of Mt. Adams and contains a good stand of sugar pine and spruce.

This property was discovered in 1901 and has been worked as a prospect off and on since that time. Idle at present.

A tunnel 125' long reaches a depth on the vein of 50'. This, with a series of prospect shafts, makes up the development work.

The deposit forms a series of parallel veins in granite. They are true fissure veins, with a quartz gangue impregnated with chalcopyrite, bornite, malachite and azurite. The maximum width of the vein is 6', the average being 2'. It strikes northeast, dips 45° NW., and has a proven length on the surface of 1500'. The ore is basic.

Plumas Mohawk Mine. (Gallagher, Rossi and Grizzly Bear.) Owner, Plumas Mohawk Gold Mining Company, Johnsville; W. H. Mayfield, Johnsville, president; M. H. Bernheim, Johnsville, secretary.

Location: Johnsville Mining District, Sec. 3, T. 22 N., R. 11 E., 5 miles northwest of Johnsville, 8 miles northwest of Blairsden by wagon road. Elevation 5800'–6100'.
Bibliography: Cal. State Min. Bur. Report XIII, pages 294–297. Lindgren, W., U. S. Geol. Survey Prof. Paper 73, page 111. U. S. Geol. Survey Folio 37, Downieville.

This property comprises seven quartz claims, the St. Joseph, Roberts, Mayfield & Gallagher Extension No. 1 and No. 2, Garabaldi, Eureka Ledge, and Rossi or Squirrel Creek; also the Grizzly Bear placer claim of 160 acres, making a total of 300 acres and covering a length along the lode of 3000'. The surface offers good tunnel sites.

Gallagher discovered the property in 1880, the claims being consolidated and purchased by the present owners in 1906. The mill was run in 1908 for a short time, 23 men working during that time. Only assessment work has been done since.

Pocahontas Mine. Owners, J. A. Hall, Brush Creek; G. M. Sparks, Oroville.

Location: Granite Basin Mining District, Sec. 12, T. 22 N., R. 6 E., 7 miles northeast of Brush Creek, 35 miles southwest of Quincy, by automobile road from Quincy via Letter Box to Granite Basin, thence by trail 4 miles, automobile road from Oroville to Letter Box and Granite Basin 45 miles. Elevation 4200'.
Bibliography: U. S. Geol. Survey Folio 43, Bidwell Bar.

The property includes the three claims, Winona, Pocahontas and Minnehaha, covering 60 acres in area and a length along the lode of 4500'. Steep cañons characterize the surface.

Locations were made in 1895 but only assessment work has been done since.

This includes a 30' shaft and a 40' tunnel on the Pocahontas, and a 40' incline on the Minnehaha. Other work consists of seven open cuts at intervals of 100'.

There is one quartz fissure vein with gouge on both walls. Samples taken from various openings are said to have averaged $5 gold, $3 silver and $6 copper. The foot-wall is Calaveras slates, the hanging wall 'porphyry' (possibly schists). It has an average width of 4', strikes northeast, dips 80° E., and has a proven length on the surface of 3000'.

A minimum of 300 horsepower can be developed from Coldwater Creek Falls, within 1000' of the property.

Transportation charges from Oroville are 1¢ to 1¼¢ per pound; wages paid, $3 and board.

The Morning Star, Granite Basin and Coquette mines adjoin.

Premium Mine. Owners, P. A. Taylor, Taylorsville; F. W. and R. Young, Crescent Mills.

Location: Taylorsville Mining District, Secs. 32 and 33, T. 26 N., R. 10 E., 1½ miles southwest of Taylorsville, thence 12 miles to Keddie, by good automobile road. Elevation 3700'.
Bibliography: Diller, J. S., U. S. Geol. Survey Bull. 353, pages 111–121. U. S. Geol. Survey Topo. sheets Indian Valley, Taylorsville, Honey Lake.

This property consists of five claims, 100 acres in area and covering a length along the lode of 4500'.

The mine was worked in the '70's by G. Standart of Greenville and is said to have produced $180,000. One hundred tons of ore removed by underhand stoping below the Premium tunnel is reported to have yielded $816. The mine has been idle since 1898, assessment work only being done.

The East and West veins are developed by open cuts only. The Premium tunnel, with a length of 460' on the vein, develops the Premium vein to a maximum depth of 135'. The Lower tunnel is 350' below the Premium tunnel and will crosscut all three veins. It is already in 155′ and has cut the East vein, which is 20′ wide and assays $1.80. The tunnel will have to be driven 200′ farther to cut the Premium vein. One shoot has been stoped to a height of 65′ above the Premium tunnel for a width of 4′ and another shoot has been stoped to the surface, 135′, for a width of 8′. Ore is said to have averaged $11 per ton.

The three veins in this property, namely, East, Premium, and West, are all quartz fissure veins in granodiorite, the vein filling being quartz and decomposed granodiorite.

The ore is free milling, being oxidized and containing very little sulphide. The East vein is 20′ wide, strikes N. 50° W., dips 70° SW., and has a proven length on the surface of 800′. The Premium is composed of two veins, 8′ and 4′ wide, striking N. 50° W., dipping 80° SW., and having a proven length on the surface of 1000′. The West vein strikes N. 40′ W., dips 70° NE., and is 3′ wide. It has a length of 400′ proven on the surface and one pay shoot 140′ long has been developed.

There is an old 5-stamp mill with 600-pound stamps on the property.

Water is obtained from Crystal Lake under a 260′ head, though a much greater head can be obtained, it being possible to secure a 3300′ head from Hough Creek.

Prospect Claim. (Cabalan.) Owners, J. S. Carter, Mrs. Maud Neer, Crescent Mills.

Location: Crescent Mills Mining District, Sec. 13, T. 26 N., R. 9 E., 1 mile northwest of Crescent Mills, thence 11 miles, by automobile road, to Keddie. Elevation 3900′.
Bibliography: Cal. State Min. Bur. Report XIII, page 289. Diller, J. S., U. S. Geol. Survey Bull. 353, pages 114–115. Lindgren, W., U. S. Geol. Survey Prof. Paper 73, pages 114–116. U. S. Geol. Survey Topo. sheets Indian Valley, Taylorsville, Honey Lake.

This property consists of one patented claim of 20 acres, covering a length along the lode of 1500′. It is situated on the ridge lying between Crescent Mills and Greenville.

The Carter family has been the owner for the past 20 years.

There is one vein, a quartz fissure vein, containing free gold developed by a 500′ tunnel and several shorter ones. It is 12′ wide and low grade, trending northwest, and dipping nearly vertical. The country rock is meta-rhyolite.

No work has been done for some time.

Adjoining mines are the Crescent and Green Mountain.

Reising Mine. (Reising Placer Mine.) Owners, H. C. Flourney, Quincy; Jerry W. Uslenghi, Twain.

Location: Butte Valley Mining District, Sec. 9, T. 25 N., R. 8 E., 3 miles northwest of Twain, Virgilia (W. P. Ry.) 4 miles southwest by wagon road and trail. Wagon road to Uslenghi Ranch, then 2 miles, by trail, up Rush Creek to mine. Elevation 3300′.
Bibliography: U. S. Geol. Survey Folio 15, Lassen Peak.

This property contains the Oriental, Reising and Pennant quartz locations and the Reising and Rattlesnake placer locations. There is a total of 130 acres, 71 of which are placer locations. The length along the lode is 4215'. Narrow ridges and deep cañons characterize the surface.

The property was worked as a placer in early days, before the claims were relocated. Assessment work only is now being done, and so far it has been of little utility. It consists of an 80' tunnel from the creek, now caved in, another tunnel run in from the ravine east of the Reising house, which to all appearances is outside of the lode proper, and prospecting 15' above the creek by a shallow open cut 300' across the outcrop.

The deposit consists of two large lodes, Upper lode, 123'; Lower lode, 157', with 150' of bedrock intervening. The lode itself consists of a highly metamorphosed quartzite, largely charged with sericitic mineral, and some calcite, impregnated with finely divided pyrite. In this vein matter irregular stringers of white quartz ramify in all directions and interbedded, well defined, large veins of quartz occur. Small fragments of slaty rock, generally well charged with pyrite, occur all through the vein matter, and pyrites are also found sparsely scattered through the vein quartz. The Upper lode is more irregular and disrupted and has less clear quartz visible. The gold seems to be associated with quartz, which may be of later origin than the quartzite as in some cases the 'vein' quartz seems to cut the cherty quartzite. Samples taken along the outcrop on the creek averaged $1.16 for a total width of 114', and on the Lower lode $1.25 for a width of 138'. These samples were taken from hard outcrop and there is no doubt but that the value of the ore could be materially increased by the selection of quartz showing greater mineralization than the whole body of the outcrop. Both the foot and hanging walls are schists and slates. These lodes have a general northerly trend and dip from 60° to 80° E. They have been traced on the surface at intervals for a distance of 3000'.

Rush Creek furnishes a large and never failing water supply, probably not less than 500 cubic feet at the lowest stage and averaging over 1000 cubic feet. Good opportunities for the storage of water exist at the head of the creek. For a large power supply the waters of the river, East Branch of the North Fork Feather River, may be utilized by electrical transmission not exceeding three miles. A flume and ditch about 2500' in length belong to the property, with the water privileges pertaining thereto.

The best gold prospects have been obtained from the quartz and stringers carrying pyrite, which have in some cases been oxidized, leaving cavities and iron-stained bands of quartz. The surface debris overlying the lower lode was sluiced off and a considerable quantity of angular gold, containing particles of quartz was recovered in the sluice boxes. The pieces of gold were in some cases quite large and the character shows that their migration has been slight, and that they were in all probability derived from the lode quartz.

Robinson Mine. Leased to United States Exploration Company, 617 Pacific Building, San Francisco.

> Location: Granite Basin Mining District, 35 miles northeast of Oroville, 25 miles southwest of Quincy.
> Bibliography: U. S. Geol. Survey Folio 43, Bidwell Bar.

Posey and Miller, representing Colorado men, took a bond on this mine in September, 1915. By the middle of October the dismantling of the 20-stamp mill and the installation of Sears-Smith rotary mills with a capacity equivalent to 40 stamps was in progress. The shaft was to be deepened and a six mile road from the basin to Junction House on the Oroville road was to be built. This is the initial step toward the development of the Granite Basin District on a large scale by the United States Exploration Company.

In the fall of 1918 it was stated that development had proven unsatisfactory and work had been suspended till after the war.

Rose Quartz Mining Company. (Kelly Mine.) Owner, Rose Quartz Mining Company, Nicolaus Building, Eighth and K streets, Sacramento; H. E. Weyl, lessee, Eclipse via Quincy.

> Location: Sawpit Flat Mining District, Sec. 3, T. 22 N., R. 10 E., 1½ miles east of Eclipse, thence 24 miles northwest by good automobile road, with steep grades via Nelson Point to Quincy. Elevation 6000'.
> Bibliography: U. S. Geol. Survey Folio 37, Downieville.

This property consists of nine claims, names unknown, none of which are patented. There is a total of 180 acres with a length along the lode of 3000'. High lava-capped peaks and deep V-shaped cañons mark the surface.

The main vein (No. 1) is developed by a 178' crosscut adit to the vein, cutting it 150' below the outcrop, and 60' driven along the vein. There is also a winze on the vein extending 30' below the tunnel level. The No. 2 vein is developed by a 60' shaft with a 50' crosscut from the bottom, and the Rose vein by a 259' crosscut adit, meeting the vein 100' below its outcrop, with 95' driven on the vein. Drilling is done by hand. The deposit consists of quartz veins evidently following a siliceous porphyry dike in slates. The workings are in the decomposed dike and no crosscuts have been run to true walls. Nos. 1 and 2 veins, parallel and 85' apart, are made up of quartz and decomposed porphyry containing free gold, auriferous arsenopyrite and galena. The foot-wall of No. 1 vein is not determined, the hanging wall is slate. It varies in width from 10' to 15'; strikes N. 7° E., dips 70° E., and has a proven length on the surface of 1000'. No 2 vein has slate walls, is 50' in width, strikes N. 10° E., and dips east. The Rose vein is a quartz vein in slates with a filling of rose quartz. It varies from 3' to 6' in width, with an average of 4' strikes north and dips east. It carries free gold and a very little galena and arsenopyrite. No. 1 vein averages $9; No. 2, where 15' wide, runs $4.80 a ton; where 30' wide, it runs $3.50. The Rose mine is a very good looking prospect, and from panning of ore appears to be well worthy of extended development. Final judgment can not be passed until the veins are crosscut and developed at deeper levels. Masses of arsenopyrite are found, which can be burned and show a large amount of gold. Free gold also occurs in the center of hard, glassy looking quartz, not associated with sulphides nor a product of oxidation. Galena in appreciable quantities is associated with the arsenopyrite.

There are on the property a blacksmith shop and cabins; a 5-stamp Hendy mill, rock breaker and concentrator to be run by a distillate engine are being installed. A tramway will be installed from the mouth of tunnel No. 1 to the mill, a distance of 300'.

Labor cost from $3 to $3.50 per day in 1914. Transportation 1¢ per pound from Quincy.

The Oro Fino, on Hopkins Creek, is the nearest mine.

Round Lake Mine. (Dixie Queen.) Owner, Round Lake Mining Company, Insurance Exchange Building, San Francisco; M. H. Miller, president and manager; F. J. Mott, San Francisco, secretary.

Location: Johnsville Mining District, Sec. 18, T. 21 N., R. 12 E., 12 miles south of Blairsden by stage road with 4 miles of steep grade. Elevation 6500'.
Bibliography: Lindgren, W., U. S. Geol. Survey Prof. Paper 73, page 111.
U. S. Geol. Survey Folio 37, Downieville.

This property consists of the Dixie Queen and the Dixie Queen Extension, locations. There is an area of 40 acres, covering a length along the lode of 3000'. The surface is characterized by rugged glaciated ridges.

It was discovered in the early days, but no ore has been stoped as yet, though it is a prospect with good chances.

There is a 300' shaft on the dip of the vein. A 100' drift east from the shaft, on the 150' level, shows the vein splitting. The main wall continues its regular course without quartz, while quartz stringers swing into the foot-wall until the strike is nearly north and the dip nearly vertical. On the 300' level, drifts are driven 100' east and 160' west under the lake. There is a 40' raise from the 300' level, and considerable ore blocked out, but the quantity has not been estimated.

The vein is a solid quartz fissure vein, oxidized in the workings so far opened, with well defined walls and a few inches of gouge on the foot-wall. It carries free gold and less than 1% of sulphides. The walls are augite porphyrite, altered augite-andesite. In some places the vein is 15′ wide, but the average is 4′ to 5′. The strike is east, and the dip is 45° N. Only a few feet have been proven on the surface, it being covered by glacial drift and extending under Round Lake. Two shoots, 50′ each in length and another under the lake, length unknown, have been developed.

Photo No. 12. View showing Round Lake Mine in center. Glacial moraine in foreground.

Ten men were employed erecting a mill in 1915. It is being built for ten 1000-pound stamps, but only five are being installed; no concentrators. An 18-horsepower Western Distillate Gas Engine hoist is being used.

The Oakland mine, now idle, adjoins.

Saint Nicolas Mine. (Bushman.) Owner, Nick Borentz, Quincy.

Location: Quincy Mining District, Sec. 34, T. 25 N., R 9 E., 5 miles, by fair wagon road, north of Quincy. Elevation 3350′.
Bibliography: Cal. State Min. Bur. Reports, XI, page 328; XII, page 214; XIII, page 288. U. S. Geol. Survey Folio 37, Downieville.

This property consists of one claim, the Saint Nicolas, a location of 20 acres with a length along the lode of 1500′. The surface is steep.

The property was located by Bushman in 1894, but was relocated in 1906 by Borentz. Three men are working at the present time.

Very little development work has been done. A shaft has been sunk 24′ on the vein and a tunnel 50′ above the shaft has been driven 60′ on the vein, but no ore has been stoped.

The deposit consists of small veins and stringers in slate, following the strike of the slates. There is one quartz vein on the surface with three parallel stringers about 6' apart. It is free milling with from 2% to 3% pyrite which goes $58 a ton. In the drift from the bottom of the shaft the vein is 4' wide. It strikes N. 48° W., dips 80° S., and is proven on the surface for 300'. The 4' vein will average $10 to $12 per ton. Assays from shaft are as high as $50.

There are several houses on the property, and a 3-stamp mill, 500-pound stamps, a 15-horsepower upright engine, but no concentrator or rockbreaker. The mill was being repaired in 1913 preparatory to mining.

Steam is used for power but it is the intention to install water power.

The Butterfly or Smith mine adjoins.

Savercool Mine. Owners, J. R. Murray, Greenville; W. T. Tuleaven, 1913 Ashby avenue, South Berkeley.

Location: Butte Valley Mining District, Sec. 5, T. 26 N., R. 8 E., 2 miles north of Seneca, by trail; 25 miles southeast of Seneca, via Greenville, by automobile road. Elevation 4000'.
Bibliography: Cal. State Min. Bur. Reports, X, page 493; XIII, page 305. U. S. Geol. Survey Folio 15, Lassen Peak.

This property consists of four patented claims, with a length along the lode of 6000'. It is located on the steep bluff on the west bank of the North Fork Feather River, and contains a fair stand of timber.

The property was located in 1877. It has been idle for the last 16 to 20 years, and the workings are either closed or inaccessible.

It was developed by a series of adits—No. 1, 75'; No. 2, 380'; No. 4, 260'; No. 5, 75'; No. 7, 500'; No. 8, 128', and No. 9, 450'; all driven on the vein. (From report of 1890, other work may have been done since.) The longest stope was in tunnel No. 4, 120'.

The deposit is made up of a quartz vein and stringers in black slate near the contact with altered andesite, containing 3% of auriferous sulphides which go $83 per ton. The walls are slate. The vein is 8' wide, strikes northwest, dips 50° SW. and has at intervals a proven length on the surface of 6000'. Three shoots have been worked for an average length of 150'.

Several cabins are on the property, and an old 40-stamp mill, now in ruins.

Water was used for power, 75" under a 440' head being available.

The White Lily and Del Monte mines adjoin.

Southern Eureka Group. (Hibernia.) Owners, J. Standart, Greenville; Mrs. C. O. Hamilton, Oroville.

Location: Crescent Mills Mining District, Secs. 11 and 14, T. 26 N., R. 9 E., 1 mile south of Greenville; Keddie is 16 miles south from Greenville, by good automobile road. Elevation 4580'.
Bibliography: Cal. State Min. Bur. Report XIII, page 297. Diller, J. S., U. S. Geol. Survey Bull. 353, pages 114–115. Lindgren, W., U. S. Geol. Survey Prof. Paper 73, pages 114–116. U. S. Geol. Survey Topo. sheets Indian Valley, Taylorsville, Honey Lake.

This property consists of five claims, the Atlantic, Pacific, Hibernia and the Green Mountain timber tract (160 acres), all patented, and the McLellan placer claim (160 acres), a location. There are 60 acres of quartz claims and 320 acres of timber and placer ground, covering a length of 1500' on the Indian Valley vein and 3000' on the South Eureka vein. It is situated on the top of the ridge south of Greenville with good timber on the property.

G. Standart purchased the group in 1890 and it has been held in the family up to the present time. Two men are working in the McLellan crosscut doing assessment work. Options have been given on this property and a number of properties adjoining and a consolidation is said to be under way.

The South Eureka vein has been devoloped by a crosscut 450' long, reaching a maximum depth of 80' and 400' driven on the vein. It has been stoped for a length of 400', a width of 12' and a depth of 80'. A tunnel 100' long has been driven on the McLellan vein, reaching a depth below the outcrop of 350', and a crosscut tunnel 300' long has been driven on the Hibernia vein and 200' x 20' x 120' of ore has been stoped. The Pennsylvania tunnel from the McLellan claim into the Hibernia, 500' below the surface, will have to be driven 200' farther to cut the McLellan vein. It will also be extended to cut the South Eureka.

The deposit is composed of three quartz fissure veins near a contact of granodiorite and meta-rhyolite. The vein filling of all the veins in quartz and gouge, the ore being oxidized and containing free gold. The South Eureka vein is 12' to 14' in width, strikes N. 30° W., intersecting the Indian Valley vein, and dips 70° NE. The foot-wall is granodiorite and the hanging wall is 'porphyry,' probably meta-rhyolite. It has a proven length on the surface of 3000'. Two pay shoots have been developed 80' and 450' in length, the ore, it is said, plating $6 to $8. The McLellan vein dips 65° E. Its walls are 'porphyry' and it has a proven length on the surface of 3500', and two 100' pay shoots developed ore which is said to have averaged $6 to $7 per ton.

A blacksmith shop comprises the only equipment.

The property was idle in September, 1918.

The Indian Valley and Droege mines adjoin, the former being idle, and the latter operating.

Specimen Mine. Owner, Mrs. Sarah Jolly, Oroville.
Location: Granite Basin Mining District, Sec. 24, T. 23 N., R. 6 E., 10 miles northeast of Brush Creek; Quincy 30 miles northeast from property; good automobile roads from Quincy or Oroville via Letter Box. Elevation 4900'. Bibliography: Cal. State Min. Bur. Reports, X, page 490; XIII, page 306.

This property consists of one claim, the Specimen, a location, 20 acres in area and covering a length along the lode of 1500'. Low hills are characteristic of the surface, and fair timber stands on the property.

The mine was located in 1880 and has been worked at intervals since that time. It was under lease in 1913 to Len Hensath of Brush Creek, who, with an assistant, was repairing the mill.

The Specimen vein has been developed by the Showshed adit of 600', driven on the vein, and the West vein by an adit tunnel of 500' driven on it. Ore has been stoped from the tunnel levels to the surface. The Showshed adit reaches a maximum depth of 160'.

There are two quartz veins in granite, the Specimen and the West, rather flat fissure veins, parallel and 300' apart. The ore contains rich specimens of free gold and also 1% of sulphides. The Specimen vein, which varies from 6" to 15", averages 1' in width, strikes northeast, dips 30° E., and has a proven length on the surface of 1000'. The West vein varies from 1" to 15" in width and strikes northeast. Pay shoots are short, but one 10' in length produced $20,000. Ore averages $12 to $14 in both veins.

Several houses furnish living quarters, and an old 4-stamp 750-pound mill, with Challenge feeder and a Gates crusher, operated by a Pelton waterwheel, comprise the reduction equipment. Water under 100' head is supplied by a ditch one mile in length.

The Robinson and Morning Star mines adjoin.

Star Claim. Owners, Lakin Estate, Tonopah, Nevada.

> Location: Johnsville Mining District, Sec. 23, T. 22 N., R. 11 E., in town of Johnsville, 8 miles west of Blairsden (W. P. Ry.) by good automobile road. Bibliography: Lindgren, W., U. S. Geol. Survey Prof. Paper 73, page 111. U. S. Geol. Survey Folio 37, Downieville.

About $1000 worth of work has been done on this property but no ore has been developed.

The Plumas Eureka mine adjoins on the north.

Summit Group. Owner, A. N. Cameron, Seneca.

> Location: Butte Valley Mining District, Sec. 2, T. 25 N., R. 7 E., 8 miles west of Twain by trail, 4 miles northwest of Virgilia (W. P. Ry.) by trail. Elevation 2850'–5000'.
> Bibliography: U. S. Geol. Survey Folio 15, Lassen Peak.

This property consists of five claims, the Summit, May, Gold Fleece, Argonaut and Bell Rose; also 40 acres of placer claims, controlling tunnel, mill and water rights. There is a total of 100 acres with a length along the lode of 6000'. It covers the ridge between Red Gulch and North Fork Feather River and contains good timber.

It was discovered in 1877 by Dan Bull, and abandoned later, to be purchased by the present owner from Lee in 1887. Assessment work only was being done in 1913.

The property is developed by three tunnels. No. 3 tunnel (lower) crosscuts 180' and follows the vein 100'; No. 2 tunnel, 350' above, is

60′ long and 50′ below the surface at the face, and No. 1, following the vein from the Deadwood side of Redwood Mountain, is 150′ above No. 2 and 180′ long. No ground has been stoped.

There are two veins, the Main vein and the Contact vein. The former is quartz and recemented breccia carrying free gold, galena, pyrite and some chalcopyrite. Both walls are slate. The vein varies from 20′ to 60′ between walls, strikes N. 45° W., and dips 70° NE. It has a proven length on this group of 2000′, and also extends through other claims. The vein carries gold throughout the 2000′, an average value of 14 samples taken from different places, being $7. The Contact vein is filled with quartz and calcite. It is 30′ wide and strikes N. 45° W. Maximum assay value $7.

Water power on North Fork Feather River up to 10,000 horsepower is available.

The Elizabeth Consolidated and Halstead mines are extensions of the Summit vein to the southeast. The Duncan, Halstead and Elizabeth Consolidated are now all under option to Camp and Snyder Brothers, Salt Lake City.

T. C. and **O. K. Claims.** Owner, Professor C. Bayless, Dubuque, Iowa.

> Location: Quincy Mining District, Sec. 34, T. 25 N., R. 9 E., 3 miles north of Quincy by good automobile road. Elevation 3800′.
> Bibliography: U. S. Geol. Survey Folio 37, Downieville.

This property includes two patented claims, the T. C. and O. K., 40 acres in area and covering 3000′ along the lode. There is fair timber on the ground.

It has been held by the present owner since 1880, but no work has been done on the claims for many years and their value is problematical.

This deposit consists of one vein exposed in a 130′ shaft, said to be the same as the Iowa vein of the Bell group. It is a quartz vein with stringers following a siliceous dike, containing free gold and pyrite. The foot-wall and hanging wall are made up of quartzite and slate. It strikes N. 15° W., and has a proven length on the surface of 600′.

The St. Nicolas and White Oak quartz mines and the Bushman drift mine adjoin.

Tefft Mine. Owner, J. U. Tefft, Quincy.

> Location: Quincy Mining District, Sec. 11, T. 23 N., R. 9 E., 9 miles by wagon road south of Quincy. Elevation 6000′.
> Bibliography: U. S. Geol. Survey Folio 37, Downieville.

This property consists of the following locations: Mohawk, Banner, Providence, Amelia B., Crescent Eureka, Center Star, Baby Modoc, and Modoc Fraction. The total area of the claims is about 140 acres and they cover a length along the strike of the lode of 4500′. The

group is situated on the northern slope of the cañon of Middle Fork
Feather River, 2500' above the river. Though sparsely timbered,
excellent timber can be had within one mile of the mine. The claims
were located by Tefft in 1906 and two men are working at the
present time.

The vein has been developed to a depth of 170' by a crosscut adit
240' in length. From the point where this adit encountered the vein,
a drift was driven north within the vein for a distance of 105' and
south for 225'. The above work blocked out 10,000 tons of ore
averaging over $7 per ton. There are also 800 tons of ore on the
dump. A lower tunnel started 180' below the upper tunnel was in
a distance of 100' in 1913. It is estimated that this tunnel will have
to be driven 250' farther to intersect the vein. If the oreshoot proves
to be of the same length and width as on the level above, a drift on
the vein will develop 20,000 additional tons of ore.

The Tefft vein lies in a narrow belt of amphibolite schist between
Calaveras slates on the east and a belt of serpentine on the west.
The vein is a true fissure vein and cuts diagonally across the general
strike of the schists and slates. Its course is nearly north and the
dip is 60° W. The average width of the vein is 5', the maximum
about 8'. Both walls are an altered schist, and a clay gouge is found
on both. The vein filling is an oxidized, iron-stained 'sugar' quartz,
which contains 'rusty' gold, and is free milling. There are three
other veins on the property, which in 1913 had only been opened by
superficial open cuts, but pan samples taken from these veins all
showed free gold. The ground stands well and very little timbering
has been necessary. There are five buildings on the property, which
include a blacksmith shop and stable. An air compressor was
installed in January, 1914.

If a mill is built, wood or oil will have to be used for fuel until
such time as water power can be developed. Transportation costs
1¢ per pound from Quincy.

The Crescent Hills Gold Mines Company of California (Oddie
mine) adjoins.

Valentine Claim. Owner, Neseman Estate, care E. N. Johnson,
Mohawk.

Location: Johnsville Mining District, Sec. 30, T. 22 N., R. 13 E., 1½ miles
east of Clio on W. P. Ry., by good automobile road. Elevation 4700'.
Bibliography: Lindgren, W., U. S. Geol. Survey Prof. Paper 73, page 111.
U. S. Geol. Survey Folio 37, Downieville.

This property is patented and lies on the low ridge rising from
Mohawk Valley on the north. There is fair mining timber on the
property.

No work was done in 1913 and only a little in 1912.

The Bullion and Antelope mines adjoin.

Wardlow Mine. (Blaine.) Owners, J. F. Wardlow, Greenville; H. D. Wardlow, Greenville.

Location: Crescent Mills Mining District, Secs. 10 and 11, T. 26 N., R. 9 E, 1½ miles south of Greenville, thence 15 miles south by good automobile road to Keddie. Elevation 4700'.
Bibliography: Diller, J. S., U. S. Geol. Survey Bull. 353, pages 114–115. Lindgren, W., U. S. Geol. Survey Prof. Paper 73, pages 114–116. U. S. Geol. Survey Topo. sheets Indian Valley, Taylorsville, Honey Lake.

This property consists of four claims, the Taft (formerly known as the Blaine), Blue Mule, Ladlee, and Roosevelt. There is a total of 75 acres with a length along the lode of 3000'. The mine is situated on the ridge south of Greenville and there is a fair stand of timber on the property.

It was worked in early days and was acquired by the present owners in 1903. Assessment work only is being done at present.

The property is developed by tunnels. The Lower tunnel is a 525' crosscut to the Ladlee vein, 600' below the surface, and 60' drifted on the vein. The Ladlee tunnel cuts the vein 100' below the surface, and is then driven 60' on the vein. The Blaine tunnel is a 100' crosscut with 700' driven on the vein, 400' below the outcrop. A small amount of ore was stoped in the latter.

The deposit is supposed to be made up of two veins, but it may be one faulted vein. It is a quartz fissure at the contact of meta-rhyolite and diorite, the filling being quartz and 'porphyry.' It is free milling and contains 1% of auriferous pyrite assaying $121 per ton, and some manganese oxide. Both hanging and foot walls are made up of 'porphyry' and granite. The vein varies from 10' to 25' in width, strikes east, and dips 80° S. It has a length proven on the surface, by open cuts, of 1500'. In the Ladlee tunnel the vein is 3' wide and assays $12.50. In the Blaine the vein is said to be 4' wide and to assay $14.

Equipment consists of a cabin, blacksmith shop and tools. Water power is available from Round Valley Reservoir.

The New York and Indian Valley mines, both idle, adjoin.

This property, together with the Southern Eureka group, Hibernia and McLellan, was purchased in October, 1915, by Geo. D. Needy and associates of Spokane, Washington, who expected to push development. The Southern Eureka Mining Company was organized by Spokane people, with a capitalization of $2,000,000, to operate the properties. The group contains approximately 450 acres of mineral ground. Geo. D. Needy, E. F. Yaeger, M. D. DeHoff, Hal J. Cole and H. R. Van Dreathen, all of Spokane, are directors.

White Oak and **Black Oak Claims.** Owner, H. P. Wormley, Quincy.

Location: Quincy Mining District, Sec. 34, T. 25 N., R. 9 E., 4 miles north of Quincy in a direct line, 5 miles by fair wagon road. Elevation 3700'.
Bibliography: Cal. State Min. Bur. Report XIII, page 288. U. S. Geol. Survey Folio 37, Downieville.

The property is situated on a ridge of gentle slope and consists of two claims, the White Oak and Black Oak, 40 acres in area and covering a length along the lode of 3000'. The timber was cut over in early days.

Wormley has owned the property for a long time, but has been doing assessment work only in the past 15 years.

A 200' tunnel has been driven on the vein and one crosscut to the east, near the face of the tunnel driven 30' through slate cut numerous quartz stringers, none, however, with well defined walls.

One vein composed of small stringers of quartz following the strike of slates and not well defined, was worked. The filling is iron-stained quartz and gouge, with some pulverized quartz containing free gold.

The stringers vary from 2" to 1', the general strike being northwest and the dip 80° E. There is a proven length on the surface of 3000'.

The Bushman drift placer mine adjoins, in which the gold has been derived in part from the erosion of the veins and stringers on the White Oak quartz property.

White Lily Mine. Owner, Seneca Mining and Milling Company, Seneca; A. P. Dunn, Seneca, president.

Location: Butte Valley Mining District, Sec. 9, T. 26 N., R. 8 E., ½ mile north of Seneca, thence 31 miles southeast via Greenville and Crescent Mills, by good automobile road to Keddie. Elevation 3700'.
Bibliography: U. S. Geol. Survey Folio 15, Lassen Peak.

This property embraces 110 acres of locations, namely, the White Lily quartz mine, Addie Bell quartz mine, Wedge Fraction, Whitlock placer (60 acres) and Madison placer (old Calliope claim). It covers a length of 3000' along the lode, and is situated on the east bank of North Fork Feather River with a steep rise to the top of a ridge. The property is well timbered.

It was located in 1896 by P. K. Dunn and has been worked ever since by the Dunn family. Suit was brought by the Del Monte Company, in 1912, because of a drift passing through the side line of the White Lily into the Del Monte property, and the White Lily people have been prevented by injunction from removing ore. The total yield of the mine to date is about $225,000. Two men are leasing and working in a part of the mine not under injunction. Negotiations are now under way for the consolidation of the White Lily and Del Monte properties. The owners are said to be anxious to sell and if satisfactory terms can be arranged there is apparently enough ore in sight to pay for the property.

The vein is made up of quartz and quartz stringers in slates, schist and gouge in a badly shattered zone near the contact with altered meta-andesite and possible diorite. The vein filling is oxidized crushed quartz containing free gold and very little sulphide, the ore being so crushed that very little powder is necessary for breaking it. The foot-wall is slate with clay gouge and the hanging wall is said to be diorite. In width the deposit varies from 30' to 60', 30' being the average width of the stopes. The strike is east and the average dip is said to be 35° N., but at the lower tunnel level the orebody appears to be lying nearly flat. Tailings are disposed of in North Fork Feather River.

The mine equipment consists of houses, barns, blacksmith shop and electric hoist. The reduction equipment includes a complete new 10-stamp 1000-pound Hendy mill. This was installed in the latter part of 1911 but on account of the suit was never operated. There is also an old 2-stamp mill which can be put into shape to run.

Water from North Fork Feather River to the amount of 2500″ under 30' head is available for turbines. Cost of treating ore with the old equipment was $2.50. Tailings vary from 50¢ to $1.25.

Whitney Group. Owner, A. W. Whitney, Crescent Mills.

Location: Crescent Mills Mining District, Sec. 23, T. 26 N., R. 9 E., 1 mile west of Crescent Mills on Indian Valley Railroad.
Bibliography: Diller, J. S., U. S. Geol. Survey Bull. 363, pages 114–115. Lindgren, W., U. S. Geol. Survey Prof. Paper 73, pages 114–116. U. S. Geol. Survey Topo. sheets Indian Valley, Taylorsville, Honey Lake.

This property consists of four locations, the Jackson, Munro, Tunnel and Lizzie (fraction), a total of 70 acres, covering a length along the lode of 3000'. It is situated near the top of the ridge back of Crescent Mills, 1000' above the floor of Indian Valley. There is a fair stand of timber on the property.

In early days rich pockets were taken out from the surface workings to a depth of 50'. It has been worked recently under bond by W. W. Robbins, but is idle at present.

The vein is developed by a 60' crosscut adit, then a drift of 50' on the vein. Pocket mining has been done for a length of 100' and to an average depth of 50'.

There is one cherty quartz vein, really a siliceous zone with no well-defined walls, impregnated with sulphides, marcasite, pyrite and a small amount of finely disseminated galena. Very little free gold has been found below the oxidized zone, a depth of 50'. Some ore containing as high as 5% sulphide, goes $200, but the best values are in ore containing galena. The walls are siliceous rhyolite. The ore zone varies from 8' to 10', but the sulphides are not equally distributed. The strike is N. 32° W., the dip vertical and there is a proven length on the surface of 300'. No distinct pay shoots developed.

There is a blacksmith shop at the mine.

This district will be supplied with power by the Great Western Power Company from their Big Meadow project.

The Green Mountain and Crescent mines adjoin.

Wolters Mine. (Fall River Consolidated Mine.) Owner, C. Wolters, Gibsonville.

Location: Granite Basin Mining District, Sec. 24, T. 21 N., R. 7 E., 10 miles from Lumpkin, 9 miles west from La Porte. Elevation 4500'.
Bibliography: Cal. State Min. Bur. Reports, XII, page 216; XIII, page 293. U. S. Geol. Survey Folio 43, Bidwell Bar.

This property consists of three claims, two of which are patented, containing 60 acres and having a length along the lode of 4500'. It is situated on the west side of Fall River and has good tunnel sites and a good stand of timber.

It was discovered in 1888 by Jack Moore and purchased by Wolters and Company in 1889. There has been a total production of about $2000.

The property is developed by a 700' tunnel to the first vein, which is then continued 150' to strike the second vein, on which there is a 50' shaft, and drifts 100' south and 250' north. Two shoots of 50' and 100' were stoped for an average width of 4'.

The deposit consists of quartz fissure veins containing free gold, chalcopyrite and pyrite. The foot-wall is porphyry, the hanging wall granite. The vein varies from 4' to 6', strikes northeast and dips 45° W. There is a length proven at intervals on the surface of 700'. The pay shoots, stoped, milled $6 to $7 per ton; and carried 4% sulphides assaying $50 to $150 per ton. Two hundred inches of water under 80' head are available from Fall River.

Snow destroyed the 5-stamp mill three years ago.

The Cayot mine adjoins.

GOLD—PLACER MINES.

Albion Claim. Owner, Edman Estate, Quincy.

Location: Edmanton Mining District, Sec. 32, T. 24 N., R. 8 E., 12 miles by automobile road southwest of Quincy via Meadow Valley. Elevation 3500'.
Bibliography: Lindgren, W., U. S. Geol. Survey Prof. Paper 73, pages 98, 99. U. S. Geol. Survey Folio 43, Bidwell Bar.

Very little work has been done on this property, and it has practically been abandoned.

Bonnie Mine. (Eclipse.) Owner, Bonnie Hydraulic Mining Company, care W. C. Moran, Berkeley, California.

Location: Sawpit Flat Mining District, Sec. 3, T. 22 N., R. 10 E., 25 miles southeast of Quincy by good automobile road to Eclipse. Elevation 6500'.
Bibliography: U. S. Geol. Survey Folio 37, Downieville.

The property contains 320 acres characterized by lava-capped hills and steep cañons.

It was formerly worked as a hydraulic and drift mine, and in 1913 there were two leasers just starting to drift.

The gold is found in recent (Pleistocene) and glacial gravels and is probably derived from the quartz veins occurring in the slates on the eastern slope of Pilot Peak.

Water is obtained from Poorman's Creek, a tributary to Nelson Creek and North Fork Feather River.

Boulder West Mine.   Owner, Frank Chapman.

Location: Sawpit Flat Mining District, Sec. 24, T. 23 N., R. 9 E., 8 miles due south of Quincy, with a total distance by wagon road via Nelson Point to ridge above mine of 20 miles, then 1 mile of fair horse trail. Elevation 4500'.
Bibliography: U. S. Geol. Survey Folio 37, Downieville.

The holdings consist of one location 20 acres in extent, covering the creek for 1500'. Steep cañons are characteristic of the country.

Surface sluicing only has been done, the values being found in shallow present creek gravels on a bedrock of serpentine. Gold probably derived from quartz and ancient channels above.

Water is obtained from Washington Creek and Middle Fork.

Adjoining mines are the Oversight quartz mine and Bainbridge (now Golden Gate).

China Gulch Mine.   Owner, M. A. Chaplin, Bucks Ranch.

Location: Granite Basin Mining District, Sec. 34, T. 23 N., R. 7 E., 5 miles south of Bucks Ranch by trail, and 30 miles from Quincy. Elevation 5600'.
Bibliography: U. S. Geol. Survey Folio 43, Bidwell Bar.

The property consists of one claim of 20 acres. It is on the north side of the Middle Fork Feather River, and has been worked for a year by Chinese. One man is sluicing.

Colombo Claim.   Owner, G. Giamboni and Company, Oakland.

Location: Johnsville Mining District, Sec. 14, T. 22 N., R. 11 E., 1 mile west of Johnsville, thence 7 miles by good automobile road to Blairsden. Elevation 6000'.
Bibliography: Lindgren, W., U. S. Geol. Survey Prof. Paper 73, page 111. U. S. Geol. Survey Folio 37, Downieville.

This property consists of a 20-acre location on glacial gravel. Some work was done on the claim in 1913.

Denning Mine.   Owner, Lee F. Denning.

Location: Granite Basin Mining District, Sec. 1, T. 22 N., R. 7 E., 7 miles south of Buck's Ranch, by trail; thence it is 17 miles northeast to Quincy, by automobile road.
Bibliography: U. S. Geol. Survey Folio 43, Bidwell Bar.

Property is situated on a branch of Willow Creek, one mile from the North Fork Feather River. Owner working alone.

English Bar Group.   Owners, Pauly Brothers, Nelson Point, and Judge Moncure, Quincy.

Location: Sawpit Flat Mining District, Sec. 11, T. 23 N., R. 10 E., 2 miles northeast of Nelson Point. Elevation 4050'.
Bibliography: U. S. Geol. Survey Folio 37, Downieville.

At the present time these claims are under option and are being prospected by a company for dredging purposes.

Fenton Group. Owners, R. L. Fenton and Wm. Dushman, Capay, Yolo County.

Location: Granite Basin Mining District, Sec. 8, T. 23 N., R. 7 E., 19 miles southwest of Quincy, by good automobile road, via Buck's Ranch. Elevation 5300'.
Bibliography: U. S. Geol. Survey Folio 43, Bidwell Bar.

Property consists of two claims, the Grizzly Gulch and Lava Gulch, both located in 1913. Assessment work only has been done, pending the securing of a right from the Forestry Bureau to run three-fourths mile of ditch from Lava Gulch.

Flannigan Mine. Owner, Wm. Flannigan, Belden.

Location: Butte Valley Mining District, Sec. 28, T. 26 N., R. 7 E.
Bibliography: U. S. Geol. Survey Folio 15, Lassen Peak.

This property is situated on Soda Ravine, tributary to Mosquito Creek. The creek gravel carries smooth coarse gold and rough quartz gold.

Forest Grove Mine. Owner, Jerry Curtiss, Twain.

Location: Johnsville Mining District, Sec. 9, T. 22 N., R. 11 E., 5 miles west of Johnsville, 10 miles southwest of Blairsden by trail. Elevation 6000'.
Bibliography: Lindgren, W., U. S. Geol. Survey Prof. Paper 73, page 111.
U. S. Geol. Survey Folio 37, Downieville.

This property comprises 20 acres, with a length of 2000' along a channel of bench gravel about 1000' above the present creek bed.

It was located in 1884 by B. L. Jones, who took out $7000 by hydraulicking. Curtiss bought it in 1891 and has taken out $3000 by sluicing. One man was working all the time in 1914, but most of the available ground had been worked out.

The deposit is bench gravel, which may have come from the country rock of slate and porphyry. It averages 8' in depth for a width of 75', and has been worked for a length of 2000'.

Equipment consists of cabin, tools, blacksmith shop, etc.

Four hundred inches of water with an 80' head is obtained with a one and one-half mile ditch from a creek on the north side of Eureka Peak.

The West Elizabeth is an adjoining mine.

Fortuna Mine. (Diana.) Owner, W. Schield and Company, La Porte.

Location: La Porte Mining District, Secs. 31 and 32, T. 22 N., R. 9 E., distant 6 miles from La Porte by good wagon road and 35 miles from Quincy. Elevation 5000'.
Bibliography: Lindgren, W., U. S. Geol. Survey Prof. Paper 73, page 105.
U. S. Geol. Survey Folio 37, Downieville.

The property consists of 150 acres of unpatented land extending three-fourths of a mile along the present stream channel.

The surface gravels have been worked at intervals since early days. It was worked by C. E. Gillette, relocated by Quigley, and in part was purchased by the present owners.

Development consists of two tunnels 150′ and 145′ in length, under the lava, and a 22′ shaft put down 150′ beyond the end of the 145′ tunnel.

The deposit represents present river gravels, eroded from rocks of the bedrock series and lava gravel, running east. Bedrock has not been reached, as too much water was encountered in the shaft. The deposit is capped with andesite and basalt. The gravel is fine, but has some large boulders in it. A portion lying on 'hardpan' to a depth of 7′ is said to have averaged 16¢ to 24¢ per yard. No test pits or drilling have been done, and until some work has been done, the value, depth, etc., are problematical. Surface gravels can only be worked profitably by dredge or dragline scraper.

Garfield Claim. (Garibaldi.) Owner, P. Laurenzi, Sonoma City.

Location: Johnsville Mining District, Sec. 3, T. 22 N., R. 11 E., 4 miles northwest of Johnsville. Elevation 5500′.
Bibliography: Cal. State Min. Bur. Report XIII, page 294. Lindgren, W., U. S. Geol. Survey Prof. Paper 73, page 111. U. S. Geol. Survey Folio 37, Downieville.

This property consists of 40 acres. Assessment work was done in 1913.

Gard and Orr. (See Sierra County.)

General Harrison Mine. (Standard Mining Company.) Owner, Chris Radcovich, Johnsville; C. A. Macomber, secretary, San Anselmo. One thousand acre location, dam and two-mile ditch.

Location: Johnsville Mining District, Sec. 19, T. 22 N., R. 11 E., 9 miles west of Johnsville. Blairsden is 14 miles northeast by good wagon and automobile road. Elevation 5000′.
Bibliography: Cal. State Min. Bur. Reports, XII, page 216; XIII, page 294. Lindgren, W., U. S. Geol. Survey Prof. Paper 73, page 111. U. S. Geol. Survey Folio 37. Downieville.

The property embraces 40 acres, covering one-half mile along Nelson Creek, held by the present owner since 1882. The mine consists of present creek gravels on a bedrock of slate. It is now worked out.

The Queen group adjoins.

Greenblower Group. Owner, H. J. Greenblower.

Location: Granite Basin Mining District, Secs. 30 and 31, T. 23 N., R. 8 W., 6 miles southeast of Bucks Ranch, by trail, thence 17 miles northeast to Quincy, by automobile road.
Bibliography: U. S. Geol. Survey Folio 43, Bidwell Bar.

This property consists of a number of claims on the south slope of Mt. Ararat, two miles north of the Feather River. Owner working alone.

Hellas Mine. Owner, Edman Estate, Quincy.

Location: Edmanton Mining District, Sec. 33, T. 24 N., R. 8 E., 2 miles southeast of Meadow Valley, thence 9 miles by good automobile road east to Quincy. Elevation 3500′.
Bibliography: Lindgren, W., U. S. Geol. Survey Prof. Paper 73, pages 98-99. U. S. Geol. Survey Folio 43, Bidwell Bar.

This property covers creek gravels, but it has practically been abandoned.

Jones Placer Mine. (Weaver.) Owner, David Jones, Waldo, Yuba County, California.

> Location: Edmanton Mining District, Sec. 7, T. 23 N., R. 8 E., 2 miles east of Bucks Ranch, by good trail, thence 17 miles northeast to Quincy, by good automobile road. Elevation 5200'.
> Bibliography: Lindgren, W., U. S. Geol. Survey Prof. Paper 73, pages 98–99. U. S. Geol. Survey Folio 43, Bidwell Bar.

One man, J. C. Kaiser, has been working on the claim, ground sluicing, for the past four years.

Joseph Group. (Emerson and McMullin mine.) Owner, A. Joseph, Quincy. Bonded to R. C. Jackson, Folsom and Twenty-second streets, San Francisco.

> Location: Genesee Valley Mining District, Secs. 2 and 11, T. 24 N., R. 11 E., 7 miles south of Genesee, by trail; 22 miles northwest of Portola, by wagon road. Elevation 5280'.
> Bibliography: Cal. State Min. Bur. Report XIII, page 292. Diller, J. S., U. S. Geol. Survey Bull. 260, pages 45–49. Diller, J. S., U. S. Geol. Survey Bull. 353, pages 111–121.

King Solomon Group. Owners, Lucky Strike Mining Company, H. O. Howard, Lovelock, Nevada.

> Location: Taylorsville Mining District, Sec. 30, T. 25 N., R. 11 E., 6 miles southeast of Taylorsville, thence 12 miles southwesterly, by good automobile road to Keddie (W. P. Ry.).
> Bibliography: Diller, J. S., U. S. Geol. Survey Bull. 363, 1908. U. S. Geol. Survey Topo. sheets Taylorsville, Indian Valley, Honey Lake.

The King Solomon group of six placer claims was acquired early in 1915 by the above company. The company took a bond on the group in 1912 and has performed sufficient work to demonstrate the presence of rich gravel. The channel has been traced for a mile, and at places is 300' wide. Most of the work consists of shafts and open cuts, but preparations are being made for more thorough development.

Little Star Mine. Owner, S. A. Pezzola, Johnsville.

> Location: Johnsville Mining District, Sec. 24, T. 22 N., R. 11 E., near border of Johnsville, 9 miles west of Blairsden, by automobile road. Elevation 5200'.
> Bibliography: Lindgren, W., U. S. Geol. Survey Prof. Paper 73, page 111. U. S. Geol. Survey Folio 37, Downieville.

This property comprises 40 acres of locations in the creek bed just above Johnsville. It has a length along the channel of 3000'.

The claims were relocated by the present owner in 1909. About 20 acres of the property was worked in early days. Assessment work only being done at present.

The deposit consists of free glacial and creek gravels, with some boulders. They are the surface gravel of Jamison Creek, the gold being derived from the erosion of the Plumas Eureka and Jamison veins. The channel courses north.

The Jamison placer and Plumas Eureka quartz mines adjoin.

McFarlane Mine. Owner, Vernon Hammet.

> Location: Edmanton Mining District, Sec. 7, T. 23 N., R. 8 E., 3 miles east of Bucks Ranch by trail, thence 17 miles northeast to Quincy by good automobile road.
> Bibliography: Lindgren, W., U. S. Geol. Survey Prof. Paper 73, pages 98–99. U. S. Geol. Survey Folio 43, Bidwell Bar.

This mine is idle at present, owner working on the Star Plumas claim.

Minerva Bar Claim.

Location: Sawpit Flat Mining District, Sec. 18, T. 23 N., R. 10 E., 3 miles west of Nelson Point. Elevation 3800'.
Bibliography: U. S. Geol. Survey Folio 37, Downieville.

Formerly owned by Minerva Bar Mining Company. Last work done by Scott Beaser, in 1911.

Nelson Creek Claim. Owners, E. C. Fish, Oroville; C. M. Root, Nelson Point.

Location: Sawpit Flat Mining District, Sec. 22, T. 23 N., R. 10 E., 1 mile south of Nelson Point, thence 11 miles northwest to Quincy, by good automobile road. Elevation 4000'.
Bibliography: U. S. Geol. Survey Folio 37, Downieville.

Assessment work only being done.

Nelson Creek Gravel Company. (See under Drift.)

New York Mine. Owner, N. H. Fries.

Location: Granite Basin Mining District, Sec. 15, T. 23 N., R. 7 E., 2 miles south of Buck's Ranch, thence 17 miles northeast to Quincy by good automobile road.
Bibliography: U. S. Geol. Survey Folio 43, Bidwell Bar.

This property consists of 40 acres, with ground owned by Gold Mountain Hydraulic and Dredging Company. Owner working alone.

Plumas Investment Company. Owner, Plumas Investment Company, W. P. Hammon, 433 California Street, San Francisco.

Location: Spanish Ranch Mining District. Elevation 3700'–3900'.

The company's holdings comprise three groups: The Mountain House No. 59, four miles northwest of Spanish Ranch in Sec. 31, T. 25 N., R. 8 E.; the Pine Leaf No. 91, one mile north of Spanish Ranch in Sec. 11, T. 24 N., R. 8 E., and the Silver Star group containing six hundred acres in Sec. 15, T. 24 N., R. 8 E., about one mile west of Spanish Ranch. The latter group takes in Spanish Creek Valley, west of the town. No work is being done on any of these claims.

Quartz Ravine Claim. Owner, H. Smith.

Location: Granite Basin Mining District, Sec. __, T. 23 N., R. 7 E., south of Bucks Ranch, thence 17 miles northeast to Quincy, by good automobile road.
Bibliography: U. S. Geol. Survey Folio 43, Bidwell Bar.

Owner is doing assessment work alone. Property is situated on Willow Creek.

Red Saddle Mine. Owner, Mark A. Chaplin.

Location: Granite Basin Mining District, Sec. 3, T. 22 N., R. 7 E., 7 miles, by trail, south of Buck's Ranch, thence 17 miles northeast to Quincy, by good automobile road.
Bibliography: U. S. Geol. Survey Folio 43, Bidwell Bar.

This deposit consists of creek gravels located south of China Gulch claim.

Rock Rim Mine.

Location: Granite Basin Mining District, Sec. 2, T. 22 N., R. 7 E., 7 miles south of Bucks Ranch, by trail, thence 17 miles northeast to Quincy, by automobile road.
Bibliography: U. S. Geol. Survey Folio 43, Bidwell Bar.

Situated on Willow Creek, one mile from Middle Fork Feather River, near the China Gulch mine. Owner is doing assessment work alone.

Woods Ravine Mine. Owner, R. Gifford, Spanish Ranch.

Location: Spanish Ranch Mining District, Sec. 7, T. 24 N., R. 9 E., 1½ miles northwest of Spanish Ranch, 9 miles to Quincy, by good automobile road. Elevation 3800′.
Bibliography: Lindgren, W., U. S. Geol. Survey Prof. Paper 73, pages 98–99. U. S. Geol. Survey Folio 43, Bidwell Bar.

This property consists of 40 acres in a ravine fed from the Badger and Gopher Hill mines and the tailings are reworked. No work has been done in the last few years.

DREDGING.

Gold Mountain Hydraulic and Dredging Company. (See under Hydraulic.)

Mountain Meadow Dredging Company. Owner, same, Chicago; E. E. Stirling, in charge.

Location: Crescent Mills Mining District, 8 miles from Susanville.
Bibliography: Diller, J. S., U. S. Geol. Survey Bull. 353, pages 114, 115. Lindgren, W., U. S. Geol. Survey Prof. Paper 73, pages 114–116. U. S. Geol. Survey Topo. sheet Indian Valley, Taylorsville, Honey Lake.

This property consists of 3000 acres located by Lloyd Baker of Chicago. It was reported that a dredge was to be installed during 1915, but the project did not materialize.

LIMESTONE.

Pyramidal Placer Mine. Owners, H. C. Flournoy, Quincy; D. W. Johnson, 742 Market street, San Francisco; C. J. Lee, Quincy.

Location: Butte Valley Mining District, Secs. 6, 7, 8, 16, 17, 21 and 28, T. 25 N., R. 8 E., 4 miles northwest of Twain; Virgilia (W. P. Ry.) 2 miles south. Elevation 3000′–5500′.
Bibliography: U. S. Geol. Survey Folio 15, Lassen Peak.

Property consists of 940 acres. High ridges with steep slopes to watercourses characterize the surface.

The ground was first located in 1896, was relocated by the present owners in 1908. Assessment work only has been done. The deposit is crossed by the Western Pacific Railway at Virgilia, and if it will average $CaCo_3$, as the sample shows, it is undoubtedly of commercial value.

A 142′ open cut across the deposit is the only work that has been done, and so far this has not encountered the west wall.

The following analysis of the rock was made by F. C. Pioda of the Spreckels Sugar Refinery from a sample taken by Mr. Flournoy:

SiO_2	4.71%
Fe_2O_3 and Al_2O_3	0.37
$CaCO_3$	93.63
$CaSO_4$	Trace
$MgCO_3$	.98
Undetermined	.31
	100.00%

MANGANESE.[1]

Braito Mine. Owners, Fred E. Braito and T. J. Mason, Crescent Mills. Comprises one claim in Sec. 26, T. 26 N., R. 9 E., M. D. M., near Crescent Mills.

The ore body lies in schist and strikes northwest. It is developed by open cuts and a tunnel, which showed mixed ore for a width of 4' to 7'.

During 1917 the property was under lease to the Noble Electric Steel Company. They employed 30 to 40 men and up to January 1, 1918, had shipped 20 carloads of ore to their Heroult smelter.

Burch and **Woody Prospect** is near the line of Secs. 21 and 28, T. 26 N., R. 9 E., four miles west of Crescent Mills. When the property was visited in 1917, a small amount of manganese oxide, which was too siliceous to sell, had been taken out.

Crystal Lake Manganese Group, known also as the Mt. Hough, is owned by H. A. and R. L. Kloppenburg and H. S. Myton of Quincy and leased to Smith Brothers of Taylorsville, who bought the lease from Allen and Robinson.

The group comprises three claims in Sec. 8, T. 25 N., R. 10 E., on Mt. Hough, five miles east of Indian Falls. Half a mile of road was required to reach the deposit.

Allen and Robinson shipped ten cars of ore from the property before selling their lease. Smith Brothers report shipments of seven or eight carloads during 1918, and expect to keep up production during 1919.

The ore could be traced for 200' along the strike, N. 42° W. When visited, an orebody 6' wide and pitching 80° SW., was exposed. It is said that the ore from this property carries from 50% to 54% metallic manganese, which would make it equal in grade to any in the state. It has been sought after for use in dry batteries.

[1]From Bulletin 76, Calif. State Mining Bureau, August, 1918.

Diadem Lode is one of a group of three claims which include 20 acres in Sec. 33, T. 24 N., R. 8 E., fourteen miles southwest of Quincy. Manganese oxides and rhodonite are reported to occur in a quartz vein on this claim associated with iron oxide. The vein strikes N. 37° W. and dips 60° NE.

No development work for manganese had been done at time of visit and it is believed that the deposit is only superficial.

Iron Queen Claim was located by Chas. Devlin and A. F. Smith in Sec. 8, T. 26 N., R. 9 E., about six miles northwest of Crescent Mills. Two small, short open cuts had developed a little good ore, but most of the manganese oxide was too siliceous.

The **Penrose Mine**, on Mumford Hill, three miles southwest of Meadow Valley, near Edmanton, shows an occurrence of manganese oxides in the gossan of a quartz vein similar to that at the Diadem lode. The deposit is probably superficial.

MOLYBDENUM.[1]

The **Dufay** and **Eyhi properties** near the Mohawk mine (about eight miles northwest of Chilcoot) have been worked for copper ores which are said to carry some molybdenite. Some ore was shipped by Dufay in 1915, but apparently no use was made of the molybdenite contained.

Mohawk Mine. The ore at this copper property, which lies eight miles by road northwest of Chilcoot, is said to carry a small amount of molybdenite, but none of it has been recovered separately.

Murdock Mining Company. The property contains nine claims located nine miles northwest of Chilcoot and a mile beyond the Mohawk. Shoots of molybdenite ore occur here in quartz veins which carry principally bornite and chalcopyrite. Two tons of high grade molybdenite were picked out of the dump and shipped by lessees in 1916, but no production has been reported since. The vein principally developed is 3′ to 4′ wide, and it is said that it can be traced for over half a mile. A more detailed description of the mine is given under **Copper**.

SILVER.

Indian Valley Silver Mine. (See under Gold—Lode.)

---

[1]From Bulletin 80, Tungsten, Molybdenum, Vanadium, Nickel. Cal. State Mining Bureau (in preparation).

STONE INDUSTRY.

The **Chilcoot Granite Company.** R. B. Myers, manager, 204 Bacon Block, Oakland, owns a granite quarry near Chilcoot on the Western Pacific Railroad, but it has not been operated recently.

Paul Sonognini, at Chilcoot, has a granite quarry which he has operated in a small way for several years past, but it was idle in 1918.

The **Western Pacific Railroad,** at several places along their right of way in Plumas County, but principally near Chilcoot, utilizes granite for rubble and ballast. A ditcher, Rodger's ballast, and flat cars are used.

INDEX.

O